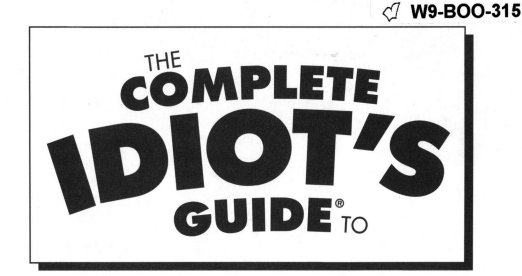

THE COMPLETE IDIOT'S GUIDE® TO

The Vietnam War

by Timothy P. Maga, Ph.D.

alpha books

Macmillan USA, Inc.
201 West 103rd Street
Indianapolis, IN 46290

A Pearson Education Company

Publisher
Marie Butler-Knight

Product Manager
Phil Kitchel

Managing Editor
Cari Luna

Acquisitions Editor
Randy Ladenheim-Gil

Development Editor
Michael Thomas

Production Editor
Billy Fields

Copy Editor
Faren Bachelis

Illustrator
Jody P. Schaeffer

Cover Designers
Mike Freeland
Kevin Spear

Book Designers
Scott Cook and Amy Adams of DesignLab

Indexer
Angie Bess

Layout/Proofreading
Darin Crone
John Etchison
Paula Lowell

Contents at a Glance

Contents

Foreword

Vietnam is a country I prefer to remember as I first saw it in 1963 when my wife, Lila, and our infant daughter, Heidi, visited on our way home from Peace Corps service in the Philippines. Although there were horrible things happening there at the time, few people knew about them.

Certainly we didn't. In fact, most Americans knew next to nothing about Vietnam and couldn't even find it on a world map. For our young family in 1963, the French flavor of Saigon, the beauty of the countryside, the fine food, and the friendly people are all still clear mental images.

After ten years had passed, and America was in an embarrassing withdrawal, my visions were the opposite—not only of Vietnam, but of Cambodia and Laos as well. I sometimes wondered if the friendly Laotians, Cambodians, and Vietnamese I once knew were still friendly—or if indeed were still alive. The Vietnam War was something I wanted to forget and put behind me—perhaps not consciously, but really nevertheless.

And so it is with many of my generation, and the one that followed as well; it was painful to think about, and no one wants to think about painful things. Consequently, there was a dearth of scholarship about Vietnam, Cambodia, and Laos, with very few studying and trying to understand the politics, economics, and social issues of Vietnam and the effect of the American presence there.

The result was that millions of Americans, and our erstwhile allies as well, were ignorant of the war and of the country that was the battlefied. Our veterans were silent about their experiences, and some had great troubles getting readjusted after returning home.

James F. Dunningan and Albert A. Nofi have written an important book, *Dirty Little Secrets of the Vietnam War* (St. Martin's Press, 1999). Early in their book they make the point that all wars are complicated affairs, and that since the Vietnam War was highly politically charged, it was an even more complex phenomenon, more difficult to understand.

Tim Maga now appears on the historical literary stage with *The Complete Idiot's Guide to the Vietnam War*, enlightening us on Vietnam. He goes a long way in filling large gaps in our knowledge and thinking about the war.

People of two generations owe him appreciation and gratitude. He has given us a book that stands on its own as an important contribution, but also is a companion book to many others that have appeared, and that will continue to appear in the years to come.

The Vietnam War can never be erased from the American experience, but thanks to Tim Maga, it can be much better understood.

Dirk Anthony Ballendorf
Guam, August 2000

Dirk Anthony Ballendorf is professor of History and Micronesian Studies at the University of Guam's Micronesian Area Research Center. He was in Vietnam and Cambodia in 1963, and in 1973 was in Laos, Cambodia, and Vietnam.

Introduction

Americans love an underdog. The little guy who takes on the big guy and wins has always been the hero in American folklore. The Vietnam War messed up the folklore, messed up Americans, and messed up America—and, years later, many are still asking why.

By all rights, little Vietnam should have been considered a good buddy to U.S. policy 50 years ago. It fought a revolution against a nasty European master just as the Americans had, had a national leader who compared himself to Washington and Jefferson, and had a maverick, independent streak that rivaled that of any hotheaded New Yorker. In fact, Ho Chi Minh, that national leader, once lived in New York. So what was the problem?

The problem was the U.S. government's die-hard anticommunism policy at the time, the desire to have an easy place to demonstrate that policy, and a basic ignorance of things Vietnamese. For years, few Americans could find Vietnam on a map, and when they did, they could never agree on whether their country should be involved over there or not.

Without question, the Vietnam War wins the prize for being America's most convoluted, complex, and downright mystifying overseas venture. This slim volume is not the last word on the subject, but it will get you involved in all the dirty secrets, ugly revelations, and contradictory politics. Separating politics from the Vietnam War is not possible, so don't even try. A lot of it looks pretty goofy in hindsight, but remember, you're reading history here and not hindsight.

Today's leading American politicos are all products of the old Vietnam War debates. To understand the present, you have to take a stab at understanding the past. Take the challenge here, and you won't regret it. From the complexities of Ho Chi Minh to the twenty-first century objectives of Douglas "Pete" Peterson, the new U.S. ambassador to Vietnam, it's quite a story.

America lost its innocence in the Vietnam War. So much has changed because of it. *The Complete Idiot's Guide to the Vietnam War* charts those changes for you. Maybe you'll learn something about yourself and your own family here. I hope so.

How This Book Is Organized

The Complete Idiot's Guide to the Vietnam War is broken into five parts.

Part 1, "The Not-So-Good War," examines the origins of the Vietnam conflict, the key personalities involved, and what made them tick. The good guys weren't always that good, and the bad guys weren't always that bad.

Part 2, "How to Make a Quagmire," analyzes the tough decisions that led to America's role in the Vietnam nightmare. A lot of mistakes were made here. Too bad nobody noticed—until it was too late.

Part 3, "Escalation," takes a look at the slow buildup of American troops in Vietnam, the government they were supposed to defend, and why the other side almost always won.

Part 4, "No Light in the Tunnel," chronicles the darkest days of the war for the United States. The Tet Offensive, the Cambodian invasion, and the Watergate scandal were all part of the misery. The Vietnamese died by the thousands. The Americans became a bitter, divided people.

Part 5, "Defeat and Renewal," accents the lessons learned from this endless war. From Congress to Hollywood, everyone had something to say about Vietnam's legacies. Unfortunately, much of what was said continued the divisions and emotions that characterized the war years themselves. Time tempered the debate. By the beginning of the twenty-first century, the newly reestablished U.S. Embassy in Vietnam was doing its best to heal old wounds.

Extras

You'll find a number of sidebars throughout this book. They're meant to give you, as longtime WGN Radio commentator Paul Harvey used to say, "the rest of the story." In short, they include some interesting tidbits and facts relevant to the Vietnam tale.

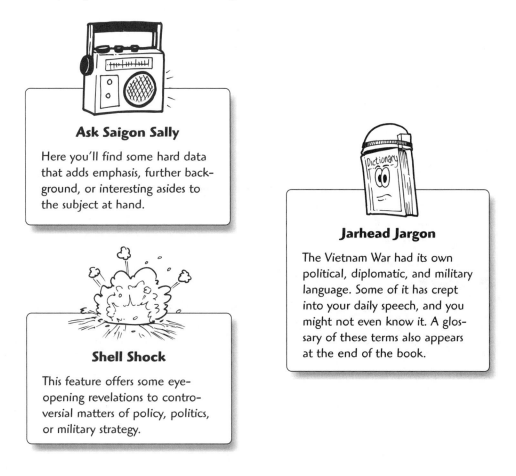

Ask Saigon Sally

Here you'll find some hard data that adds emphasis, further background, or interesting asides to the subject at hand.

Jarhead Jargon

The Vietnam War had its own political, diplomatic, and military language. Some of it has crept into your daily speech, and you might not even know it. A glossary of these terms also appears at the end of the book.

Shell Shock

This feature offers some eye-opening revelations to controversial matters of policy, politics, or military strategy.

Tales from the Front

This sidebar contains interesting war lore, data on military operations, and bios of combatants.

Acknowledgments

I would like to thank author Alan Axelrod for introducing me to *The Complete Idiot's Guide* series. Even more thanks goes to Randy Ladenheim-Gil and her editorial team for "guiding" me through the *Guide* work. But the super thanks goes to the "Executive Assistant," my wife Patsy, for hunting down photos, offering solid advice, and putting up with yet another book project.

Special Thanks to the Technical Editor

The Complete Idiot's Guide to Vietnam was reviewed by an expert who double-checked the accuracy of what you'll learn here, to help us ensure that this book gives you everything you need to know about the Vietnam War. Special thanks are extended to Dr. James Weland.

Dr. Weland is professor of history at Bentley College in Waltham, Massachusetts, where he teaches courses on modern China, Japan, and Vietnam. He is a retired Air Force intelligence officer who spent eight years in East and Southeast Asia, including tours to Vietnam in 1964, 1965, and 1968.

Trademarks

All terms mentioned in this book that are known to be or are suspected of being trademarks or service marks have been appropriately capitalized. Alpha Books and Macmillan USA, Inc., cannot attest to the accuracy of this information. Use of a term in this book should not be regarded as affecting the validity of any trademark or service mark.

Part 1

The Not-So-Good War

Who was Ho Chi Minh and what did he want? The French in Vietnam asked this question quite a few times, and never cared much for the answers. The Americans were destined to do the same thing.

Ho could sound like Thomas Jefferson on Tuesday and Joseph Stalin on Wednesday. A communist, nationalist, opportunist, and die-hard revolutionary, Ho Chi Minh was a complicated guy. But to the leaders of the French Empire, he was simply the opposition. He and his freedom fighter friends had to go. This was not an easy task.

Neither the French nor the American governments spent much time studying up on things Vietnamese. Until their soldiers started coming home as the honored dead, they barely noticed tiny Vietnam. While the French fought their losing battle to hold on to their abused, nineteenth-century colony, the Americans decided to champion their anticommunist cause in Southeast Asia. It was a deadly decision.

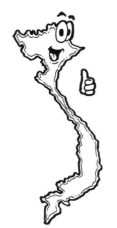
Discovering Vietnam

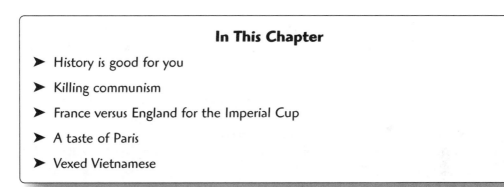

In This Chapter

➤ History is good for you

➤ Killing communism

➤ France versus England for the Imperial Cup

➤ A taste of Paris

➤ Vexed Vietnamese

History hurts. It's the study of dead people and old stuff, a university student once told me, and it offers little relevance to today's fast-paced world. I beg to differ. True, what our forebears did or did not do can seem downright mystifying. And yes, the past can even appear rather alien. People acted so differently back then. But this does not mean history is irrelevant, and the Vietnam War is an especially large case in point.

In today's America, the political leadership owes its very interest in politics to the Vietnam War. Most of our politicians fought in it, protested it, or otherwise avoided it. To these aging baby boomers, Vietnam is not a footnote in a history book. "May it never happen again" tends to be their motto, and modern U.S. foreign and domestic policies trace their roots to the Vietnam debates of the 1960s and early 1970s. Understanding yesterday's Vietnam War means understanding present-day America. And knowledge never hurts.

Why Vietnam?

Since April 1975 and the end of the Vietnam War, most Americans have wondered whether the conflict was necessary. In hindsight, this 30-years-long bloodbath appears terribly sad and unfortunate. But 50 years ago, during the strident days of the Cold War, the confrontation between capitalism (represented by the United States) and communism (represented by the Soviet Union) was a simple fact of life. Like baseball, Chevys, and apple pie, the Cold War, most believed, was here to stay. Winning it was America's destiny. But was Vietnam the place to lead this crusade?

Tales from the Front

Of the 58,000 names carved on the Vietnam War Memorial Wall in Washington, D.C., only one belongs to an Army Nurse. First Lieutenant Sharon Lane was killed in hostile action while on duty at the 312th Evacuation Hospital in Chu Lai on June 8, 1969. She was one of eight American women killed in Vietnam. During 1993, Vietnam-era nurses were honored for their service when a special Vietnam Women's Memorial was dedicated in their memory near the larger Vietnam Memorial Wall in Washington, D.C. The memorial depicts three nurses and a wounded soldier. Thanks to strange compilation methods, politics, and other reasons, the estimates vary over how many women served in Vietnam. The range is 7,000 to 21,000.

Hit by typhoons, soaked by monsoons, and including some of the poorest communities on earth, Vietnam was a French colony from the 1880s to 1954. Because the leader of the anti-French resistance in the late 1940s and early 1950s, Ho Chi Minh, accepted limited military assistance from both Soviet and communist Chinese sources, Washington regarded him as nothing less than a communist agitator, puppet, and all-around nasty guy.

In 1954, the American secretary of state, John Foster Dulles, made it quite clear that if a foreign leader like Ho was not 100 percent behind U.S. policy, he was 100 percent against it. In Dulles's view, and in general U.S. Cold War policy-making, no one could accept even token assistance from a communist and be regarded as an American friend. Interestingly, although Ho had violated this golden rule, he never formally became a Soviet or Chinese ally either. Playing the *nonalignment* game was a popular sport for Ho.

Roughly the size of the state of Delaware, but with tropical weather, Vietnam's geography ranges from endless rice fields separated by dikes in the north to high mountains in its center to a swampy river delta in its far south. In short, it was a lousy location to fight a war over Cold War commitments. Be it intelligence agents, military advisors, or millions of troops, six American presidents (Truman, Eisenhower, Kennedy, Johnson, Nixon, and Ford) would place U.S. government personnel in harm's way there.

After the casualty figures began to roll in, as early as the mid-1940s, it became difficult to extract America's Cold Warriors from Vietnam without achieving the goal of crushing communism. But who were the communists? Were they just Ho Chi Minh supporters? Washington had a hard time distinguishing between the good guys and the bad guys over there.

Buddhist activists, French-influenced reformers, Vietnamese nationalists, and ambitious generals and colonels, as well as socialists and humanitarians of all shapes and sizes, clouded America's understanding of Vietnamese politics. Rather than try to puzzle it out, it was better and easier to support an anticommunist strongman within the country—one who may or may not have been a supporter of democracy, but who definitely knew how to oppose communism. In those expedient days of the Cold War, all that mattered to both the Democratic and Republican occupants of the White House was the strength and competence of anticommunism in Vietnam. The potential for a democratic state there would be something to figure out after the communists were beaten.

The U.S. government marched into Vietnam because it feared the growth of communism in a region next door to communist China. Years of sometimes rabid anticommunist rhetoric from American political leaders suggested that something had to be done. Besides, the Washington politicos believed, marching into tiny Vietnam was no big deal anyway.

After World War II, the U.S. dollar dominated global business, the American military seemed unassailable, and like never before in their

Jarhead Jargon

Championed in the early 1950s by Gamal Abdel Nasser, leader of the first post-British colonial government in Egypt, the term **nonalignment** was invented to describe a newly independent government that determined its own destiny and thumbed its nose at both Washington and Moscow in the Cold War.

Ask Saigon Sally

During the late 1940s, the Truman Doctrine was born. Championed by the U.S. government all the way to the 1990s, this policy supported anticommunist regimes around the word. Being democratic was not a prerequisite for that support.

history, most Yanks believed their country had a duty to influence international events. Beating back a communist challenge in a faraway Southeast Asian nation would be easy, they said, and total victory in the Cold War loomed on the horizon. They were wrong.

Saigon Is Not a Detroit Suburb

In 1952, during the U.S. presidential campaign between Democrat Adlai Stevenson and Republican Dwight Eisenhower, a terrorist bomb was exploded in a crowded hotel restaurant in downtown Saigon in southern Vietnam. The hotel was frequented by French military officers, American journalists, and other Westerners, making it an obvious target for Vietnamese freedom fighters. The soon-to-be secretary of state, John Foster Dulles, was asked by CBS News about his reaction to the bombing in Saigon. He answered that he wasn't sure where that town was, and joked that it could be a suburb of Detroit. Oops.

America's so-called foreign policy experts of the early 1950s knew little about Ho Chi Minh's war for independence. Quite simply, Vietnam had never been a priority concern for U.S. diplomats. In a few short years, Washington's ignorance of the place would seem inexcusable to American voters wondering how their country had gotten into the Vietnam mess. Vietnam had always been a matter of concern for the French government, it seemed, and even fewer Americans knew how the French had gotten there. The story was not a pleasant one.

Shell Shock

In 1919, President Woodrow Wilson was called before the Senate Foreign Relations Committee to explain why the United States was readying for war with Japan over a place called Yap (a small island in the Western Pacific). Although Wilson admitted that he could never find Yap on a map, he explained that whenever and wherever U.S. interests were in peril, the American government must respond with force. Years later, the White House explained its Vietnam interests in the same way.

A Short History of French Rule

France's involvement in Vietnam stretched over the centuries. French and even Portuguese Catholic missionaries had made the first foreign inroads in Vietnam in the 1620s. A number of trade missions followed, and French forces were sometimes dispatched to defend them, but this limited involvement had little impact on the big picture of French foreign policy. That changed after the Franco-Prussian War of 1870.

Chancellor Otto von Bismarck's fast, furious, and successful invasion of France even led to Germany's first kaiser, Wilhelm I, being crowned ruler of all the German principalities, in Versailles, France. This was a terrible insult to French patriots, and the postwar French government, or Third Republic, vowed revenge. Low on cash, but high on nationalism, Third Republic leaders looked beyond Europe to restore the pride and glory lost in the Franco-Prussian War.

The Third Republic's founding fathers even boasted that the French franc would be the choice of world business by 1900, and that a new French empire would be the envy of all by that same time as well. It was quite a dream, if you were a French imperialist and patriot.

In the early 1880s, after years of scandal and struggle, France made its most dramatic move to carve up planet Earth in the name of pride and glory. Nicknamed "Tonkin Ferry" by the French press, Prime Minister Jules Ferry established a protectorate over northern Vietnam (Tonkin), and invaded central Vietnam (Annam). His successful military campaign in Annam permitted him to link longstanding French trade and Catholic interests in southern Vietnam (Cochin China) with the rest of the country.

Ask Saigon Sally

Arriving in 1627, Alexandre de Rhodes, a Jesuit priest, established the first Catholic mission in Vietnam. He converted thousands to Catholicism in northern Vietnam alone.

Meanwhile, the neighboring countries of Laos and Cambodia bowed to the new era of French dominance, and in 1887 the French government officially dubbed its new Southeast Asian empire of Vietnam, Laos, and Cambodia the French Union. To "Tonkin Ferry," creating the French Union was the modern, patriotic equivalent of Napoléon I's victories in Europe earlier in the century. France was back.

Beyond the emotionalism of pride and glory, the French Union had a certain geopolitical significance. To Third Republic leaders, the new Southeast Asian empire was a counterweight to English colonization interests in the region. The French politicians talked the talk about beating the Brits in India, which Britain had colonized, and saber rattling always won them votes at home, but deliberately triggering a world war was never truly in their interest.

The First Cold War

During the late 19th century, a different cold war existed than the one that developed 50 years later, but it was a cold war just the same. It remained defined in terms of French and British competition for colonies. One was never enough. The nation with the most colonies won this deadly game, and the French never forgot that the last play was supposed be made by the turn of the century. The French remained committed to the 1900 deadline for their triumph over Great Britain in the colonial race. Time was always running out, and Vietnam remained a pawn in this bigger battle to become king of the hill.

Jarhead Jargon

The French often referred to Vietnamese political leaders as mandarins. Although the French saw nothing wrong with the label, the Vietnamese did. **Mandarin** refers to one of the nine ranks of high officialdom in old imperial China, and the Vietnamese, once colonized by China, wanted nothing to do with Chinese life, politics, and labels.

Ask Saigon Sally

In 1879, upon his return to the United States from an Asian/Pacific tour, ex-president Ulysses S. Grant told a friend in Congress that Vietnam was conveniently close to larger American trade interests in China, but that it would be a difficult place for "Americans to fight in" if the locals challenged them.

The greatest prize in France's colony-versus-colony contest with England was originally supposed to be China, and not little Vietnam. Since the 1840s and their defeat of the Chinese in the Opium Wars, England had had an on-site advantage to capture the China trade thanks to its Hong Kong colony. Vietnam, the French decided, could be France's Hong Kong. It shared a common border with China, and the French colonial governments were well aware of that significance.

A close race for the allegiance of China was seen as inevitable in Paris. Could France woo the Chinese into the French Union from Vietnamese *mandarins,* and do it before the British made a move? For the plotters and schemers who ran late nineteenth-century France, this was the stuff that dreams were made of. Just as the British used Hong Kong for their base to penetrate the rest of China, Vietnam would be the staging area for the French move into China. But reality got in the way of the dream. They also thought that Vietnam's rivers might serve as navigable gateways into China. They were mistaken.

Whereas the late nineteenth century returned pride and honor to France, the twentieth century promised the China trade and big, big money. They had to get the big money from somewhere. Vietnam, the French discovered, was worthless. No coal, no oil, no profit. There was nothing there, in terms of natural resources, to help them fuel their industrial revolution at home, and colonies were supposed to enrich the mother country.

More cash went into Vietnam than came out. In fact, there would still be no investment potential in Vietnam when the Americans arrived in the 1950s. Be it in the 1950s or the 1890s, Vietnam would always be about pride, honor, and ideology for the foreigners involved there. The profit motive was nonexistent.

Parlez-vous Français?

In 1898, French forces and British forces met face to face and armed to the teeth at the tiny oasis of Fashoda in the Sudan of East Africa. For a moment, it looked like the great war between France and England had finally arrived; however, cooler heads in London and Paris prevailed. This particular World War I was avoided. While domestic political scandals rocked France's Third Republic, focusing the nation's attention away from foreign adventurism, new colonial players entered the game.

The United States, Japan, and even Russia now wanted their own shot at an empire, particularly in the available real estate of the Asian-Pacific region. The British, embroiled in a bloody no-win war against the Boers of South Africa, seemed unable to achieve one of their own colonial dreams, to dominate all of eastern Africa on the north-to-south axis from "Cairo to Capetown." The times were truly changing and the French dreams of dominance were over, thanks to their own domestic political squabbles, fiscal mismanagement, and lack of military reform. Besides, they learned quickly, it was tough enough just administering little Vietnam. Imagine trying to administer China!

In the new, twentieth-century Vietnam, the French had to accept certain facts. Vietnam was not a stepping stone to grander dreams and policies. It was the end of the road. How to administer the colony properly now became a more important question than ever before. Sadly, proper rule came to mean oppression and misery for the Vietnamese.

Given economic crises at home, a national debate over the use of French military power, and the fact that Vietnam was not making them a dime anyway, the French government scaled back its Pacific ambitions. Its most consistent policy toward its Vietnam colony by 1900 was cutting the colonial governor's budget. With the promise of endless support from Paris long gone, colonial officials in Vietnam went about the mundane business of trying to run a poor place with an inadequate budget.

French law replaced Vietnamese law. French replaced Vietnamese as the country's official language. Buddhist pagodas were torn down to make room for Catholic churches, even though more than 90 percent of the population recognized Buddhism as their religion. Meanwhile, many peasants in agrarian Vietnam lost their land due to high colonial taxes.

By the 1930s, only 9 percent of the population in Tonkin, for instance, owned most of the cultivated land. In Saigon, the south's biggest city, French architects re-created Paris street scenes to remind them of home, and downtown curfews were sometimes maintained against the Vietnamese so they would not disturb a Frenchman's reverie. In the countryside, big plantations of freshly imported rubber trees owned by Frenchmen dotted the landscape, and the Vietnamese became a second-class workforce from north to south.

Shell Shock

The French in Vietnam encouraged collaboration by what they called indigenous colonists. The latter was a fancy way to describe the Vietnamese who willingly assisted the colonial regime and made money off of fellow Vietnamese in the process.

Ask Saigon Sally

Buddhism divided Vietnam. Northerners largely recognized the progressive, Chinese-influenced Mahayana Buddhism. Southerners welcomed the very conservative, India-influenced Theravada Buddhism.

Two Vietnams evolved under French rule. A more rural, relaxed economy developed in the south, and French colonial administrators, hoping for some sort of financial success, saw greater money-making potential there than in the north. The southern population was less dense, landholdings were spread out, and Saigon city managers even tried to create an industrial-based economy complete with a thriving middle class and working-class jobs galore.

In the north, the rice-farming economy struggled more than it thrived. Cities like Hanoi or Haiphong were heavily populated, but were not examples of twentieth-century urban life on the Western scale. Jobs and land were scarce, and both northerners and southerners predicted an orgy of violence against the French someday.

Vietnam for the Vietnamese

"Moral victories are for losers," or so said legendary Green Bay Packers coach Vince Lombardi. His marvelously defiant expression on behalf of his small-town team could be easily applied to Vietnamese history. The Vietnamese have been especially proud of their fearless reputation for taking on much bigger, more threatening foes and always emerging triumphant. Total victory was their only goal, and their history has included a pantheon of amazing successes in the face of impossible odds. Compromise, calling it a draw, and negotiated deals were never part of the Vietnamese political vocabulary.

Ask Saigon Sally

In the effort to convince the Vietnamese that resistance against French rule was useless and foolish, the colonial government stationed French forces even in the most remote regions and countryside of the colony.

The Vietnamese had endured Chinese invasions earlier in their history and prevailed. Now the French were next, and they would never know what hit them. Considering the Vietnamese to be racially inferior, the French did not study Vietnamese history and they knew little about Vietnam's previous triumph over China. Like the Chinese before them, the French had little tolerance for Vietnamese protests against their rule. Retaliation against the Vietnamese was swift and cruel, and the real bloodbath began.

In 1930, more than 5,500 peasants from Nghe An, a central Vietnam province and the country's poorest, descended on the provincial capital of Vinh. They wanted an end to unfair taxes and rents, and they demanded a dramatic new land redistribution policy.

The French responded with an air strike, killing hundreds of the demonstrators. They even opened fire on the relatives of the dead who arrived on the scene. A ruthless display of power, the French believed, was needed to demonstrate their superior position in Vietnam. The locals would never dare demonstrate against them again—or so they hoped.

Facing a full-scale revolt, and in the middle of a major economic crisis at home (the Great Depression), the French rounded up their real and imagined opponents across Vietnam. The worst that could happen to a suspected and captured anti-French activist was a sentence to the prison on Con Son Island. The length of sentence rarely mattered there, for few left the island alive.

Shell Shock

Although the Vietnamese were quick to denounce French oppression, they were not immune from terror tactics themselves. After the French defeat, the new South Vietnamese government reopened the old French-run tiger cages on Con Son island in order to both jail and terrorize their own political rivals.

Tales from the Front

In 1947, a young American diplomat in Vietnam named William Sullivan ran into a Viet Minh combat unit by accident. Its leader, also an aspiring diplomat, was Tran Van Dinh. The latter spared Sullivan's life. Fifteen years later, Sullivan was the U.S. Ambassador to Laos and one of the State Department's top experts on Southeast Asian politics. Tran Van Dinh moved to the United States and became a leading activist on behalf of democratic civil rights/civil liberties in South Vietnam.

It was on Con Son where the "tiger cages" were used. Within small, cramped, stifling cages, prisoners were forced to stoop, squat, and survive in their own filth. The horror of the place, the French reasoned, would make a potential anti-French agitator elsewhere in Vietnam think twice about resistance activities. In fact, the infamous tiger cages might have *won* more Vietnamese to the anti-French cause than anything else. But turning that cause into an effective, winning resistance movement required disciplined organization and leadership. It would not be an easy task.

Just Shoot Me

This was just the beginning for Ho Chi Minh. His day would come in the 1940s, and he was the first anti-French activist to learn from the mistakes of his predecessors. The most obvious, glaring mistake had been the arrogance and elitism of the early twentieth-century resistance leaders. They ignored the peasant majority, stayed near big cities, and seemed more influenced by the political tactics of the French or Chinese than by those of the Vietnamese.

Ho and his closest colleagues realized that foreign domination could never be lifted if the majority of their countrymen believed a resistance movement was irrelevant to them. Recognizing this simple fact was the first step to success. But who was this Ho Chi Minh, and why was he a winner? The French, the Japanese, and the Americans would find out soon enough.

The Least You Need to Know

➤ The impact of the Vietnam War lives on in today's U.S. political community.

➤ Just as Vietnam was a pawn within the anticommunist agenda of the United States, Vietnam was a pawn in the late nineteenth-century colonial race between Britain and France.

➤ Two Vietnams began to emerge under French rule.

➤ The French colonial regime in Vietnam was oppressive.

➤ Early anticolonial demonstrations in Vietnam were not tolerated by the French.

Chapter 2

Ho, Ho, Ho Chi Minh

In This Chapter

➤ Ho who?

➤ "Ism" politics

➤ From Hong Kong with love

➤ Ho, Hoover, and Franklin D.

Ho Chi Minh remains one of the more complex, confusing, and fascinating politicians of the last century. Obsessed with creating a George Washington–like image for himself early in the war of liberation against the French, Ho was particularly successful in myth-making, folklore, and misinformation. For years, Western political leaders and even historians were never sure how old he was, what his background was, and what his political agenda was. Who was the real Ho Chi Minh?

Leftists said Ho was a champion of anticolonial causes and, because of that "fact," deserved respect, support, and even devotion. Right-wingers said he was an annoying troublemaker and die-hard communist who deserved nothing less than total defeat. Meanwhile, moderates were not sure how to react to him.

Was Ho Chi Minh a doctrinaire communist? To this day, the answer depends upon whom you read, what film documentary you view, or what side you take in the continuing debate over the legacy of the Vietnam War.

A George Washington for Vietnam

It would be one of history's grand ironies that a man who once quoted Thomas Jefferson in the 1940s Vietnamese Declaration of Independence would later be the mastermind of a bloody crusade against the "tyranny" of the United States. Born Nguyen Tat Thanh, and also known as Nguyen Ai Quoc, Ho would become Vietnam's most beloved national leader. Brilliant, dedicated, and a political junkie by the time he was in his teens, Ho left Vietnam as a seaman in 1911. He would not return home for more than 30 years.

There are few candid shots of Ho Chi Minh. Most surviving photographs are formal, heroic, and posed. This one was taken in the late 1940s.

National Archives Still Pictures Unit, College Park, Maryland.

During his years of wandering, Ho once insisted, he enrolled (illegally) in some of the world's finest institutions of higher learning, including New York's Columbia University. According to this tale, Ho studied American politics and democracy under the great Constitutional historian and peace activist Dr. James T. Shotwell. Some said that he even mastered the English language with a New York City accent. Most of these stories of Ho, the transplanted and gifted political intellectual, were spread during the 1940s when he was trying to win allied recognition for his fight against the brief Japanese occupation of his country.

In reality, Ho's political mentor was not Thomas Jefferson. It wasn't Karl Marx either. Those Western figures had little relevance to the Vietnamese. Ho's first political hero was Phan Boi Chau, the founding father of the modern Vietnamese nationalist movement.

The Influence of Phan Boi Chau

To Phan Boi Chau, Vietnamese independence from the French could never be won on Vietnamese terms alone. The country was too poor and struggling to prevail. Instead, Vietnam needed to create an intellectual and political vanguard. It needed Western technology and economic investment. It needed to create the proper environment to challenge the French on their terms and win. Ho would grow up to be the type of political leader that Phan Boi Chau had once dreamed about.

Phan Boi Chau rejected the existing monarchy of Vietnam and all of its political leaders who fraternized with the French. Over time, if Vietnam moved in his desired direction, Phan expected great success. In 1904, he founded the Modernization Society to begin the long march to independence. Men, women, and even different religious and political groups were always welcomed in it.

Referring to the French as "The Invaders," Phan expected his Society to represent national interests. He downplayed wild-eyed revolutionary rhetoric. As a nation of farmers, Vietnam was a conservative place. At the least, they could all agree that the foreign presence was bad, and that it had to go.

The Modernization Society represented a mountain of contradiction, and Ho would follow this example, too. For instance, Phan Boi Chau talked of "Vietnam for the Vietnamese," but he sought foreign assistance to get the job done quicker. At first he turned to Japan (which was beginning to depict itself as a potential "liberator" of Asian-Pacific peoples) and was rejected. Then he turned to Sun Yat-sen's Revolutionary Party in China. Although China had been a hated traditional enemy to Vietnam, the Revolutionary Party had overthrown the aged Manchu dynasty in 1911 and dreamed of a new democratic republic for China. But Japan had entered the colonial race itself at this time.

Ask Saigon Sally

Founded by the Indochinese Communist Party in 1941, the Viet Nam Doc Lap Dong Minh Hoi (or Vietminh Organization) dedicated itself to the principles of independence once outlined by the Modernization Society.

Phan Boi Chau even asked disaffected supporters of the Vietnamese monarchy to speak on his behalf to the upper-class Vietnamese who were suspicious of his movement. These newcomers offered a certain high and mighty profile to the Modernization Society, but this annoyed many of the people Chau hoped to win to his cause. Decades later, Ho Chi Minh engaged in the same kind of nonalignment policy-making.

A Legend Begins

Whereas much of the legend of George Washington, the president who could never tell a lie, was created after his death, Ho's legend of invincible, saintly, Uncle Ho leadership

Shell Shock

In 1925, after years of failing to organize the Vietnamese, Phan Boi Chau was arrested by the French when he was living in exile in China. Found guilty of sedition, he lived under house arrest in the old Vietnamese imperial capital of Hue until his death in 1940.

Ask Saigon Sally

According to Vietnamese myth-makers, Ho Chi Minh influenced world events from the moment he first arrived in France in 1918. Indeed, many of the tall tales, portrayed as history, in the Vietnamese accounts of the life of Ho Chi Minh, appeared in one book, Truong Chinh's *President Ho Chi Minh: Beloved Leader of the Vietnamese People.* This interesting mix of propaganda and history confused historians and others for years.

was created during his lifetime. Keeping his own past a shadowy mystery was part of the process, for the Vietnamese independence movement, in Ho's view, had always lacked powerful, unassailable leadership. Through his personal guidance, the long dream of freedom would come true. If it meant begging, borrowing, and robbing various political ideologies to accomplish this, then Ho would do it.

Nationalism, Communism, Opportunism

Understanding Ho Chi Minh is especially important to understanding the Vietnam War. What do historians truly know about Ho Chi Minh and the early years? Although sketchy, there is a real Ho Chi Minh who emerges from all the propaganda and political folklore.

The Real Ho Chi Minh

We know Ho worked as a cook's assistant on a French steamship after he left Saigon in 1911. We know he jumped ship in the United States, worked in Boston and New York, and even wandered the U.S. South. It was there that he learned the difference between the promise of democracy and a working democracy. American democracy, he discovered, didn't work very well for African Americans. In a fit of disgust, he would later write about this unfortunate contradiction.

When World War I began in 1914, Ho headed to London, and, apparently, it was there that he first studied the works of communist guru Karl Marx. When World War I ended, he moved into the heart of enemy territory for a Vietnamese nationalist—downtown Paris, France. It was here that he changed his name to the outrageous-sounding Nguyen Ai Quoc (Nguyen the Patriot).

By late 1919, Ho was a member of the Parti Socialiste de France (PSF), and he said that he loved the Parti's boundless energy to champion the cause of workers everywhere. The love affair ended quickly. Ho discovered that the PSF's commitment to workers was only to workers in France, and its foreign policy was as procolonial as most French conservatives. In 1920, Ho attended what would soon be a legendary event for European leftists, the creation of the French Communist Party in Tours.

At first Ho did not understand the appeal of the successful leader of the 1917 Russian Revolution, Vladimir I. Lenin. The latter seemed most interested in the troubles of urban workers, the miseries of Russian poverty, and his own career. But then Ho read Lenin's *Theses on the National and Colonial Questions*. It was in this study that Lenin linked the struggle of European workers to the plight of Asian colonials.

According to Lenin, misery was misery, and an auto worker in Paris had more in common with a rice farmer in Vietnam than he realized. Together, they could change the world forever, and the new French communists endorsed the notion. This was Ho's kind of party.

Ho and Lenin

After writing a series of prodecolonization articles in obscure Paris-published newspapers, Ho saw himself as Lenin's chief spokesperson on behalf of colonized Asia. Few might have read his work in Paris, but he did not go unnoticed by Lenin's regime. By 1923, he was studying Marxism, and was sponsored by the Soviet government in Moscow. Yet these were confusing days for the young Ho. Few Soviet officials, he learned, really supported Lenin's decolonization message, and even fewer had any intention of aligning colonists and European workers for a grand revolutionary cause.

Whether he was suffering from ideological fallout or not, Ho welcomed the chance to help set up a pro-Soviet organization in southern China. It was the closest to home he had been in years, and in 1924 he was ready to tap into the growing anticolonial sentiment of the region. Far away from the Soviet Union, Ho could make up his communism as he went along and the locals would not know the difference.

But how long could Ho represent a government that, in fact, did not exist? If he hoped to return home as something of the conquering hero, he had to move fast. The nearby French authorities in Vietnam already had a price on his head, and in 1924, when one of his more radical colleagues, Pham Hong Thai, attempted—without Ho's endorsement—to kill the French colonial governor, things got worse for Ho and his friends.

Pham Hong Thai was killed by the French police, and although Ho eulogized the failed assassin as a great patriot and hero, it was obvious that something better than hit-and-run attacks on French officials was required. But what?

The RYL

On the organizational front, Ho formed the Revolutionary Youth League, or RYL. The RYL was designed to spread Ho's revolutionary message from China to Vietnam itself, and it represented something of the homecoming for the struggling Ho Chi Minh. The RYL looked communist and acted communist, but rarely talked communist. The RYL insisted that the average Vietnamese was not yet ready to accept his revolutionary responsibility. The French had deliberately kept him in the dark, and he couldn't have cared less about the ambitions of a communist ideologue in Russia or China.

Thanks to its discipline and Ho's leadership, the RYL hoped to change things sooner rather than later. It became the first truly working example of organized resistance to the French in Vietnam. Yet it broke apart in 1929. The RYL's strength had been in northern Vietnam, and especially in Ho's home province, alone. Some RYL members were by-the-book communists, and they argued over who was more loyal to the cause than others in their group. A few were ready to march away from communist influence entirely, while another faction thought communism was okay as long as the Vietnamese defined their own unique brand of it.

Ho told each faction what it wanted to hear, and the result was chaos and confusion. As Vietnam entered the 1930s, it seemed like Ho Chi Minh and his anti-French colleagues were their own worst enemies. Nevertheless, Ho still promised an *"inevitable French defeat."*

Jarhead Jargon

In his pamphlet *The Revolutionary Path*, authored in the mid-1920s, Ho Chi Minh made predictions, too. At a time when French power seemed invincible, Ho predicted an **"inevitable French defeat."** He asked for support and patience from the colonized Vietnamese.

Shell Shock

Contrary to public image, Ho did not act alone. Born in central Vietnam in 1906, Pham Van Dong would be a lifelong associate of Ho Chi Minh. He helped coordinate the anti-French Revolutionary Youth League in the 1920s, and he remained a master organizer for Ho throughout the wars against the French, the Japanese, and the Americans.

Ho's Hong Kong Honeymoon and Hoover's Depression

The RYL broke apart into squabbling, divided factions, and Ho's faction still claimed ideological leadership. It could not claim dominance, however, and Ho was forced to flee again. Ho traveled to Siam (today's Thailand) to start a new version of the RYL, but the locals questioned his motives, objectives, and his connections to any larger authority. These were not Ho's best days.

In 1930, the struggling Ho packed up for Hong Kong. Housing one of the largest populations of Vietnamese refugees and immigrants in the world, Hong Kong was an excellent location in which to make a grand statement against the evils of French colonialism. First of all, the British in charge of Hong Kong had no problem with a Vietnamese radical belittling the French. The Crown Colony of Hong Kong had long enjoyed a spirited competition with nearby French Vietnam. The governor generals of Britain's far-flung colony usually regarded Vietnam as an example of French colonial failure, and the flow of Vietnamese to Hong Kong seemed to prove the point. It was in this atmosphere that Ho authored what would soon be called his Hong Kong Platform.

The Hong Kong Platform

According to later Vietnamese accounts, Ho's self-proclaimed platform was the equivalent of America's Declaration of Independence, Constitution, and Emancipation Proclamation rolled into one. That legend would serve Ho well in the years to come, especially in the 1940s effort to appeal to the Americans. In reality, Ho's Hong Kong Platform was a rehash of Moscow-generated propaganda and his own interpretation of anticolonial communism.

Specifically, Ho called for the creation of a new Vietnam-based party of liberation that would be run by a coalition of common workers, common farmers, middle-class folks, and even sympathetic businessmen and wealthy industrialists. In short, anyone who opposed the status quo of French rule was welcome in Ho's coalition.

The Platform's rhetoric was communist-like in tenor and tone, but Ho's coalition could never be truly communist if it included the middle class and wealthy. Its membership suggested more of the democratic mission than the communist one, but Ho did not describe it that way in the early 1930s. Holding this diverse group of folks together required a certain no-nonsense leadership, and, of course, Ho positioned himself to be that leader. He described the conference that produced the Hong Kong Platform as the greatest gathering of Vietnamese patriots in history.

Ho had high hopes for this new coalition. First of all, he hoped the Soviet government would finally respect his efforts to marry the anticolonial movement to the communist movement. That never happened. Second, he hoped all those who questioned his objectives, such as the small Vietnamese middle class, would welcome their own valuable role in the liberation campaign. That

Ask Saigon Sally

In early 1921, the incoming secretary of state in the just-elected Warren Harding administration, Charles Evans Hughes, was asked by the press about the health of the post–World War I French empire. It was okay to ignore the French and their imperialist struggles, he said, and the French empire must never become an American concern.

never happened, either. Third, Ho hoped the world press would now begin a discussion of Vietnam's problems, leading to sympathetic support from countries such as the United States. But the Western press rarely covered Vietnam matters, and few Americans cared about French colonial troubles.

Ho always kept his eye on world developments, the United States particularly, and watched for any political trend that could positively influence his cause. The early 1930s provided plenty for Ho to watch, and much of the action was provided by Washington, D.C. Would America ever develop an interest in the plight of Vietnam?

The American Home Front

In the early 1930s, Americans had bigger fish to fry. The Great Depression influenced everything, including U.S. foreign policy. With more than one-quarter of the workforce out of work, international trade at a standstill, and U.S. industry simply trying to survive the worst economic crisis in 100 years, Americans had little time to consider the struggles of Vietnamese colonials. Nevertheless, their president, Herbert Hoover, talked a lot about Asia, and many wondered whether that might lead to a new era of U.S. involvement in Asian/Pacific matters.

Shell Shock

Although it took nine years, the Vietnamese government published *The Complete Works of Ho Chi Minh* in 1989. Despite the fact that these writings fill 10 large volumes, Ho Chi Minh, the man, the leader, the mover-and-shaker, remains an elusive story. Even in death, the myth and mystery surrounding Ho Chi Minh remains an important part of his legacy.

Although on a much smaller scale in comparison to Ho, there were certain myths and legends associated with Herbert Hoover. One of them involved his claim to be the country's top expert on China and the Asian mainland. This was not the case, but it enhanced his image of the brilliant president. The claim was first made during his 1928 race for the presidency, and not even his Democratic opponent, Al Smith, the governor of New York, bothered to challenge him on it.

Inaccurately predicting a continued boom for the "Roaring Twenties" economy, Hoover, a proud Republican conservative, promised to push U.S. business away from Europe and toward the Asian mainland. Because of his years in the engineering business in China, Hoover claimed to know what Asia wanted, and he offered some interesting, although cryptic, comments about the struggling European empires there.

To much of the Asian/Pacific world, Washington's do-nothingism over Japanese aggression said an awful lot about U.S. foreign policy. America had emerged from World War I a dominant world power, but both its government and its people were not sure what that meant. During the 1931 Japanese invasion of Manchuria, the Asian/Pacific region's biggest crisis since World War I, the Hoover administration scolded Tokyo, refused to recognize Japanese colonial policy, and did little else.

To Ho Chi Minh and other decolonization activists across Asia, the U.S. inaction meant several things: that it had bowed out of Asian/Pacific responsibilities; that Hoover's interest in things Asian had little meaning; and that the decolonization cause in Asia might be, as it always had been, a matter for Asians to resolve in Asia. Meanwhile, Ho's difficult life got more difficult.

The Arrest of a Radical

At the time of the Manchurian crisis, the British government in Hong Kong was under heavy pressure from London, and from strong law-and-order advocates in the colony, to eliminate radicalism, dissent, and political agitation in the name of presenting a united front against Japanese aggression. Ho was arrested for radical activities.

Ho's maverick, independent style of communism finally came under heavy, merciless attack by the Soviet government, too, and his Hong Kong support group went the route of the RYL. It broke up into squabbling, angry factions. According to Moscow, Ho was not a good communist, and they had a point. But Ho endured.

Franklin Roosevelt—A Ho Chi Minh for America?

While a lonely, depressed Ho Chi Minh tried to get his act together following his release from a Hong Kong jail, Americans fell in love with the always-together Franklin Roosevelt. Although confined to a wheelchair, Roosevelt told the voters that he had triumphed over his affliction. Under his leadership, the entire nation, he promised, would triumph over its affliction of the Great Depression. And he intended to do things his way, even though his country remained enthralled by *isolationist* achievements like the *Kellogg-Briand Pact.*

Jarhead Jargon

The symbol of U.S. retreat from world responsibilities in the 1920s remains the **Kellogg-Briand Pact.** According to this 1928 diplomatic arrangement, the United States and France were to lead the world in the effort to "outlaw war as an instrument of national policy." In other words, war was declared illegal (except in matters of self-defense), and that was impossible to achieve. Within a few short years after its creation, the Pact was signed by Germany's Nazi government, Italy's fascist government, and Japan's militarist government. They were not sincere.

Jarhead Jargon

Isolationism refers to America's post–World War I foreign policy of disarmament, endless peace talks, and general "take care of America first" politics. It was abandoned only after Japan's December 1941 attack on Pearl Harbor.

Like Ho Chi Minh, Roosevelt broke political rules and built his own coalition. His strategy for victory in 1932 involved an appeal to the most suffering, the most struggling, the most forgotten. Again, like a man he never heard of, Ho Chi Minh, Roosevelt didn't care about the rules, and his promises of three "Rs" ("relief, recovery, and reform") resounded across the nation.

Although the two men came from different backgrounds, cultures, and countries, and an easy comparison could never be made, Ho Chi Minh and Franklin Roosevelt were masters of their respective causes. They saw diversity as a plus in the uphill battle for victory, and they were destined to win the adulation of their countrymen before the job was done. Without question, the two were also destined to match wits, but 1933 was not the time. Roosevelt remained leashed by congressional isolationism and Ho still faced a French-administered Vietnam.

Shell Shock

During the 1932 election, Franklin Roosevelt deliberately claimed a certain ignorance about colonial matters in Asia and other foreign affairs issues. He was masking a grand interest in global politics, but that was a liability in this isolationist era election.

As the World Turns

Upon his release from the Hong Kong prison, Ho Chi Minh headed back to Moscow. Because of his political position on colonial freedom, he received a very lukewarm welcome there. The Soviet government no longer practiced what it preached, and his very presence reminded them of that fact. Ho worked at low-level administrative jobs for the Communist party and watched the changing world anticommunist movements now dominated global politics, and to Moscow's Communist party bosses, it was time for expedient policies to defend the nation. Organizers like Ho were needed for the fight.

Ho Chi Minh was now applauded for having attempted to win many different voices to his anticolonial cause. He was asked to go back home and resume his efforts, but Ho remained suspicious of the new, expedient attitude of the Soviet communists. In any event, this new commitment to winning anybody to the general communist cause, and not to ideological purity, began to effect procommunist inroads in Vietnam.

In the very heart of France's "Paris of the Orient," the southern Vietnamese city of Saigon, the local city council elected communist councilmen for the first time. Some of the reasons for this success involved Moscow's new open-door attitude, but most involved the Great Depression: When America's economy sneezed, even French Vietnam caught a cold. The Saigon communists promised a great deal of economic remedies, and voters responded.

In spite of the Saigon success, Ho's suspicions about Moscow's insincerity were proven correct. By 1935, even though anticommunist movements (like Adolf Hitler's Nazis and Benito Mussolini's fascists) were stronger and more threatening than ever, Ho endured another reprimand from Moscow for advancing his own kind of communism. A depressed Ho Chi Minh could only hope for a better day, and world events were soon to deliver it on a silver platter.

The Least You Need to Know

➤ Ho Chi Minh was a new breed of freedom fighter.

➤ Communism was an interpretive and flexible ideology to Ho Chi Minh.

➤ Ho's independence movement was plagued by organizational and ideological rifts.

➤ Ho's success also depended upon world developments; therefore, the position of the American government was important to Vietnam's future.

➤ World tensions did not necessarily make Ho Chi Minh a trusted ally of the Soviet government.

Chapter 3

Uncle Ho Meets Uncle Sam

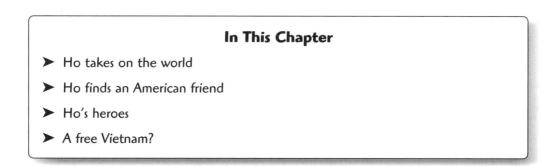

In This Chapter

➤ Ho takes on the world

➤ Ho finds an American friend

➤ Ho's heroes

➤ A free Vietnam?

Ho Chi Minh never knew when to quit. If he had, the histories of his country, Japan, France, and the United States would be very different today. World War II was a great turning point for him and for all of Vietnam. Things would never be the same again.

In the summer of 1940, to the world's surprise, Hitler defeated France in less than six weeks, and Vietnam's sovereignty switched from French colonial protectorate to Japanese-occupied "Co-Prosperity Sphere." A pro-Japanese, pro-Nazi government run by Frenchmen co-existed side-by-side a Japanese occupation army for the next five years. The Allies eventually helped Ho beat back the Japanese, and by the fall of 1945, Ho's dreams had come true. In downtown Hanoi, in northern Vietnam, he stood before an excited crowd and declared his country free.

Ho Gets Charisma

It was during World War II that Ho became Ho. For years, he preferred to be called Nguyen Ai Quoc, and it had brought him nothing but bad luck. So much for being

Jarhead Jargon

More than a sleepy resort town in central France, the word **Vichy** became synonomous with collaboration and treason during World War II. Later Vietnamese who sided with the French during the French phase of the Vietnam War would be labeled Vichyites by fellow Vietnamese who supported Ho Chi Minh.

Ask Saigon Sally

Whereas the Germans had Hitler and the Italians had Mussolini, the Japanese had no single dominating figure as head of state during World War II. American wartime propaganda turned the prime minister at the time of the Pearl Harbor attack, General Hideki Tojo, into something of the great fascist dictator, but that was never the case.

Nguyen, "The Patriot." Now he was Ho Chi Minh, "He Who Enlightens." Good luck was headed his way, but he would not experience it immediately.

Following the French government's surrender to the Germans in late June 1940, French Vietnam was left in limbo. Hitler was already planning his dream invasion of the Soviet Union. He needed every trooper he could find. Fully occupying a country as large as France was not only out of the question, but unnecessary considering the healthy number of pro-Nazi Frenchmen on hand.

Deciding to occupy only the industrial heartland of France, Paris, and strategic ports in the north and the west of France, Hitler left the rest of the country to a Nazi collaborationist government headquartered in the old resort town of *Vichy*. He also left the Vietnam issue up to Vichy and its chief, World War I icon Marshall Henri Philippe Pétain.

The Nazi führer fully expected Vietnam to fall under the administration of his Far Eastern ally, Japan, and, of course, Pétain did not disappoint him. The ruthless Japanese occupation government in Vietnam would be a rude awakening to those Vietnamese who once saw Japan as a potential liberator. The Japanese had as much interest in liberation and Vietnamese freedom as the French.

In May 1941, Ho answered the new Japanese challenge with his League for Vietnamese Independence, or Vietminh. Dedicated to overthrowing the Japanese presence, Ho this time said virtually nothing about communist interests. The rhetoric and the commitment of the Vietminh remained in the realm of raw, naked nationalism. Ho, sounding more like an American Republican Party stalwart than anything else, stressed the need for a new, moral Vietnam. And when he wasn't touting the need for justice and morality, he spoke of New Deal–like economic reforms that would result once the foreigner was gone.

In what appeared to be an imminent victory for fascists everywhere, Ho's newest tactics had little impact. But though the tactics failed, Ho himself impressed. For the first time, he talked and acted like a worthy national leader. The Vietnamese, who once never gave him the time of day, now described him as charismatic. Ho was on his way to the big time. Too bad the Japanese were in the way.

Let's Dance! Ho Chi Minh and Franklin Roosevelt

Following the establishment of his Vietminh organization, Ho headed to China looking for anyone who might be interested in fighting alongside him in Vietnam. He was arrested for his efforts, and spent a year in prison. Chinese prison life was less than sanitary, and he nearly died from the experience. Released in 1943, Ho learned that the Chinese now saw great value in his anti-Japanese cause. China's war against its Japanese invaders had been bogged down since that invasion began in 1937. A desperate Chinese government now accepted help from all quarters.

Ho had spent his months in prison wondering how the Vietminh could ever prevail. The key to success, he concluded, was that country he had visited as a youth, the United States. At the time, Ho knew little about Franklin Roosevelt and his war aims for America following Japan's December 1941 attack on the U.S. fleet at Pearl Harbor, Hawaii, U.S. Naval Station-Guam, and the lingering U.S. colony of the Philippines. In any event, he would soon discover that President Roosevelt was more complex than communist propaganda suggested, and that maybe the American government could welcome the liberation cause that other governments did not.

Without question, Franklin Roosevelt had been busy presenting a favorable picture of the United States to Asian/Pacific region residents. Japan's "Asia for Asians" propaganda had created something of the Cold War between the United States and Japan for the allegiance of certain Asian/Pacific peoples. For the Philippines, the 1934 Tydings-McDuffie Act countered Japanese policy by promising independence in a little over a decade. For Guam, citizenship rights and territorial status had been discussed, but not granted, at a White House conference with two Guamanian rights activists who had made their own way to Washington in 1936. Francisco B. Leon-Guerrero and Baltazar J. Bordallo made international headlines because of their difficult trip, and Japan answered by holding naval war games off the coast of Guam.

In October 1937, Roosevelt tested the still deep isolationist waters in his country, and thereby risked his career, by responding to the Japanese invasion of China with an angry speech that criticized Japan (but not by name) as an "aggressor nation." Roosevelt's later denial of "strategic exports" to Japan that might be used as war material in China was described by the White House as a "humanitarian act" to protect Chinese citizens.

Shell Shock

Like so much in the story of Ho Chi Minh, the details of Ho's 1943 release from a Chinese prison remain unclear. His release was ordered by Zhang Fakui, a Chinese military officer. Most historians believe that General Zhang knew of Ho's communist past, and that he released him with the proviso that Ho must organize an armed resistance against the Japanese in Vietnam.

Ho had to consider these developments as a possible shift in U.S. policy-making that might benefit Vietnam, but a further learning experience was required. His Vietminh had conflicting views of America. Which one was the best one to exploit for his cause?

Ask Saigon Sally

Most of the original Japanese Imperial Army occupation forces on Guam were transferred to Vietnam, and because of it, they would be spared from the bloody 1944 U.S. military liberation of the island. Most of Guam's Japanese defenders were killed.

Jarhead Jargon

In Vietnamese, *thoi co* means waiting for the right moment to make the right move. Ho Chi Minh was a master of *thoi co*. Throughout the twentieth-century wars in Vietnam, *thoi co* became part of a winning military strategy against an always-impatient enemy.

One view of America came straight from Moscow—that America was the running dog lackey of imperialism and oppression. The other view involved the evolution of the Roosevelt administration itself. Roosevelt moved from the victim of Congressional isolation to the leader who assisted democratic causes in the Philippines, Guam, and even China. And when the United States entered the war in December 1941, Ho learned of another fascinating development.

The Atlantic Charter was announced to the world press shortly after the Pearl Harbor attack. It had been negotiated several months earlier in great secrecy. During the summer of 1941, Franklin Roosevelt had told the White House press corps that he would be going fishing for awhile.

During these olden days of a polite press, which, in the name of respect, never photographed the president in his wheelchair, no one questioned Roosevelt's fishing story. In reality, Roosevelt went fishing for a diplomatic deal with the British prime minister and an old friend, Winston Churchill. They met in Newfoundland in a top-secret and code-named location to agree on joint American-British war aims for World War II.

It was at this meeting that Roosevelt insisted that Woodrow Wilson's dreams of decolonization had to be realized. A new world association of nations or United Nations organization could handle the specifics of the effort. Once America entered the war, and, at this time, Roosevelt believed it was truly a matter of "when" and not "if," the United States planned to assist any resistance movement against fascism. This meant helping out Ho Chi Minh as well. Beautifully written, the Charter became the symbol of democracy's best intentions during World War II, and it served as an excellent ideological counterpunch to the ruthlessness of the fascist cause.

Ho Chi Minh never cared about Roosevelt's motives. The bottom line for him was America's Atlantic Charter commitment to wartime resistance movements and post-war decolonization. It was something of a broad-based commitment, similar to his

Vietminh's appeal to anyone, including all Frenchmen, who opposed the Japanese presence in Vietnam. Ho later noted that it was easy for him to accept the basic mission of the Atlantic Charter. It reminded him of his early days in the United States, and he remembered his studies about the promise of American democracy.

The Atlantic Charter, Ho believed, brought the Americans back to their Thomas Jefferson–styled, anticolonial roots. He had no intention of abandoning his own definitions of a communist-led world, but he welcomed the return of an ethical United States. Whether he was sincere or not, Ho would claim to his dying day that the Atlantic Charter represented America's best moment of the twentieth century.

The Beginning of a Beautiful Friendship?

Being used became an "in" thing in Vietnam. Ho Chi Minh planned to use U.S. assistance to bring himself to power—if, of course, the Japanese could be defeated. Picking the right time and method to achieve power, or *thoi co,* was important to Ho. Meanwhile, the wartime version of the postwar Central Intelligence Agency (the OSS, or Office of Strategic Services) shipped munitions to Ho's anti-Japanese resistance movement. The OSS was well aware of Ho's communist background, but first things—ejecting Japan from Vietnam—stayed first. Ho's real use to the O.S.S. involved intelligence gathering and helping downed U.S. pilots.

Ho proved to be quite the nice guy, at least when he was in the presence of OSS officers. One revealing OSS report described Ho as a "sweet old man," and years later OSS personnel still remembered Ho's ever-present grin, helpfulness, ill-fitting pith helmet, and concern for the OSS men who were so far away from home. This Uncle Ho image was carefully crafted on Ho's part, and it would always surface in the debate over foreign involvement in Vietnam. In short, why should a country like America wage war against such a gentle, friendly fellow like Ho Chi Minh?

Being America's good little buddy carried a price. Ho promised that his Vietminh would report on Japanese troop maneuvers and assist downed allied pilots or escaped POWs. In return he wanted thousands of guns to carry on the fight himself. While making these promises and requests, Ho also wrote letters to the White House, and he expected the OSS to deliver them. The message was always the same.

Shell Shock

William Donovan, the director of America's World War II intelligence agency, the Office of Strategic Services, took pride in his outfit's commitment to objective analysis. In reality, Donovan (nicknamed "Wild Bill") integrated strong personal opinions into many of his reports on resistance movements to the White House.

Ho insisted that his movement represented the best possible post-French regime in Vietnam, and he presented a confusing, damning picture of any other Vietnamese movement that threatened his destiny to rule postwar Vietnam. In fact, most of the reports on political activity in Vietnam were provided by Ho's Vietminh to the OSS Archimedes Patti, Ho's last and best OSS contact near the end of World War II, who knew that the Vietnamese political scene differed from Ho's analysis of it, but he sent Ho's various missives to the White House anyway.

Ho's appeal to Franklin Roosevelt first and then to President Harry Truman always accented the point that his Vietminh was a prodemocratic government in waiting. Nothing was ever mentioned about communist influences, but much was said about humanitarian needs, "hands across the sea," and America's own revolutionary, anticolonial past, which Ho compared to Vietnam's current struggle.

The letters reached their destination, but there has never been any solid evidence to suggest that they were read. Ho always thought as much. Hence, his growing belief throughout the middle and late 1940s that America would never truly care about a tiny place like Vietnam.

Shell Shock

In 1945, one reason Ho Chi Minh received U.S. aid but not U.S. troops was the planned American invasion of Japan. In the days when the atomic bomb had yet to be proven and tested, Operations CORONET, DOWN-FALL, and other plans were being drawn for an assault which, according to Pentagon chief General George C. Marshall, might kill one million American soldiers.

In 1943, following Roosevelt's first meeting with China's leader, Chiang Kai-Shek, the American president had more to say about resistance movements and the future of Asia. In Cairo, Egypt, Roosevelt reaffirmed his administration's commitment to assist antifascist, prodemocratic groups. To Ho, Roosevelt's comments at Cairo were the stuff that dreams were made of.

As the loyal resistance movement leader beneath the umbrella of the Atlantic Charter and its welcomed reaffirmation at Cairo, Ho wanted the Vietminh armed and fully supported by the American government. The OSS worried that Ho, like Chiang of China, planned to use any significant military support for a war against political opponents at home. Chiang was getting away with it. Ho might follow his example. No way, Ho shouted back to Washington. He insisted that he was not a Chiang Kai-Shek, but it was irrelevant whether the OSS believed him.

More than 5,000 guns were airlifted to the Vietminh by the OSS. Ho had to fight the Japanese first, if he was to establish a position against the return of the French. To the OSS, Ho was assisting U.S. policy, and that was all that mattered. An armed Vietminh could be a French problem, if the French were lucky enough to survive World War II and attempt to return to Vietnam. That was a big "if," even in early 1945.

Free Vietnam!

By April 1945, the Japanese were fighting for their lives. On April Fools' Day, U.S. troops landed on Okinawa, the 79-mile-long island just to the south of Japan proper. The kamikaze suicide flights against the American invasion fleet and the fanatical "never surrender" approach of the Japanese ground troops would haunt Americans for years. Were all Asians this crazy? Years later, the battle of Okinawa would be compared to battles fought between the Americans and the Vietnamese.

In contrast to the war in Vietnam, the United States would prevail on Okinawa. After fighting inch by inch on an island U.S. occupying troops would soon nickname "The Rock," the Japanese surrendered in June 1945. The heavy fighting foreshadowed the great battle to come in Japan, or so the White House feared. But it would be a battle without Franklin Roosevelt. The president died at his retreat in Warm Springs, Georgia. For many Americans, the four-term president had represented American life and politics for a good part of their lives. A certain sense of security was now gone, and the new president, Harry S Truman, was a mystery. Ho Chi Minh felt just as apprehensive.

Eleanor Does Vietnam?

Franklin Roosevelt might have been gone, but the former First Lady's career was just beginning. Soon to be the U.S. ambassador to the United Nations, Eleanor Roosevelt had been more visible than her husband throughout much of the New Deal and World War II. Often claiming to represent her husband on a variety of issues, she instead frequently represented herself first. That fact confused a lot of people, and Ho Chi Minh was no exception.

In 1943, Eleanor Roosevelt had traveled to the Pacific. There had been reports that U.S. troops on Pacific islands and elsewhere had worse-than-necessary living conditions and inadequate medical provisions. America's Pacific allies, particularly New Zealand, had even refused to help their guest U.S. troops. The First Lady was outraged by it all, and she even scolded and threatened the New Zealand government. President Roosevelt, Eleanor told the New Zealanders, was most upset with them. This was not the case. The First Lady carried no diplomatic authority, but her husband later backed her up.

Eleanor's speeches during this grand swing tour of the Pacific also stressed the sufferings of Pacific region residents, how the United States would soon relieve that suffering, and that peace would bring a caring America into their lives. It was classic Eleanor Roosevelt, and Ho, especially after Franklin Roosevelt's death, did not want to lose touch with her.

Connecting himself to her humanitarian concerns, Ho wrote sickly sweet letters to her. Dripping with sentiment, he waxed poetic about a pending new era of American-Vietnamese friendship. If Mrs. Roosevelt had been a diabetic, she would have died from reading them. Whether she read these letters or even received them remains a matter of historical debate.

Eleanor Roosevelt, America's champion of the downtrodden. As the U.S. ambassador to the United Nations, she would remind this world association of nations that commitments to decolonization, justice, and peace were important.

Franklin D. Roosevelt Library, Hyde Park, New York.

Ho Meets Harry

In the spring of 1945, Ho and his fellow Vietminh were divided over tactics. Now armed by the Americans, how should they assault the Japanese? Some were in favor of a great decisive battle. Japan was on the ropes. They could be beaten, and the political impact of the battle would play well in the years to come. But the Vietminh were a guerilla movement, and the Japanese could kill thousands in that one great battle. Ho argued that the Vietminh needed every man for the larger contest to come against the French. His position won out, and guerilla warfare continued.

If Ho was banking on a French return, he must have lost hope in the power of America's Atlantic Charter and other promises. Indeed, during the last days of his life, Franklin Roosevelt had decided not to oppose the British and French demands for colonial-like "trusteeships" after the war was over. Whether he would have continued that slide from the Charter was unclear, but Harry Truman would slide further and further away.

Truman was a different political animal from Roosevelt. Known for his no-nonsense approach to politics, salty language, Midwestern manners, and moderate views on Roosevelt's New Deal, Truman, nevertheless, had been a strong Roosevelt loyalist. Given his humble roots, no one would ever call him, as they did Franklin Roosevelt, the "patrician politician," but he was an experienced politician with an interest in foreign policy-making.

Publicly, Truman presented a stronger confrontationalist stance against communism than Roosevelt ever had. It would take a while for the public Truman to catch up to the private, policy-making Truman. In the meantime, he, too, got letters from Ho Chi Minh, and they were tailored, of course, to the new president's style. Ho accented precise military and diplomatic matters with Truman, and grand praises of American-Vietnamese ideological harmony were avoided. As always, none of this meant Ho would ever be answered, and he never was.

In August 1945, two American atomic bombs finished Japan, but the pro-Japanese collaborationist puppet leader of Vietnam, Bao Dai, expected to continue his rule. Bao Dai was Vietnam's emperor, and he had no intention of being its last. On liberation day, August 17, 1945, Bao Dai called for a rally of supporters in Hanoi. More than 150,000 people crowded Hanoi's streets, but nearly all of them were Vietminh supporters. Oops.

Ask Saigon Sally

Harry and Bess Truman brought a first kid into the White House, a teenage daughter named Margaret. Young Margaret dreamed of becoming a pop singer someday, but the critics panned her every note. Even foreign leaders, such as the head of France's brief postwar Provisional Government, Charles de Gaulle, criticized her singing ability.

Bao Dai's days were numbered, and he abdicated the throne only one week later. On September 2, 1945, Ho addressed his people, quoted America's Declaration of Independence, and asked the band to play the U.S. National Anthem. "We are free," Ho shouted.

He was wrong.

The Least You Need to Know

➤ The Vietnamese fight for independence was always linked to international events.

➤ The Vietminh represented Ho Chi Minh's own mixture of communism, nationalism, and opportunism.

➤ Franklin Roosevelt and his Atlantic Charter offered hope and solace to decolonization activists like Vietnam's Ho Chi Minh.

➤ America's Office of Strategic Services (OSS) assisted the Vietminh.

➤ Ho Chi Minh thought his country had reached full independence in 1945.

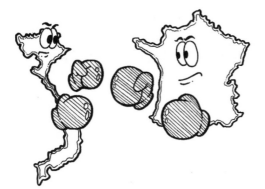

Chapter 4

Thirty Years War, Act One

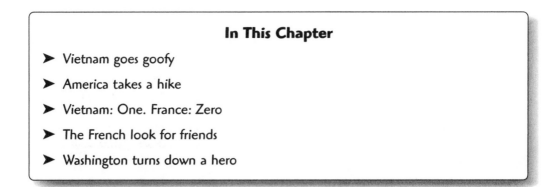

In This Chapter

➤ Vietnam goes goofy

➤ America takes a hike

➤ Vietnam: One. France: Zero

➤ The French look for friends

➤ Washington turns down a hero

In the months following World War II, U.S. foreign policy was hard to define. To most Americans, foreign policy meant getting their loved ones home safely from some far-away place. The Second World War was over, and they wanted their families reunited and the good life to return. And that good life was to be had! During the war, U.S. industry promised tons of consumer goodies once "the Jap [sic] was beat." America entered the late 1940s not only with its economy intact, but booming. The Great Depression was a distant memory, and few wanted to hear about death and misery in Vietnam for a while. Or did they?

Harry, Goofy, and Dewey

In late 1945 and 1946, U.S. troops came home to a different country than their counterparts did after World War I. Many Americans now believed that it was their long love affair with isolationism that triggered the Second World War. They were pretty hard on themselves about it, too.

According to the polls, a majority of them believed that the German Nazis, the Italian fascists, and the Japanese militarists would not have had a chance to achieve power if the United States had flexed its muscles during the 1920s and '30s. Instead, the American government had reduced its military and criticized those who had opposed it. Guilt swept the country after World War II.

Hitler and his pals, most Americans now said, had been given a green light to strut their stuff around the world, and it was America's sons and husbands who later paid the price. The once-vaunted Kellogg-Briand Pact of the 1920s was viewed as downright stupid, and the neutrality legislation of the 1930s was considered even worse. Americans now felt enlightened, worldly, and ready to take on all comers.

Ask Saigon Sally

Whereas the Vietnamese welcomed the return of the French in 1945 with a force of arms, the Japanese welcomed the American occupation of their country with open arms (1945–52). In Japan, the desire for fast reconstruction combined with new anti-militarist politics and even war guilt helped to create a cordial U.S.–Japan relationship. Labeled the "American Caesar," the former commander of allied forces during the war in the Pacific, General Douglas MacArthur, also established a reform-minded occupation government in Japan.

In 1946, 50 percent of Americans polled by the Gallup organization said they favored some sort of military response to halt communist expansionism, but 74 percent said they wanted "the boys home" and a president who concentrated on domestic issues. Would the real America please stand up?

Truman and Chiang

Harry Truman was not immune from this confusion. America's China policy, for instance, did not jive with the new opinion to halt communism. Isolationism was now a thing of the past, and most Americans agreed that their country had a moral responsibility to safeguard the world against evil ideologies. With the fascist powers defeated, the last evil ideology was communism. But the new nuclear age made warfare more horrible than ever before. If nuclear weapons were used, halting communism could mean halting human life on planet Earth. The American people could agree that communism was bad and must be halted wherever it expanded, but they disagreed on how to achieve this goal. It was a frustrating dilemma, especially when

America's allies seemed to invite their own communist takeover. Chiang Kai-Shek's government was a classic case in point.

Truman had never liked, trusted, or cared to support Chiang Kai-Shek. The man had bilked his last dollar from the United States, Truman once told freshman Congressman John Kennedy, and that was that.

As far as Truman was concerned, Chiang had lost the support of his people years before, and had already lost his battle with the Chinese communists by the time of Roosevelt's death. Chiang had not committed his troops to stop the Japanese, and he suspected that any U.S. military expedition to save his government from the communists would put America in the lead role. It could also force a Soviet military response, and World War III would follow hard on the heels of World War II.

Just like the old soldier, Chiang would fade away. In his view, he ran straight into a do-nothing U.S. policy that had general *bipartisan* support. He was right, but he had no one to blame but himself. Mao Tse-Tung and his peasant communists would prevail, and diehard American anticommunists would accuse Harry Truman of being "soft on communism." The "political correctness" of the day demanded that Truman prove his own anticommunist credentials somewhere or just keep his mouth shut.

Jarhead Jargon

It was one of the great semantic inventions ever to come out of Washington, D.C. In the early 1950s, the term **bipartisanship** became a household word. No matter what party occupied the Oval Office, bipartisanship politics encouraged Republican and Democratic cooperation and unity in the march to Cold War victory.

Report from Vietnam

In the midst of all this big picture stuff was the ongoing nightmare in Vietnam. Early in the Truman administration, A. Peter Dewey provided the depressing Vietnam reports for the president. As the OSS's top on-site analyst and field agent in Vietnam, his opinion was valuable. But the benefit of the doubt belonged to an Englishman, General Douglas Gracey.

During September 1945, Gracey had arrived in Vietnam with nearly 20,000 British troops. He was soon joined by 10 times that number of French forces and 200,000 Chinese troops. A supporter of Churchill and empire, Gracey had no love for things French, but he hated communists more.

Considering Ho and his Vietminh a group of terrorists and renegades, Gracey passed out guns to French citizens in Saigon and elsewhere. Indeed, Ho had begun a guerrilla war against the French who had remained in Vietnam during the Japanese occupation. Women and children were not immune from their attacks, and Frenchmen in Saigon had even rioted in the effort to convince Gracey to hand over those guns.

At first the Vietminh spent most of their time concentrating on the Chinese troops. The Chinese were a sad, ragtag bunch, and they had entered Vietnam under starvation conditions. They were not averse to killing a Vietnamese family for their food, and the Vietminh avenged such Chinese-instigated violence.

Suddenly trapped in an orgy of violence, Gracey concluded that extra firepower would do the trick, especially after the Vietminh blew up the electric power stations in Saigon. This situation brought Saigon to its knees for weeks, and even Ho apologized for all the extra misery. But it was the last straw for Gracey, who even armed Japanese POWs in the effort to provide the order part of law and order. Of course, arming yesterday's enemy was a controversial decision, and for years both the British and the French denied it ever took place. They lied. The Japanese occupation had been ruthless in Southeast Asia, and the Vietnamese were shocked at how quick and easy the European colonials kissed and made up with a former regime that committed war crimes.

The odd coalition of British, French, Chinese, and Japanese troops achieved the opposite of what Gracey had hoped for. Ho's liberation cause could not have been clearer or nobler to the Vietnamese at this time. Dewey pointed out Ho's winning ways to Washington. The foreigners in Vietnam were their own worst enemy, he insisted. He was quick to criticize Gracey as "goofy," and to his face now and then as well.

Dewey's policy recommendations stressed a U.S. denunciation of the Gracey approach, a lukewarm endorsement for the Vietminh, and a demand that the United States stay away from the place in the future. Predicting victory for the Vietminh and a horrible defeat for the French, Dewey would later be praised for his powers of analysis and crystal-ball accuracy.

Sadly, Dewey had little time to make his point and prediction. He was killed by Vietminh troops near Saigon in late September 1945. Ho claimed it was an accident and offered his sympathies for this "friendly fire" mistake to Washington. Accidental or not, A. Peter Dewey, the voice in the wilderness, was America's first battle casualty on a casualty list that would stretch all the way to April 1975. Vietnam was on its way to becoming America's only Thirty Years War.

Gone with the Wind and Brother Charles

Although Ho Chi Minh never stopped asking the United States to see things his way, the Truman administration had little interest in seeing anything at all. Until the United States truly had a working foreign policy, Ho could not expect a helpful answer from the United States. This would be something of the kiss of death for Ho. The late 1940s were critical years for the Vietminh and their continuing fight for independence. Without any outside assistance, it was going to be a lonely battle. America seemed gone with the wind to Ho. He was right, but when the United States finally blew into Vietnam, it would not be in his favor.

In the late 1940s, the Truman administration announced its Truman Doctrine. This was supposed to answer all the questions about America's role in the post–World War II era, for the doctrine was dedicated to uplifting anticommunist regimes anywhere around the world. Noncommunist governments were tumbling like *dominoes,* or so the Truman team concluded. A little expediency was required, for the world was not easily divided into democratic and communist states. There were quite a few dictatorships out there that were anticommunist, but not democratic. U.S. policy was on their side now, and it would stay that way for many years.

Ho Chi Minh made expedient conclusions, too. In the late 1940s, one of his more intriguing opinions involved France's famous Charles de Gaulle. Ho liked the guy. During the 1940 Battle of France, de Gaulle's troops were among the few to stand their ground against the advancing Nazis. Eventually fleeing to England while he had the chance, de Gaulle used his already growing reputation as an anti-Nazi hero to form the Free French.

Jarhead Jargon

In 1946, President Truman dispatched a State Department expert on Asia, Abbot Low Moffat, to evaluate the Vietminh and its leader Ho Chi Minh. Moffat reported that Ho was "probably" a passionate communist, and that Vietnam, Laos, Cambodia, and Thailand would soon fall like **"dominoes"** to communism.

Heavily supported by the British government, the Free French were dedicated to ridding France of Nazi occupation. They had little use for the many pro-Nazi French collaborators either. Unfortunately for de Gaulle, it was difficult to organize a resistance movement against the Germans while living in England. The Nazi Occupation was a brutal one, and de Gaulle's patriotic encouragement over BBC radio rarely convinced a Frenchman to risk his life.

Tales from the Front

For thirty years after he left Washington as chief of the National Security Council for the Johnson administration, Dr. Walt W. Rostow remained an unreconstructed hawk in his economics and history classes at the University of Texas–Austin. The "domino theory" was correct, he said, for communism succeeded in Laos, Cambodia, and Vietnam after U.S. troops were withdrawn. To Rostow, the Vietnam War was America's most important front line against advancing communism.

When the U.S. military and Free French units liberated Paris in August 1944, de Gaulle made sure he was there to witness the event. He had an excellent claim to be the postwar leader of France, but the OSS and the Roosevelt administration had grave doubts about him.

Ask Saigon Sally

After World War II, The French high commissioner for Vietnam, Georges Thierry d'Argenlieu, made headlines with the suggestion that Hitler's success over France in 1940 had been pure, naked luck. The Vietnamese, he vowed, would never be that lucky.

Without question, de Gaulle's politics were way out in right field. OSS chief "Wild Bill" Donovan joked that the only real difference between Hitler and de Gaulle was that de Gaulle spoke French. Franklin Roosevelt found de Gaulle to be a "strutting egotist," unfriendly toward the United States, and a strong believer in somehow restoring lost French pride, honor, and glory. In any event, de Gaulle nosed out his political opposition, Truman did not share the same objections as Roosevelt, and the Free French leader emerged as France's first postwar leader.

By all rights, Ho Chi Minh should have hated de Gaulle simply because he was a French nationalist and patriot. But that kind of emotional response got in the way of Vietnamese policy-making and common sense. Ho saw a lot of himself in de Gaulle. In battle, they had both gone up against impossible odds, and then saved their strength to fight another day. Both were master organizers, slowly, methodically eliminating all opposition while making the right moves to achieve full power. Both had loyal lieutenants who adored their every action. Both insisted that morality and right were on their side, and in the face of very real forces of evil. Both saw themselves as the living destiny of their respective nations, and both were arrogant guys with a long list of real and imagined enemies.

Given these endless comparisons, Ho expected to wheel and deal with de Gaulle, brother resister to brother resister. But it takes two to tango, as they say, and de Gaulle, who learned of Ho's brother resister views in 1946, thought the Vietnamese independence leader must be nuts.

de Gaulle didn't see any comparisons at all. To the French leader, Ho was a communist, a traitor to the empire, and it was outrageous and insulting to be considered the man's brother. Nevertheless, Ho was shocked that the two might never develop a dialogue, or so he later said.

de Gaulle saw colonial Vietnam as one of the last symbols of French pride, honor, glory, and prestige. Most Frenchmen agreed with him. Yet he was ousted from power at the time of the French escalation of the war in Vietnam. Preferring a sort of Napoleonic-style government in order to rebuild his war-torn country efficiently, de Gaulle had opposed the creation of a Fourth Republic and the Constitution that governed it. As outrageous as ever, de Gaulle declared that the country would pine over him after he was out of office. The French would regret their silly Fourth Republic, he predicted. Thanks to France's disastrous Vietnam War, and a resulting rerun of the same type of colonial challenge in Algeria, de Gaulle would be proven right. With a loud "I told you so," de Gaulle returned to power in 1958.

France Fights the Last War

Observing France's military nightmare from the comforts of his "American Caesar" position in Japan, General Douglas MacArthur once joked that the French had an amazing knack to employ the tactics of old wars in new ones, and then, when they start losing, blame everyone from Satan to Mickey Mouse for their own incompetence. Always known for his candor, MacArthur never had any apologies for his remark. President Truman disassociated himself from the general's "recklessness," but just about everybody in Washington agreed with MacArthur's assessment of the French misery.

The madness truly began in the fall of 1946. At that time, Ho Chi Minh told French prime minister George Bidault, once a strong de Gaulle stalwart, that patience and commitment remained on the side of Vietnam. France was tired, and Vietnam would not rest until all Frenchmen were back in France. Ho had been in Paris to get a final word from the French, but what he received was a complicated, twisted plan to maintain French sovereignty over Vietnam. Ho even added his signature to the French plan, stimulating a firestorm of controversy.

How could Ho agree to a continued French presence in Vietnam? There were two reasons. First, if he didn't sign the French plan, he could be arrested as an anti-French terrorist and jailed for years. By signing, Ho left for home as a respected negotiator. Second, while various Vietminh factions argued over regional leadership, Ho had just told the French to go to hell and he left the country in one piece. In the eyes of many Vietnamese, this was true national leadership, and the continuing image of the unassailable Ho kept him above squabbling local politics.

Shell Shock

Whereas most historians agree that the first shots of the American Revolution were fired in April 1775 at Lexington and Concord, few agree on where the first shots were fired in the Vietnamese war of independence against the French. Some books will tell you that the French naval bombardment of Haiphong by the warship *Suffren* constituted those first shots in November 1946, but there had been skirmishes between the French and Vietminh for months.

The French Offensive

Through massive firepower and technology, the French military in Vietnam, after the British and Chinese were gone, hoped to quickly eliminate any Vietminh challenge.

Britain had its own empire to worry about, and the Chinese government was fighting for its life at home. After all Japanese troopers had been evacuated from the region, the British and Chinese began their withdrawal, and the French were left to fight their own colonial war. Their first offensive was in November and December 1946. Led by French naval forces, the major northern cities of Hanoi and Haiphong were bombarded. French strategy involved a simple effort to drive the Vietminh out of these cities and restore full political leadership there to French rule. It worked. Ho Chi Minh and some 39,000 Vietminh supporters were forced out into the jungle. But many neighborhoods across Hanoi and especially Haiphong were left in rubble.

Jarhead Jargon

Concerned about losing the isolated sections of the country to the Vietminh, the French built military installations in those same sections. Called **hedgehogs,** these bases were supposed to destroy Vietminh supply lines and organizational efforts.

The French now occupied a shell of what once were major urban centers, and, of course, they won the hatred and animosity of those Vietnamese residents who had never considered taking a stand against the French. Hit-and-run terrorist attacks on French soldiers and civilians in those cities and elsewhere constituted a certain Vietnamese revenge, and the French seemed powerless to halt them. While the French government claimed that the enemy was on the run, Ho and his senior military advisor and general in the field, Vo Nguyen Giap, patiently organized for a long wearing-down campaign against the French.

Strategically, the French were caught in a difficult position. Being in control of the cities in an agricultural country like Vietnam did not mean all that much. The Vietminh claimed the major rice-growing areas of southern Vietnam as their own, and they were right. Meanwhile, the Vietnamese borders near Laos and China were fairly open to the arms trade, and the French had to do something about it fast. Keeping both rice and arms away from the enemy was the key to success, claimed the French. Hence the creation of the *hedgehogs.*

Manned by some of the best troops in the French military, the hedgehogs were staging areas for depriving the Vietminh of food, guns, and any safe haven in the countryside. This was easier said than done. The French were in an alien environment, were very visible, and were often put on the defensive by determined Vietminh guerrillas.

Even the weather was hostile. The Mekong Delta region of southern Vietnam, where many of the hedgehogs were located, received some of the highest totals of rainfall in steamy Southeast Asia. Given the stormy weather, calling in for artillery or air support often was not possible for French ground troops. The misery factor remained high for Westerners unprepared for endless heat, rain, and strange tropical maladies. Military technology, and clever, sweeping, blitzkrieg tactics studied in the war colleges had little relevance for a guerrilla war fought in a swamp.

General Giap's patient war of wearing down the French paid off. Finding French recruits to head out into the killing fields of Vietnam became more and more of a challenge for Paris. French Foreign Legion troops, a controversial collection of crude but highly trained war lovers and mercenaries from a variety of nations, often carried the brunt of the war wherever an especially isolated hedgehog was located. Because some of their ranks included ex-Nazis, and because reports of their torturing of Vietnamese prisoners made the news even in the United States, Vietnam quickly won a reputation as the world's dirtiest ongoing *"brushfire war."*

Overseas *brushfire wars* were not supposed to hurt a domestic economy, but by the early 1950s France was feeling the pain. Although it was difficult for the proud French government to conclude, it was in their interest to seek an American rescue of some kind. But as early as 1950, the United States was giving off mixed signals about Vietnam involvement. Was America ready to prove how pro-French and anticommunist it really was?

Jarhead Jargon

Brushfire war is a military confrontation in the Third World that avoids the use of nuclear weapons, strives to keep casualty figures low, and makes a political statement at the same time. The Americans put Vietnam in the brushfire category, and the Soviets put their 1979 invasion of Afghanistan in that same category as well.

A French Foreign Legionnaire in the Red River Delta between Hanoi and Haiphong (circa 1953).

National Archives Still Pictures Unit, College Park, Maryland.

Ask Saigon Sally

In 1949, the French made an agreement with Bao Dai, the last of the Vietnamese monarchs. Formally and legally, the French now considered themselves in charge of Vietnam's foreign and military policies. Local government authority was left to Bao Dai.

Shell Shock

Although pro–Ho Chi Minh propaganda downplayed this fact, both during and after the war against the French, there were thousands of Vietnamese who fought *with* the French. Called the Vietnamese National Army (or VNA), these French-trained troops were in the field as early as July 1949.

An Appeal to America

In 1951, General Jean de Lattre de Tassigny, the overall commander of French forces in Vietnam, visited the U.S. Congress and made a loud, eloquent appeal on behalf of his government. He added specifics to the general French government request for American aid. Playing into America's fears of communist encirclement, de Lattre de Tassigny predicted a country-by-country collapse of Southeast Asia in a matter of months. The communist cause of the Vietminh, he said, was soon to be carried through Laos, Cambodia, and Thailand. Then, the Vietminh would link up with the insurgents in Malaya, win the support and, eventually, the oil of the Dutch East Indies, and finally move on to challenge the American-defended Philippines and Guam. Japan would bend to this new "east wind," he insisted, and Australia and New Zealand would be the last holdouts of "civilization." This was a similar offensive to the one launched by the Japanese in December 1941, de Lattre de Tassigny concluded. It would just move a little slower.

Like America's flamboyant Douglas MacArthur, the French general was a master of theatrics and overgeneralization. It worked for MacArthur—why not for an honored French guest and patriot?

Thanks to these strident days of the Cold War, de Lattre de Tassigny's doom-and-gloom vision was seriously analyzed and discussed by American policymakers. Otherwise, his thesis of an Asian/Pacific takeover by the Vietminh had as much plausibility as a *Godzilla* film. The U.S. government rejected his appeal. At the time of de Lattre de Tassigny's visit, America was embroiled in the Korean War. One war at a time was enough.

The Least You Need to Know

➤ In the name of pride, honor, and glory, the French fought to continue their imperial rule over Vietnam.

➤ During the late 1940s, U.S. foreign policy was in a state of flux until the creation of the Truman Doctrine.

➤ Ho Chi Minh tried to negotiate with de Gaulle to avoid a war with the French.

➤ French military power often prevailed in the cities, but not in the countryside.

➤ The de Lattre de Tassigny mission to gain American help in Vietnam failed.

Chapter 5

Destiny at Dienbienphu

> **In This Chapter**

➤ Playing dominoes is not fun

➤ "The Forgotten War" is remembered in Vietnam

➤ Washington looks for Vietnam and can't find it

➤ The French are smart, but the Vietminh are smarter

➤ The end of the line at Dienbienphu

In 1952, John Wayne went to "paradise" and had a terrible time. Filmed in what Republic Pictures called "the paradise of Hawaii," *Big Jim McLain* starred the Duke as a commie-hunting congressional investigator hoping to win the Cold War all by his lonesome. It was classic Wayne, albeit in a suit instead of a saddle—one man facing off against many (communists this time instead of Native Americans). At the time of the film's premier, the domino theory had truly taken hold in Washington, and, on Main Street, USA, the fear of an international communist conspiracy was growing. Hollywood saw pay dirt, and John Wayne, one of its biggest stars (both in height and box office sales), was an excellent choice to explore the problem and cash in on the fear.

As a staunch Republican conservative, Wayne and his politics were well known to moviegoers. In *Big Jim McLain*, a film partially funded out of Wayne's own pocket, the die-hard conservative tried to prove that no corner of the United States was safe from communist conspirators, agents, and saboteurs. That included the then pristine-looking U.S. Territory of Hawaii, a dreamland of palm trees, surf, and good living. To Wayne's "Big Jim" character, Asians made especially nasty commies, and Hawaii was full of them. If wedded to communist plots, the "alien culture" and "mysterious ways" of Asians, even in Hawaii, put the United States in an unfortunate position. At least heroes like "Big Jim" would try their best to keep the Asian communists at bay in Hawaii and far away from the American Mainland. Or so this film suggested.

The Red Menace was reaching across the Pacific. We needed more fighters like "Big Jim," this film told us, and less hesitation in Washington. If the politicos did not do more to stop the communists in Asia today, then these same communists would be dictating terms in America tomorrow. "Big Jim" even said so in the film, and in a rambling, tough-guy way to costar James Arness. The latter's character was killed by Asian communist agents near the end of the film, and "Big Jim's" warnings were supposed to ring true to all who heard them.

Big Jim McLain was not the blockbuster *Star Wars* of 1952, but it ended up being a decent box-office success for Wayne and Republic Pictures. Those movie patrons who hoped to escape the always bad news coming out of the Korean War came to the wrong movie here. The communist threat was about to get worse, this movie implied, and close to home, too.

Shell Shock

In 1950, both the Soviet and the Chinese governments extended full diplomatic recognition to Ho Chi Minh's Vietminh movement. The State Department's official response noted that Ho had now exposed his "true colors" as a leading, recognized communist.

At least, some said with a sigh of relief, the Truman Doctrine was now being enforced in Korea. How far should it go? Must Vietnam be added to the agenda, or were the naysayers correct? The latter always said that Vietnam was a colonial nightmare for the French, and never really part of the larger communist-versus-anticommunist tale. In any event, the time for decision, a D-Day, had arrived. But for the French, *D* stood for Dienbienphu.

Why Dominoes Are Scary

The man who made it "in" to dream up communist conspiracies was an unlikely character to have done so. Senator Joseph McCarthy had been a World War II hero who had gone to Capitol Hill as a liberal Republican from the liberal, progressive state of Wisconsin. But the national Republican Party was a conservative one, and it kept moving more and more to the right on both domestic and foreign policy issues. On top of that, the Republican Party was the country's minority party and hadn't occupied the White House since Herbert Hoover left in 1933. Appointed to the Agricultural Committee upon his arrival in the Senate, McCarthy felt lost and useless.

While the Truman administration and some of his own Senate colleagues struggled to define American foreign policy, McCarthy was discussing skim milk and cheese curds with Wisconsin farmers. As U.S. foreign policy began to look impotent in the face of Mao's rise to power, McCarthy seized the moment. He had an answer for America's collapsing position on the world stage. The issue, he said, wasn't the power and winning determination of the communists. The issue was treason and sabotage right here at home.

Ferreting Out the Red Menace

Charging, at first, that some 57 bureaucrats in the State and Defense departments were either communist agents or communist sympathizers, McCarthy offered a simple explanation for America's loss of ground in world influence. The enemy was under our beds, he insisted, and we needed to root him out and destroy him if we ever hoped to sleep securely again.

The revelations of a junior member of Congress did not dazzle the press, which compared McCarthy's list of 57 traitors to a bottle of Heinz 57 ketchup. They also joked that there could be booze in that ketchup bottle instead of the red stuff. (McCarthy was known to keep the company of Jim Beam and Jack Daniels.) But what might have become a public relations nightmare was turned around by McCarthy and his staff.

Un-American Affairs

Finding a groundswell of public support to investigate the State and Defense departments, McCarthy broadened his list to 200 spies and nasties. Finally, the Senate Un-American Affairs Committee, which had been a World War II special committee to investigate German Nazi, Italian fascist, and Japanese militarist espionage activities in the United States, was reactivated with McCarthy as its new chairman. The committee had been disbanded in 1945, and its membership given the Medal of Freedom, the U.S. government's highest civilian award for great service to the nation.

McCarthy claimed that 1950s America was in greater danger than it had been in World War II, for the communist movement was well en-

Jarhead Jargon

During early 1945, President Roosevelt made concessions to Stalin at the Yalta conference. In fact, some said that he made too many concessions. To American anticommunists, the term **Yalta sellout** was synonymous with treason, appeasement, and unpatriotic behavior.

trenched in U.S. government service. From the *Yalta sellout* to American defeats in the Korean War, the traitors were polluting foreign and national security policies from the get-go. After these evil men were discovered and punished, McCarthy predicted a slower-moving communist conspiracy and a rejuvenated United States. Consequently, he saw his work as a patriotic chore, and he urged Americans to distrust all those politicians who worried about the abuse of civil liberties during his investigations.

Innocents, McCarthy suggested, would never be called to testify before his committee. There was a reason they were called, he noted, and it involved their treasonous activities. Unfortunately for McCarthy, his own unethical and abrasive behavior led to his 1954 removal as chairman of this controversial committee.

Ask Saigon Sally

McCarthy's tactics had brought American politics to new lows. For instance, during the 1952 presidential election, he consistently referred to Adlai Stevenson, the Governor of Illinois and the Democratic presidential nominee, as "Alger Stevenson." This was a play on words. Alger Hiss had been one of the State Department bureaucrats accused of pro-communist and treasonous behavior by the Senate Un-American Affairs Committee and its counterpart in the House of Representatives. Hiss was found guilty as charged, and McCarthy implied in his "Alger Stevenson" quip that the Governor of Illinois was a communist traitor. He was wrong.

Shell Shock

In the 1950s, with Democratic party liberals calling for the liberation of all those trapped beneath oppressive regimes, and with Republican party conservatives touting the anticommunist cause more than any other political group, the die was cast for a bipartisan consensus on U.S. entry into Vietnam.

"The Forgotten War" Not Forgotten

The Korean War had been essential to McCarthy's popularity. Without it, he was nothing. To many Americans, the Korean War symbolized America's dilemma in the Cold War. In 1945, the United States had emerged victorious and unassailable from World War II. Five years later, it couldn't beat a Third World army with its hands tied behind its back. It was upsetting, and McCarthy thought he could ease the pain. His thesis of down-home country treason was easy to accept, simplifying America's foreign policy troubles for a lot of people.

During recent years, from Hollywood to Harvard, there has been a fascination with both World

War II and Vietnam. America's amazing victory in the Second World War and its amazing defeat in Vietnam are justly deserving of all the attention. But in the middle stands what some veterans and authors call "the forgotten war" of Korea.

The June 1950 North Korean invasion of South Korea finally swung the Truman Doctrine into action, and, at first, the United States rescued its anticommunist ally of South Korea. But in 1951, everything changed. China entered the war on the side of North Korea, and the allied commander, General MacArthur, supported a massive U.S. assault on the Chinese. MacArthur was fired for continuing to advocate this assault, for his commander in chief, Truman, preferred a limited engagement. By 1953, the battle raged where it had begun, straddling the 38th parallel that separates North Korea from South Korea.

The Korean War never really ended. A 1953 armistice agreement created the ugliest, scariest Demilitarized Zone (DMZ) in the world. The guns went silent, and that was it. No peace treaty was signed. Border clashes between U.S. troops and North Koreans would be commonplace for years, including a bloody, horrifying 1976 assault on an American position by ax-wielding northern troops.

Ask Saigon Sally

Although never a fancy policymaker or strategist, Sergeant William Weber enjoyed a unique distinction. He served in the U.S. Marine Corps in World War II, Korea, and Vietnam. Once asked why his country fared so poorly in Vietnam, he claimed that "any fool" knew the answer. It wasn't that the U.S. military was "so bad," he said, it was the Vietnamese who were "so good!"

The thesis of limited war left a bad taste for many Americans. More than 33,000 Americans had died in Korea. For what? The next war, some suggested, should be fought to the bitter end. Yet in the new nuclear age, the bitter end could mean the end of life on planet Earth.

In 1953, the new presidency of Dwight Eisenhower promised a "happy days" economy and continued commitments against communists. After the years of misery in Korea, most Americans heard the "happy days" part of the Eisenhower message, and his 1952 landslide (repeated in 1956) over Adlai Stevenson, the governor of Illinois, proved the point. America's Korean hell was over, but in Vietnam the French hell lived on.

Given America's own troubles, the press had not covered the early '50s Vietnam tale all that well. Ho Chi Minh could have been the name of an exotic restaurant as far as many Americans were concerned. Could France bow out of Vietnam the way America had bowed out of Korea?

Jarhead Jargon

During 1947, terrorist tactics represented the heart and soul of the Vietminh war against the French. Many unique booby troops were employed, and the most popular one was the **punji stake.** A sharpened bamboo pole tipped with poisons and even "night soil" (human manure), the punji stake was concealed near jungle trials, rice paddies, or wherever French troopers walked on patrol.

Ask Saigon Sally

Vietnam was an armed camp during the late 1940s and early 1950s. The French Union Forces (FUF) alone, a French army that welcomed Vietnamese fighters, grew from 70,000 at the beginning of the Franco-Vietnamese War to more than 500,000 in 1954.

Foolish Frenchmen

As early as 1950, the Vietminh were ready to launch a major offensive against the French. The days of relying on *punji stake* defenses were over. The first target was Dong Khe, a hedgehog near Highway Route 4 in northern Tonkin province. The French hedgehog's position enabled the French to keep a close watch on the China border where the Vietminh often received supplies. During the middle of a drenching monsoon, General Giap's newly raised army attacked Dong Khe following two days of concentrated artillery fire. Cut off from their supply line by the advancing Vietminh, the French were forced to surrender.

When the weather cleared, French paratroopers recaptured the base, but the Vietminh attacked again in the fall. The French were soon surrounded in northern Tonkin and forced to abandon most of their positions there. The battle for possession of Route 4 was over. The China-Vietnam border was now secure for the Vietminh supply line, and nearly 6,100 French troops had been captured.

Giap compared the Route 4 battles to the seesaw campaigns going on between the North Korean/Chinese and the South Korean/American troops far to the north. The difference was that there would never be any deals or cease-fires with the French, he said. France was destined for defeat. Such statements, as usual, were meant to influence public opinion in France and elsewhere. Giap always took into consideration the political priorities of his opponents, and those priorities, he knew, never included the desire for a long, bloody war in Vietnam.

General Raoul Salan joked that he was "one foolish Frenchman" who was going to prove Giap wrong. A cautious man, with postwar political interests, Salan replaced de Lattre de Tassigny. The latter had died of cancer, but not before losing his own son in Vietnam.

With much of the war now being fought by the French Foreign Legion and volunteer Vietnamese troops, Salan had a hard time saying that he was in charge of a French army. By 1953, Salan's tired troops controlled only isolated areas near Saigon, Hanoi, and Haiphong, and his hold-the-line tactics did not sit well with the French government. He was replaced by General Henri Navarre, a dashing clone of de Lattre de Tassigny, who brought his fine champagne collection with him to Saigon. A portrait of confidence, Navarre promised total victory. The French in Saigon and Hanoi had not heard the victory promise for years, and, for a while, they truly wanted to believe their handsome new military leader.

The key to success, Navarre believed, was billions of dollars in U.S. economic aid and the new Eisenhower administration's latest military hardware. That welcomed American contribution would be combined with new French divisions formed under his command, and with the Vietnamese volunteers playing the minor instead of the major role. If it worked it would be a dream

Ask Saigon Sally

In his 1952 race for the presidency, the Democratic party nominee and Illinois governor, Adlai Stevenson, suggested that the United Nations should intervene and force an end to the French nightmare in Vietnam.

come true. But Giap did not grant Navarre the luxury to put his plan together. A surprised Navarre was forced to live up to his talk of victory, and a make-or-break final battle was his answer.

Dienbienphu

Navarre was horrified by the possibility of the Vietminh linking up with another anti-French guerrilla force, the Pathet Lao, in Laos. In late 1953, that possibility seemed a strong one, and Navarre was convinced that the linkup would be the kiss of death for the French in Vietnam. Even if it meant dividing his own forces to do it, he was determined to keep the Pathet Lao and the Vietminh apart. In reality, such a linkup would have taken a great deal of time, and Navarre exaggerated its military significance.

In any event, the situation provided an opportunity to go after the Vietminh in a big way. By setting up a large base near tiny Dienbienphu, Navarre hoped to fan out and patrol the routes to and from Laos. He also hoped to cut off the opium trade that was important to the region. Both the Vietminh and the Pathet Lao were buying weapons with drug-trade money.

France Folds

The Dienbienphu base was a massive one, separated by open fields. The enemy would have to assault it without much cover. Defended by as many artillery pieces as the French could muster, the base enjoyed a tiered system of fixed defenses, tanks, and mobile troops. It was a *Maginot Line* with a 360° range of fire. But would the enemy dare attack? Navarre assumed that the Vietminh were as tired of the war as the

French. A decisive battle just had to be in Ho's interest, he argued, and his troops would be wiped out as they tried to destroy the great base at Dienbienphu.

Shell Shock

Named after Andre Maginot, the French Defense Minister after World War I, the **Maginot Line** was a massive and fearsome system of fixed defenses, mines, and tank traps that ran across the west bank of the Rhine River. Completed in 1931, it was meant to hold back a possible German invasion of France. When that invasion came in May 1940, the Germans bypassed the Line through Belgium, and attacked from the west while the French guns pointed east. Considered the height of foolishness by military experts in America and elsewhere, the Maginot Line approach to defense was given a second chance by the French commanders at Dienbienphu.

Providing round-the-clock support, a newly built airfield at Dienbienphu would be the French lifeline to their primary supply center at Hanoi. Navarre was confident that his troops could hold out at the base for a long time. It was the Vietminh, he believed, who had the supply problems. Ho and Giap were doomed.

In 1954, the Eisenhower administration spent more than $1 billion shipping supplies and raw cash to the French. Some of that money and materiel was put to good use at Dienbienphu. Navarre's command could now afford to extend their base defenses throughout the valley in which it was located. Named after the three mistresses of Navarre's second-in-command, Colonel Christian de Castries, firebases Gabrielle, Beatrice, and Isabelle now provided decent artillery cover for both the airfield and the French command center of Dienbienphu.

Navarre fully expected a frontal assault on that command center. It would be too tempting for the Vietminh to avoid, he believed, and it would be the last thing they would ever do. In early 1954, Navarre predicted total victory by Bastille Day.

France's frenetic activity to build a grand European-like fortress in the middle of a Vietnamese valley was a bizarre development to Giap. He had no intention of leading any banzai or cavalry-like charges against Navarre. Furthermore, the French had obviously never taken Geography or Meteorology 101. Heavy rains were destined to turn the valley of Dienbienphu into one large mud hole. Planes would be unable to land or take off, and the many tanks that represented the lifeline between the three "mistress" firebases would be bogged down in the mud.

As for Navarre, he had assumed that because the hills above the Dienbienphu valley were virtually impassable, the Vietminh would be unable to place any offensive weapons up there. He doubted that the Vietminh had many big guns anyway. This was true, but Giap did not need many if he enjoyed the full advantage to fire down upon a flooding base stuck in the mud.

As it turned out, the high ground above Dienbienphu was not impassable to the Vietminh. Giap also got lucky. The Chinese had captured American mortars and howitzers during the Korean War, and some of these weapons were transferred to the Vietminh at the Chinese border. To a very real degree, the battle of Dienbienphu would involve American weapons shooting at American weapons.

The Giap strategy for the siege of Dienbienphu was a simple one. First he would shell the airfield into a useless mass of muddy craters. Then he would take out each of the "mistress" firebases one by one during the worst possible weather for the French. With its defenders exhausted and hungry, he would finally use every weapon he had to go after the main command base. A confident Giap began this assault convinced that victory was inevitable and that the French had, indeed, become "fools."

Shell Shock

Vietnamese propaganda has usually suggested that the Vietminh acted with little or no assistance from the Chinese. But there was a Chinese connection, and a Sino-Vietnamese Agreement solidified it all in 1950. Starting slow, with only 400 tons of military materiel shipped to the Vietminh per month, the Chinese were sending up to 10,000 tons of military hardware by 1954.

This Is the End

In March 1954, after only two weeks of fighting, the French government admitted to the Eisenhower administration that Dienbienphu was lost. But that did not mean the war was lost, and America was once again the key to that conclusion. Although he cultivated his grandfatherly, slow-moving image in public, Eisenhower was still the decisive, no-nonsense decision-maker who won World War II in Europe. Influenced, if not infected, by the dedicated anticommunism sentiment of the day, Eisenhower did not want to be accused of being the president who let the Southeast Asia domino fall to the communists. Yet his administration was at odds over whether to help the French at all.

Eisenhower had been a senior military officer most of his life. He doubted that U.S. military aid, at this late stage in the war, could reverse what appeared to be an inevitable French defeat throughout Vietnam. President or no President, he was not alone in the White House, and his view was based on military sense and not anticommunist politics. The latter was all-important at the time, and Eisenhower engaged in pro-French political maneuvers that defied his own grasp of the military situation.

In Haiphong harbor, the USS Montague takes on Vietnamese refugees fleeing the success of the Vietminh (August 1954).

National Archives Still Pictures Unit, College Park, Maryland.

Secretary of State John Foster Dulles was on record for supporting nuclear strikes on the major suppliers of brushfire wars, namely China and the Soviet Union. But that seemed extreme. The French would be offered two atomic bombs to deal with the Vietminh problem, but the offer reflected a basic American misunderstanding of French goals in Vietnam. The French wanted to hold on to the place, not bomb it back to the Stone Age.

Tales from the Front

Pressured by the strident anticommunist politicians in the Eisenhower cabinet, General Matthew Ridgeway kept his cool. During the top-secret cabinet discussions over the possibility of a U.S. military rescue of the French at Dienbienphu, Ridgeway offered no apologies for being an "old-fashioned infantryman." No nuclear weapon could help the French, he said. No World War II–like bombing mission would do the trick either. Some seven U.S. Army divisions might make a difference (or twelve if the Chinese entered the war), he argued, but Washington was avoiding an obvious point. The French had already lost the war, he said, and President Eisenhower agreed with him. Secretary of State Dulles and Vice President Nixon refused to accept this "defeatism." They tried to get Congress to pressure Eisenhower into a French military rescue, but the Senate Majority Leader, Lyndon Johnson, supported Eisenhower and Ridgeway. A military solution, Johnson noted at that time, was not the answer.

Although Eisenhower welcomed advice from all corners of his passionately anticommunist cabinet, the bottom line remained with him and Dulles. For a while, a code-named Operation VULTURE was considered. Operation VULTURE involved a massive military rescue on the part of the United States, stressing air power first and, possibly, ground troops later.

Eisenhower's polling of friendly congressmen suggested that the legislature would not support U.S. troops in Vietnam so soon after the Korean War. The key to VULTURE or any devised rescue plan, Eisenhower said, would be international involvement. It would be an international crusade just like Korea, but, this time, with *real* international involvement. That was easier said than done, but Dulles tried to remind America's allies that it was time to put their own anticommunist rhetoric into action. And Eisenhower threw in a twist of his own. After the Vietminh were beaten back by a new international police force, the French, Eisenhower insisted, would be required to set Vietnam free. It was a bizarre plan, but it kept Eisenhower on the right side of the anticommunist effort. It was also irrelevant, for Eisenhower's original assessment was correct. The French surrendered Dienbienphu on May 6, 1954.

Ho had finally won independence for his country. But the celebration would be short-lived.

Ask Saigon Sally

In the spring of 1954, the last great battle of the Franco-Vietnamese War took a heavy toll. The carnage at Dienbienphu left nearly 8,000 Vietminh dead and 15,000 wounded. Close to 2,100 French troops were killed and 5,600 wounded.

The Least You Need to Know

➤ The strident anticommunism of the early 1950s tainted America's view of the Franco-Vietnamese War.

➤ U.S. foreign policy-makers saw little difference between a war in Korea and a war in Vietnam.

➤ The Vietminh maintained a patient strategy against the French.

➤ The French mistakenly believed that they could destroy the Vietminh at the battle of Dienbienphu.

➤ The United States strongly opposed a Vietminh military victory, but did little to stop it.

Part 2
How to Make a Quagmire

To the American government of the 1950s and early 1960s, the best commie was a dead commie. Many Americans believed that after the death of German Nazism, Italian fascism, and Japanese militarism, there was one evil "ism" left out there: communism. It was them or us, some said, and the White House shared this view. No place was exempt from anticommunist sword-rattling, and there could be no dealing with devils. Ho Chi Minh was considered one of those devils.

This heyday of anticommunist zeal looks very alien from the hindsight of the twenty-first century. But it made perfect sense to an America that saw its military, economy, and global interests as absolutely invincible. Sadly, Vietnam did not fit into this view very well. Its politics, culture, and needs were very different from the American scene, but few bothered to figure this out.

Arrogance, elitism, and callous decision-making won out over reason and common sense in America's early Vietnam policy-making. Thousands of Americans and Vietnamese would pay with their lives for that unfortunate approach.

Chapter 6

Thirty Years War, Act Two

In This Chapter

➤ Anticommunism doesn't need Joe McCarthy

➤ The big guns gather in Geneva

➤ The White House discovers South Vietnam

➤ Americans learn how to spell Ngo Dinh Diem

➤ Senator Kennedy shows his "profile"

William Proxmire had a hard act to follow. Taking over Senator Joseph McCarthy's Senate seat following the latter's untimely death in the mid-1950s, the shy, lanky Proxmire was quite a contrast to the firebrand McCarthy. A product of a special election in Wisconsin, Proxmire was a Democrat with a "different message."

In a way, Proxmire was Wisconsin's apology to the nation for the excesses of their late senator and chairman of the Un-American Affairs Committee. Called "Just Plain Bill" in some of his campaign brochures, Proxmire said the Cold War had gotten way out of hand. Young, handsome, and a physical-fitness nut, Proxmire called for a new, progressive foreign policy. He would become part of a small group of naysayers in the Democratic party who looked alike, dressed alike, and talked alike about the direction of U.S. foreign relations. But even a different message had its limits.

At this time, no politician who wanted to remain a politician stood up and said the Cold War was a mistake, that winning a Cold War threatened total nuclear destruction, or that Vietnam held no security or economic interests for the United States. In the mid- and late 1950s, few Americans doubted the sanctity of their government's anticommunist commitment. Those doubts would come later, and only after body bags were filled with American dead. For the moment, policy-makers debated over the proper, winning tactics. And open debate was difficult in the Red Scare era.

Ask Saigon Sally

World diplomats have always loved pretty Geneva, Switzerland. The town not only hosted the 1954 Geneva Conference on Asia, where key decisions on the future of Vietnam were made, but also welcomed dozens of other diplomatic gatherings throughout the twentieth century.

Shell Shock

Vietnam was a confused place after the battle of Dienbienphu, and some historians and Western observers have misinterpreted the situation. Dienbienphu was not the last battle of the Franco-Vietnamese War. The French were finished, but fighting did continue.

The Bao Dai Boogie

If Ho Chi Minh was unacceptable to the White House, somebody else had to be picked for the George Washington role. To hear it from John Foster Dulles, you would think it was the role of a lifetime. Sometimes Dulles said Vietnam was America's new last stand against advancing communism. Sometimes he said it was America's new first line of defense. Whatever he said, few Americans were listening.

When the world press gathered at Geneva to report on the international community's decisions on Vietnam, there were 10 times more European newsmen than American newsmen present. During the Franco-Vietnamese War, the madness overseas had always been French madness, and that was that. The Geneva Conference received scant attention in the United States, and years later, Americans would still be wondering what took place there. Meanwhile, John Foster Dulles, angered by the success of Ho Chi Minh, was on his worst behavior in Geneva. With few American reporters there to question his antics, it didn't matter anyway.

As early as February 1954, while meeting in Berlin, Dulles and the foreign ministers of Great Britain, France, and the Soviet Union had agreed to meet in a special Geneva-hosted conference to talk about Vietnam and other Asian matters. With grand reluctance, Dulles consented to a Chinese presence at the meeting, as long as everyone understood that the United States would never recognize the existence of a communist China. Indeed, Mao's right-hand man, Chou En-lai, arrived in Geneva when Dulles did, and the secretary of state refused to shake his hand. That simple gesture, he insisted, could be interpreted as American diplomatic recognition of "evil."

Frankly, Chou had arrived to win diplomatic recognition and respect from all those gathered in Geneva. His government had been in power for five years, and it had yet to be welcomed to significant diplomatic gatherings. This was the new China's first day in the sun, but Dulles preferred to keep Chou in the shadows.

The Geneva Conference

Nineteen nations sent delegations to the Geneva Conference on Asia. Opening in late April 1954, the conference's first agenda item was Korea. The conference was supposed to be a fast and furious one, but Dulles's lack of cooperation with the agenda delayed the progress of the meeting.

Upset over communist presence at the conference, including a North Korea delegation in the conference room, Dulles often refused to attend meetings. Staying in his hotel or with the U.S. ambassador to Switzerland, Dulles received the minutes of the meetings far away from the conference site. He would jot down his thoughts on the proceedings, have a runner take them back to the conference, and then have his comments read into the record, debated, and discussed. It was a long, bizarre process.

Eventually, Dulles bolted the entire conference, leaving his deputy, Walter Bedell Smith, in charge of the U.S. delegation. Sadly, a decision on a real peace for the Korean situation failed.

The discussion on Vietnam did not even begin until May 8, 1954, or hours after the French gave up at Dienbienphu. It took until the end of July to get some sort of agreement on the new Vietnam, and Ho Chi Minh hated the delay.

One problem with the long agenda was that some delegations preferred to talk about more "important" matters. The British delegation, for instance, would have loved an assurance from the Americans that their government would assist them should one of their own colonies go the way of Vietnam. To the British, the Americans had done too little, too late in Vietnam, and they did not want to be lost and forgotten like the French. The British-American discussions were distracting to Pham Van Dong, the Vietnamese delegate at Geneva. But there was little that he could do about it.

Tales from the Front

"Leave Vietnam with a University education." This was not just a U.S. military recruitment slogan. It was true. Founded in 1956, the University of Maryland's Far East Division enjoyed a special Pentagon-arranged contract to provide a full range of courses to U.S. military personnel throughout Southeast Asia. Fully accredited and concerned about standards, Maryland's Far East Division maintained curriculum requirements similar to its home campus of College Park, Maryland. But their classrooms could be tents and quonset huts at bases across South Vietnam. Its faculty enjoyed the equivalent rank and privileges of a Lieutenant Colonel, and they came under fire just like their students. No known deaths were ever recorded; however, in University of Maryland lore there are plenty of tales (mostly unconfirmed) of selfless, dedicated professors (called "lecturers" in the Far East Division) who taught their classes during enemy attacks or even after being wounded.

Ask Saigon Sally

The U.S. delegation to the 1954 Geneva Conference on Asia was left in good hands with Lieutenant General Walter Bedell Smith (1895– 1961). Smith served as General Eisenhower's chief of staff during World War II, and he helped plan the North Africa, Sicily, and Normandy invasions.

Although it might not have mattered to an old Cold Warrior like Dulles, Chou and Ho were not blood brothers. In fact, there was plenty of bad blood between the two. Chou went to Geneva in the name of national self-interest, and not to stand in solidarity with the Vietminh.

To Chou, Ho and his supporters presented certain problems. First, if the American domino theorists were right, and Ho created a link of communist movements under his command across Southeast Asia, Ho's brand of maverick communism would become a threat to Mao's claimed leadership of "peasant communists" everywhere. Second, if Ho just became the leader of a free, united Vietnam, there would still be potential trouble for China.

Reminiscent of some of the gloom-and-doom conspiracy theories heard in the United States, Chou had a worst-case scenario of his own. To Chou, Ho was a potential screwup. His Vietminh, from the Chinese view, were a poorly disciplined mob, and Ho would be inheriting a lousy economy in a destroyed, impoverished country. A Vietnamese civil war looked more than possible to Chou, and the United States would, most likely, influence the result. It was not far-fetched to propose, Chou allegedly said, that Ho's days were numbered and that a pro-American government was around the corner for Vietnam. That would mean U.S. military bases and U.S. weaponry all pointed toward Vietnam's neighbor, China.

Again, if Dulles and the American delegation had been aware of any fallout between Ho and Chou, it would not have mattered a bit. A commie was a commie, and their disagreements were irrelevant. Today's State Department would wheel and deal in such a situation. In 1954, at Geneva, there were only raw deals for the Vietnamese. But one Vietnamese truly lucked out.

Enter Bao Dai

Emperor Bao Dai, the Geneva delegations ruled, was now in charge of Vietnamese territory south of the 17th parallel. The Vietminh would rule the north. Modeled, to a degree, on the 38th parallel partition on the Korean peninsula, this divide-and-rule decision was meant to be temporary. Nationwide elections were scheduled for 1956 to decide the future government and bring about national unification.

Depending on the day of the week, Dulles and Eisenhower either supported or regretted this arrangement. On the one hand, they believed that Ho in a free election could never win even the post of dogcatcher in Vietnam. Of course, they could be wrong, and in these strident days of the Cold War, the Eisenhower administration preferred to play it safe. Any decision that would prevent a Ho victory in a free election was deemed the best U.S. policy. Hence, the White House hoped to play a heavy hand in the upcoming elections. America was the great master of democratic campaigning, after all. Complete with bumper stickers, TV and radio ads, and endless visibility efforts on behalf of our boy, whoever he turned out to be, the American-influenced campaign in Vietnam would be a winning one. And the Eisenhower administration fully expected landslide results after they were fully involved in the election process.

On the other hand, they despised the fact that Ho Chi Minh had won a home for his Vietminh in northern Vietnam, even if it was only for two years. It suggested American recognition of communist expansionism, and the Eisenhower team refused to endorse that contradiction. Consequently, they never signed the Geneva Accords, which were partially negotiated by one of their own people, Bedell Smith.

In addition to the big-picture issues of partition and elections, the Geneva *Accords* also prohibited Vietnam from entering into military alliances with Laos and Cambodia. It could never seek military aid beyond basic self-defense requirements. Foreign forces would be leaving Cambodia and Laos immediately, and no new forces were to be introduced in Vietnam.

A cease-fire permitted French forces to withdraw from the north and for Vietminh fighters in the south to head north. An International Control Commission, consisting of Canadian, Polish, and Indian representatives, were given the thankless task of enforcing all of this. The Americans, at least, promised not to trouble the arrangement with the "use of force," and Washington considered this vow a considerable generosity given its refusal to sign the accords.

The only other government that refused to sign the Geneva Accords was the one ruling the new South Vietnam. Ngo Dinh Diem, the newly

Jarhead Jargon

The term **accord** in what is known as the 1954 Geneva Accords has an official U.S. diplomatic definition. If a president wants to negotiate a foreign affairs arrangement, but avoid the Constitutionally mandated treaty, his administration can negotiate an accord. This is based on "executive privilege" and does not require Congressional approval. Hence, America's earliest commitment to South Vietnam was done without formal Congressional approval.

Shell Shock

In the mid-1950s, the commandant of the Marine Corps, Lemuel Shepherd, said he did not have to give any reasons why he opposed a U.S. military intervention in Vietnam. The very thought of it, he noted, was "completely insane."

65

elected anticommunist head of state, made this decision after John Foster Dulles told him it was the right thing to do. Meanwhile, Frenchmen in South Vietnam still dreamed of restoring their tarnished "pearl of the Orient" back to mother France, but it was not to be. The symbol of power in South Vietnam was now Bao Dai. And that was about all he was—a symbol.

The Violence Continues

Violence and misery ruled South Vietnam. Pro-independence Vietnamese sought revenge against pro-French Vietnamese. The economy remained tied to France, but the French were broke and already worried about a possible colonial war in Algeria. With French colonial paternalism gone, rural South Vietnam had little direction in any field of endeavor, and Bao Dai maintained a low profile through it all. Having led the Japanese collaborationist government, at least in name, and having spent years living the good life in the south of France, Bao Dai was not loved by his people.

Ask Saigon Sally

In 1954, some 580,000 Catholics were said to live in the new South Vietnam. Well educated and well connected to the French business world, the Vietnamese Catholics represented power and privilege.

Known for his interest in fine clothes, fine wine, and sleazy women, Bao Dai still tried to live up to his royalist obligations in public. His efforts to look and act like an elitist Vietnamese fell flat, for most of his countrymen knew better. As long as the emperor tried to act like a leader, the Eisenhower administration heaped tons of praise upon him. If the man was applauded in America, the White House believed, maybe the South Vietnamese would give him a second chance. But it was already too late for second chances.

The new South Vietnam faced a host of challenges. Various Buddhist sects competed for the allegiance of South Vietnamese farmers and city residents, region by region. Most were anticommunist, but they were also anti-Western and anti–Bao Dai. Pro-French Vietnamese took advantage of the chaos, promising peace and order, and that stirred up leftover Vietminh troops and supporters.

Our Man Diem

Implying that Ngo Dinh Diem symbolized a powerful, determined, last-ditch defense against evil and oppression, Eisenhower praised the South Vietnamese leader as "the Churchill of Asia." At least that was what he said publicly. Privately, Eisenhower worried about the confusion of South Vietnamese politics. Could any one anticommunist leader ever compete with the legendary Ho Chi Minh? The right answer included massive U.S. aid to Diem, the White House decided. But Diem's liabilities, ranging from oppression to corruption, would eventually become glaring.

A devoutly religious Catholic, Diem once studied to be a priest but turned to a government career instead. To Diem, the Vietminh represented chaos, confusion, and the ultimate collapse of Vietnam should they succeed. Order and stability were important to this disciplined man. So was family, and the Vietminh had already executed Diem's nephew and older brother.

At the end of World War II, when Ho began to appeal to anything that walked to join his movement, Diem had been offered a leadership role in the Vietminh. Diem turned down the offer, saying that he would never work for murderers. He then spent the next several years wandering, thinking, and praying. In contrast to Bao Dai, Diem had no vices, and this would win him great respect in Washington. He even spent three years in a seminary in New Jersey, avoiding debates over the future of his country. But as the Vietminh began to humble the French, anticommunist lobby groups in the United States, such as the American Friends of Vietnam, began to spread Diem's name around Washington, D.C.

Suddenly Diem was the "real George Washington" in waiting—an honest, religious man of principle who could provide leadership and guidance for Vietnam. Diem later quipped that he was never sure who the Americans were talking about at this time, but it certainly wasn't him. Indeed, Diem had little use for democracy.

To these refugees in 1955, life in Diem's new South Vietnam was not sweet.

National Archives Still Pictures Unit, College Park, Maryland, and the American Red Cross.

A strong authoritarian government would be good for Vietnam, he argued. He also had limited use for Western life and culture. He liked its money and its religious institutions, but the West had been "a poison," he insisted, in Vietnam; less and not more Western influence was needed there. But in those heady early days of the Truman Doctrine, Diem's dislike for democracy and Western traditions was not considered a liability for U.S. policy. It was his longtime opposition to communism that mattered.

Jarhead Jargon

After the 1954 Geneva Accords, not all Vietminh activists moved north to form a new government. Those truly loyal to the new North Vietnamese regime were expected to stay put and work with the **Committee for the South** (an outgrowth of the Vietminh-run Central Office of South Vietnam, or COSVN, during the Franco-Vietnamese War) in the heart of South Vietnam.

Shell Shock

One of the reasons President Eisenhower might have been skeptical over the future of Ngo Dinh Diem had to involve Robert McClintock. As the number-two man in charge of the U.S. mission in Saigon, McClintock reported to the White House that Diem had "little respect or support" anywhere in South Vietnam.

Lightning Joe and Colonel Ed

Did Diem have a chance? The answers varied. J. Lawton Collins suggested that American confidence in Diem might be misplaced. Known as "Lightning Joe" by his troops on Guadalcanal during World War II, Collins was the former commander of the 25th Infantry Division who rose to be army chief of staff in the early 1950s. Eisenhower sent him to South Vietnam to serve as the American special envoy.

For all effective purposes, Collins was the chief military advisor to Diem's struggling little military. From the *Committee for the South* to Buddhist protestors to unhappy rice farmers, Diem, Collins could see, had a long list of detractors and a short list of supporters. The man lived too well in the face of horrible poverty and a war-torn economy, he told Eisenhower. It was unlikely that he could overcome the ill will and distrust leveled at his administration. Because of these simple facts, Collins urged the White House to look for a different leader to champion the anticommunist cause in South Vietnam.

But the Eisenhower team could not easily go back on all of that "Churchill of Asia" rhetoric, and they were confident that the man only needed a little more time. Collins, on the other hand, remained impatient with Diem. Foreign leader or not, Collins lectured Diem, shouted at him, and generally disliked the guy. The feeling was mutual. Diem found Collins abrasive, racist, and forever trying to remake South Vietnam in the image of the United States.

In his own way, Edward G. Lansdale echoed Collins's concern. Lansdale, America's CIA boss in the new South Vietnam, was less abrasive and more cynical than Collins. Nicknamed Colonel Ed by some of his South Vietnamese admirers, Lansdale liked his work. He thought Collins and his supporters should chill out and enjoy the ride. Intelligence work was exciting stuff to Lansdale, and he added his own brand of worldly humor to the task. He considered Diem an idiot, but he was *our* idiot. And that was the point.

Lansdale engaged in a variety of counterintelligence programs, including forays across the 17th parallel to attack North Vietnamese munitions depots. Lansdale told the Vietnamese involved in this covert operation that the North Vietnamese planned horrible atrocities against their friends and neighbors. It was a lie, but it motivated the South Vietnamese like nothing else at the time.

A New, Sexy Profile

Just as Diem was fast becoming a symbol of America's hard-nosed commitment to the expedient Truman Doctrine, writers were putting out best-selling books that slammed the Truman Doctrine. It has been rare when American political and foreign policy books occupy the top of both the fiction and the nonfiction charts; however, in the mid- and late 1950s, American readers could not get enough of the stuff.

Senator John F. Kennedy was one of those trailblazing writers. In the 1950s, a politician with a fancy, cerebral book to his credit was as rare as booze at a Southern Baptist convention. Young Jack Kennedy was praised for caring enough about the voters to provide them with an innovative book that applied the lessons of the political past to the present. And it wasn't even about Vietnam. Or was it?

A Harvard political science major with a lifelong interest in historical dilemmas, Kennedy became a household name, if he wasn't already, with his *Profiles in Courage*. Assisted by speechwriter and friend Ted Sorensen, the book would go on to win the 1956 Pulitzer Prize. Years later, some would charge that the Kennedy family bribed the Columbia University School of Journalism (which administers the Pulitzer Prize) to get this award, and that Sorensen wrote every line of the book. Neither charge was true.

Profiles in Courage offered portraits of history-makers who had tried to make a difference, but who were often considered failures in their day. In most cases, Kennedy's selections were people who challenged the status quo, took on the Establishment, remained 100 percent committed and dedicated to their cause, and went the distance no matter what. This, Kennedy concluded, made them all heroes, and professional historians should reevaluate them accordingly. From Daniel Webster to John Quincy

Ask Saigon Sally

Before John F. Kennedy's *Profiles in Courage* (New York: Harper, 1956), there was his *Why England Slept* (New York: Widred Funk, 1940). The latter was a cautious but critical appraisal of British appeasement and American isolationism.

Ask Saigon Sally

Just as there had been a China Lobby, there was a Vietnam Lobby of congressmen, businessmen, and religious groups. The American Friends of Vietnam was pro-Diem, pro-Vietnamese Catholic, and passionately anti-communist.

Adams, Kennedy hailed those who had favored a different path in history. What a better country it might have been had we only listened to them.

Kennedy, following the examples in his book, called for a change in anticommunist politics. He urged men of courage to come up with a better plan than helping Western colonial powers keep their empires. Helping postcolonial dictators was distasteful, too.

These were outrageous statements to the Eisenhower team, but Kennedy was a senator from Massachusetts, a state that often expected a certain degree of outrageousness from its elected officials. His comments also suggested that he was a good friend to the Third World struggle for independence and freedom. He welcomed the label, always implying that this particular stand represented his own "profile in courage."

But Kennedy was a mixed bag. He had been a member of the American Friends of Vietnam, which always praised Diem to the heavens, and he never had any trouble alternately denouncing and even praising John Foster Dulles. On the other hand, he insisted in one eloquent speech after another that no matter how much aid and encouragement were offered to dictators like Diem, he would still be a dictator. It was time to tie some strings of democratic reform to American aid. Otherwise, the United States was financing oppression as well as triggering the very uprisings that American foreign policy was trying to prevent.

As a World War II–Pacific veteran, Kennedy claimed to have a lingering personal interest in the fate of the Asian/Pacific region. Other writers would soon focus on the reformist message and hammer away at it, too, but only Kennedy would have the power to do something about it. Would a doubting, questioning young senator see things differently if he made it to the White House? Kennedy's true profile was yet to be seen.

The Least You Need to Know

➤ America's anticommunist cause had many different champions.

➤ The Geneva Conference on Asia divided Vietnam at the 17th parallel, and it led to America's anticommunist commitment to the South Vietnamese government.

➤ The Eisenhower administration saw no alternative to a Ngo Dinh Diem government in South Vietnam.

➤ U.S. government officials served as senior advisors to the early Diem regime.

➤ America's 1950s Cold War and Vietnam policies did not go unquestioned by a future president, John F. Kennedy.

Chapter 7

Kings of Corruption

In This Chapter

➤ Vietnam: Yes. World War III: No

➤ Dulles says "peaceful coexistence" is a commie trick

➤ Ngo Dinh Diem takes on family values

➤ Americans are "ugly" as sin

➤ Whatever happened to Ho Chi Minh?

America would never fight in Vietnam, said James Reston in the late 1950s. And his view was important to the millions of Americans who shared their morning coffee with him. At the time, Reston was one of America's most read political columnists. His editorials on U.S. politics and diplomacy appeared in hundreds of newspapers across the country. Although no expert on Vietnam, Reston had a knack for explaining the twists and turns of U.S. foreign policy to interested readers.

Frankly, Reston was more concerned about nuclear war than brushfire war. If he had to choose between Vietnam and World War III, he'd take Vietnam over World War III any day. But he hoped the Eisenhower administration got the message from his editorials that the choice was Vietnam or nothing. Rescuing the downtrodden in Vietnam made better sense than blowing up the world, and this represented the enlightened "liberal view" to many people.

Don't You Trust Them Commies!

In February 1956, at the Twentieth Communist Party Congress, Nikita Khrushchev stunned the world with his announcement that his predecessor, Joseph Stalin, had been less than ethical. Implying that the economy was in a mess because of communism itself, Khrushchev said that he wanted to "liberalize" the Soviet system. He also said that he was saddened by the long bread lines in Moscow. Stalin had cared too much for power and not enough for the Soviet people.

In his own way, Khrushchev was saying that his country had spent too much on defense. They had a First World military in their struggling Third World country. Perhaps it was time to tone down the goals of Soviet expansionism, reconsider domestic priorities, and restore confidence in the original communist dream. All of these potential reforms, hopes, and ambitions were wrapped up in what Khrushchev called "peaceful coexistence."

Ask Saigon Sally

One of the press's earliest opponents to the U.S. military role in Vietnam was columnist Walter Lippmann. He won the Pulitzer Prize on two different occasions in his long career, and his columns appeared in newspapers across the United States from 1938 to 1974.

Khrushchev was a crusty, overweight bear of a man who had once worked as a coal miner. Working his way up through the Soviet system's most representative body, the Central Committee, Khrushchev was well aware of the concerns of regular folks in his native Ukraine and elsewhere.

Given his up-from-the-roots rise to power, Khrushchev was something of the textbook-perfect communist. But he inherited the house that Stalin built, complete with a huge bureaucracy that disagreed with his "liberalization" promise. The hard years of the Stalin era, they asked, had been for nothing? Whatever Khrushchev truly and specifically proposed to do fascinated both Soviet-occupied Eastern Europe and Washington politicos. For a brief, wonderful moment in the mid-1950s, it looked like the Cold War was subsiding.

In North Vietnam, Ho Chi Minh claimed that the new Soviet position was a reflection of his own approach to communism over the years. No one heard this boast outside of Vietnam, and, most likely, Ho only expected North Vietnamese to hear it anyway. Still coping with a war-ravaged economy, along with lousy rice-farming weather, Ho's most efficient policy since founding his North Vietnam government involved punishing as many pro-French Vietnamese as he could find. His wartime message of unity and tolerance did not ring true.

Meanwhile, the news from Eastern Europe was disheartening for communists everywhere. For a while, it seemed like the communist world would be shrinking and not expanding. In Poland, for example, Khrushchev's de-Stalinization program led to anti–Red Army riots as the locals concluded that independence was truly around the bend. In Hungary, students and young workers formed rebel groups against the Soviets. Things had gotten out of hand. Pressured by Stalinists to retaliate, Khrushchev feared that his entire liberalization plan was now in jeopardy. His new version of communism with a human face would have to wait, and Red Army rule returned to Eastern Europe.

Shell Shock

Nikita Khrushchev confused the U.S. State Department. His denunciation of Stalin, temporary Red Army pull-out of Eastern Europe, insistence on domestic economic reform, and love of American pop culture suggested a thaw in the Cold War to many journalists and international relations experts. In 1956, the Policy Planning Division of the State Department began to study the impact of an imminent collapse of Soviet communism and what that might mean for the rest of the world. They were thirty years ahead of their time, and Secretary Dulles halted the study once he learned about it.

All the commotion in Moscow and Eastern Europe caught the White House off guard. Was the Cold War going through a January thaw, or was this long, messy winter over for good? The American press wanted to know. Secretary of State Dulles told them not to be fooled by this latest communist ploy.

As always to Dulles, it was irrelevant what kind of communist a person was. Khrushchev, like Ho Chi Minh, was a communist and that was that. America, he vowed, would stay the course, and he urged Americans not to be taken in by the developments in Europe. Communism still lived. It just had a different champion. President Eisenhower stood by his secretary of state's analysis; however, the American people read the news carefully. Times were changing. Right?

Ask Saigon Sally

John Foster Dulles was born in 1888 to a Washington, D.C., family with a long history of government and missionary service. He was named after his maternal grandfather, John W. Foster, who was President Benjamin Harrison's secretary of state.

Jarhead Jargon

Beginning with Eisenhower's 1954 State of the Union Address, the **New Look** became the official expression to describe 1950s U.S. defense policy. Its elements included a heavy reliance on nuclear weapons, a reduction in both ground and naval forces, and an emphasis on cost-cutting and strict fiscal conservatism.

Ask Saigon Sally

A generous Hungarian Refugee Act resulted from the quick Red Army defeat of the young rebels in the 1956 Hungarian Revolt. One of the young Hungarians who came to the United States was Tom Lantos. He later became a California congressman and a tireless opponent of U.S. military involvement in the Vietnam War.

All in the Family

He ain't heavy, he's my brother. Or so the song goes, one that Ngo Dinh Diem might have known well. While the Eisenhower administration carried the burden of *New Look* defense policies and difficult world power responsibilities, Ngo Dinh Diem carried his family. The key positions in his government were held by family members, and Diem made no apologies for his decisions.

Claiming that the reasoning behind this pseudo-monarchy involved Confucian ideas of trust, discipline, and coordination, Diem insisted that his regime had nothing to do with dictatorship and corruption. It had everything to do with Vietnamese tradition, he said.

Naturally, many Vietnamese didn't think the Catholic Diem knew much about Confucian tradition. The Eisenhower administration had similar doubts. But from the beginning of the Diem era, the Eisenhower team tried to be sensitive to Diem's sense of independence. The White House begged Diem to be more democratic and American-like, but he never budged on the family rule issue.

The Can Lao

If asked, Diem said that he was a member of the Can Lao, or Personalist Party. In reality, the Can Lao was the creation of Diem's brother, Ngo Dinh Nhu, and the top party members were members of the Ngo family, including Diem's sister, Madame Nhu.

Madame Nhu, nicknamed the "Dragon Lady" by the Western press, enjoyed political influence across the country. Her father held a cabinet post, her uncle was the foreign minister, and a cousin was the minister of education. Meanwhile, Diem's brother, Ngo Dinh Canh, controlled the provinces near the old imperial city of Hue, and Diem never even gave him a title. Most people simply called him "The Chief." Another Diem brother, Ngo Dinh Thuc, was a Catholic bishop, and he was appointed director of the Vietnamese Catholic Church. The Diem regime never offered any apologies for its flaunting of Catholicism in the face of Buddhist Vietnam.

Photographed just hours before his assassination in November 1963, President Diem (second from right) poses with his family.

Courtesy of Corbis.

One of Diem and Nhu's early accomplishments involved a top-to-bottom purge of the armed forces. More than 6,000 army officers were stripped of their titles and replaced by men who owed their full allegiance, or so they said, to the Ngo family. Other soldiers were urged, if not forced, to join the Can Lao Party. Believing that an active, working military would keep his soldiers away from antigovernment politics, Diem and Nhu eliminated the civil service and replaced government bureaucrats with armed troops.

The New South Vietnam

Under Diem, South Vietnam slowly became an armed camp, and the first order of business for this new, involved military was protecting the Diem family. Fighting communists came second, and the Eisenhower administration disliked these mixed-up priorities. Nevertheless, Diem made it illegal to be a communist in South Vietnam, and the punishment for this crime was usually death. He also put free speech to death by closing down all anti-Diem newspapers and killing or jailing all those who spoke out against his government.

The White House estimated that by 1958 Diem had incarcerated close to 50,000 political offenders and executed 12,500 more. And American taxpayers paid the bill, for two-thirds of Diem's operating budget came directly from Washington. Dulles always said that the American people should be proud of their contribution to "development" in South Vietnam, but more than 75 percent of U.S. aid went straight to Diem's military as well as to the family coffers.

As always, the Truman Doctrine required only that an ally be anticommunist, not necessarily democratic. Diem tried Washington patience, but, at least in the late 1950s, his government seemed to have managed to beat back communist threats. That, of course, was what he was supposed to do.

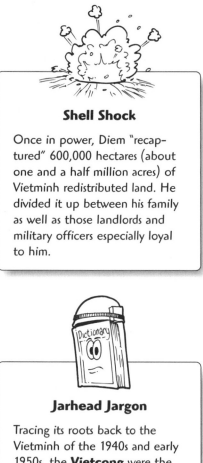

Shell Shock

Once in power, Diem "recaptured" 600,000 hectares (about one and a half million acres) of Vietminh redistributed land. He divided it up between his family as well as those landlords and military officers especially loyal to him.

Jarhead Jargon

Tracing its roots back to the Vietminh of the 1940s and early 1950s, the **Vietcong** were the Hanoi-backed armed opposition to the South Vietnamese government. American GI slang, such as Victor Charlie, VC, or simply Charlie and Chuck, comes from this title. The term Vietcong is slang even in Vietnamese. The official title for the anti-Saigon regime forces is National Liberation Front, or NLF.

To make sure his family stayed in power, Diem dedicated the South Vietnamese government to destroying leftover remnants of the Vietminh. In 1957, Diem deliberately sent his troops into communist-held regions of South Vietnam, where they prevailed. U.S. military advice came in handy during this offensive, but there were other reasons for the communist defeat. The communists themselves were divided.

Ho Chi Minh had established pro–North Vietnamese cells in the communist holdouts of South Vietnam, but their primary role was "political awareness." Given the fact that Buddhists and Western-styled supporters of democracy all had grievances against Diem, Ho believed that these other noncommunist agitators could topple Diem on their own. Then, his own tightly disciplined group would take power.

Ho miscalculated here. Longtime southern Vietnamese communists wanted to act and act now, and many of them resented Ho's lofty leadership from afar. In any event, the communists of the south were reduced to terrorist operations and murdering senior Ngo family officials, just as the Vietminh had killed French officers and their friends shortly before the full-blown Franco-Vietnamese War.

Ho the Terrorist

Terrorism, some believe, is the last tactic of the desperate. To both Diem and the Eisenhower administration, Ho's acts of terrorism meant the communists were finally on the run. All they could do was make trouble and not mount great offensives. That was good news, it seemed, to the White House and the Ngo family.

Diem had a catchy name for all those who took up arms against his government. He called them the *Vietcong*. The title would stick for years, and it would confuse people for years as well. For all effective purposes, the Vietcong included anyone who was ready to kill South Vietnamese government representatives and their foreign backers.

The Vietcong had a solid communist core. They remained a Southern-based organization, but they were influenced by the larger unification agenda of Ho Chi Minh up north. Suffice it to say, the Vietcong and the North Vietnamese were not enemies. They both wanted Diem, now nicknamed "The Mandarin," and his American friends out of Vietnam.

SEATO

Hated by his own people or not, Diem felt pretty secure in the 1950s. One reason for his confidence involved the South East Asia Treaty Organization (SEATO). The result of a Dulles-championed effort and the product of a Southeast Asian security arrangement signed in Manila, this military collective security agency was a *paper tiger*. Created in 1954, it had no resemblance to Europe's North Atlantic Treaty Organization (NATO). NATO had real troops, real bases, and a real military mission. SEATO had anticommunist rhetoric.

Like NATO, SEATO was supposed to represent the combined militaries of the anticommunist cause in a certain region. Dulles and other Washington politicians always talked about it in that kind of light. Just as Americans would be confused over who and what the Vietcong were, they would also be confused over what SEATO did and did not do.

Despite all the Washington-generated comments about how Ho had to watch out, for SEATO was watching him, SEATO was all brag and no fact. Three of Southeast Asia's more significant nations, Indonesia, Burma, and India, refused to have anything to do with it. Meanwhile, Diem's South Vietnam, along with Cambodia and Laos, could not belong to it because of specific stipulations imposed at the Geneva Conference on Asia.

The SEATO security agreement signed in Manila bound the United States, Australia, Great Britain, New Zealand, Pakistan, Thailand, and the Philippines to "consultative arrangements" on defense issues. If the communist threat in South

Ask Saigon Sally

On June 8, 1954, during the Geneva Conference on Asia, *The Washington Post* published a political cartoon showing a nervous-looking and gun-toting Uncle Sam marching off into a dark, scary place labeled Vietnam. The caption read: "French Mistakes in Vietnam. How Would Another Mistake Help?"

Jarhead Jargon

Often applied to U.S. diplomacy issues during the heyday of the Cold War, the term **paper tiger** referred to threatening rhetoric, international agreements, and angry domestic politics focused against the communist enemy. It was not a flattering term, for it implied that meaningless rhetoric and do-nothing legal arrangements were being substituted for action, force, and victory.

Vietnam, Laos, and Cambodia were to present a "common danger," the SEATO gang would "consult" each other during that crisis. It was all very vague and interpretive. In any event, SEATO provided an easy means for key Asian/Pacific nations and Great Britain to permit a large U.S. military intervention out there somewhere. It also told Ho Chi Minh that the United States, backed by other Asian/Pacific countries, was ready to march against him.

Ho Chi Minh knew a paper tiger when he saw one. NATO was scary to communists. SEATO was not. No one except the Americans were obsessed with the anti-communism cause, and Diem welcomed anything that might help him breathe a little easier.

Ask Saigon Sally

As early as 1957, Assistant Secretary of Defense Neil Hosler Mc-Elroy assured the U.S. Congress that if the U.S. military moved into South Vietnam, its technology and firepower would provide an immediate victory.

Why Americans Are "Ugly"

"The Mandarin?" "The Dragon Lady?" These were America's allies? American voters were becoming upset with U.S. foreign policy. And it took some moxie to be upset. Given the reality of the Red Scare era, whether Joe McCarthy was still part of it or not, you had to be careful when you criticized American diplomacy. You didn't want to give that wrong "comsymp" (communist sympathizer) impression, you know.

By 1958, there were plenty of Americans who were weary of this tiptoeing around. The time was right to rock the boat. Authors William J. Lederer and Eugene Burdick did just that. Their book *The Ugly American* became the surprise, runaway best-seller of the late 1950s, and it continued to sell thousands of copies into the early 1960s. Hollywood made a loosely based movie version of it, putting the versatile Marlon Brando in the title role.

The Ugly American was a novel about U.S. foreign policy in Southeast Asia, but many bookstores sold it as nonfiction. The story takes place in the made-up country of Sarkhan, but it seemed to be a mixture of South Vietnam and Thailand rolled into one. Lederer and Burdick brought years of journalism and U.S. Navy intelligence experience to their tale, and they pulled no punches. Whereas John Kennedy cautiously and vaguely alluded to big problems in current policy-making in his *Profiles in Courage,* Lederer and Burdick had an obvious ax to grind. They also weren't running for any elective office. And there was the precedent of *The Quiet American.*

The Quiet American

The Quiet American was a 1956 Graham Greene novel about America's "lost innocence" in South Vietnam. Sort of. Greene's major character, Alden Pyle, was something of the Edward Lansdale, but even more cynical and complex. A fine piece of literature, Greene's book turned on the critics, but it was not a book that you took to the beach. Greene had a long list of complaints about the United States, and his own cynicism rubbed existing critics of American policy the wrong way. Nevertheless, even this work was turned into a movie of the same name. Audie Murphy, the World War II Congressional Medal of Honor winner turned B-movie actor, starred in the cheap, black-and-white film version. It was viewed by the Murphy family, film critics, and few others.

The Ugly American indicted U.S. diplomacy, but it also preached working alternatives to existing policy. Its authors had a great deal of faith in America's potential to do the right thing. Hence their story came across as a positive, upbeat, and exciting one for a general audience looking for something both entertaining and challenging to read. The later Marlon Brando version of it would be a box-office smash.

Ask Saigon Sally

During a 1959 goodwill tour of the United States, Nikita Khrushchev was denied entry to Disneyland because of "inadequate security." The Soviet premier joked that the real reason he was not allowed to meet Mickey Mouse was because the Americans must have a secret missile base located on Disney property.

Since World War II, Lederer and Burdick wrote, America had tried its best to demonstrate its greatness to the people of developing nations. Yet American goodness had not been made clear to these same people. Viet-namese, Filipinos, and others knew where America stood in the struggle "against" communism. But what was Washington "for?"

The Good America

To Lederer and Burdick, championing the virtue of the "good" America" always remained a tactic to achieve success in the anticommunist priorities of the "great America." One of their fictional characters, a comfortable U.S. businessman, even leaves his job temporarily to help train and employ some struggling villagers in Sarkhan. The idea of volunteering your talents in the Third World, and having your hard work coordinated by a helpful government agency, became a cornerstone of John Kennedy's 1960 cry for a new U.S. foreign policy.

Kennedy read *The Ugly American*, bragged about it, and did his best to connect his own *Profiles in Courage* thesis with the concerns of Lederer and Burdick. Kennedy's opponent for the presidency in 1960, Vice President Richard Nixon, would claim that he was too busy on the job to be sitting around reading novels. That response, probably the product of long meetings with campaign staffers, was supposed to illustrate Kennedy's lack of foreign policy experience and the vice president's command of the facts. In reality, many Americans interpreted Nixon's remark differently: Nixon had not read one of the important books of his time, and, therefore, he was the dumb guy running for president.

Where Are Ye, Ho?

Isolated, facing a rice famine, and leading a government filled with bickering ex-revolutionaries, Ho Chi Minh was also doing a lot of soul-searching in the late 1950s.

During the first few years following the Geneva Accords, Ho's belief that Diem's own corruption and oppression would be the death of him remained an unshakable one. A special Party Congress had to be held in 1957 to discuss whether this assessment was correct.

Ho and his colleagues concluded that they had been kidding themselves for years. Diem would probably be around for a while, and anti-Diem forces in the south needed greater military support from the north. How to keep those southern forces loyal to Ho Chi Minh stimulated great disagreement, and no one was sure, at this early date, how discipline and order in the ranks down south could be maintained. So, first things first.

A secure land route was needed to get supplies and key military advisors south. It could take years to get a proper stockpile of weapons in the south and more years to assure a level of security for the supply line. Giap, still Ho's senior military man, had no problem with the extended calendar, and Ho had always preached that good communists are patient communists.

Soon nicknamed the Ho Chi Minh Trail, the North Vietnamese government's supply line to the south hugged the Laotian border and became, in effect, a secret military highway. Although well defended, the supply trail to the south was an elaborate maze through jungle areas that made it difficult for South Vietnamese and American aircraft to spot.

Ho and Giap anticipated certain losses when it came to the arrival of supplies at their southern destination. If Giap shipped 1,200 men with ammunition cartridges south, he expected only 1,000 of them to make it. In fact, the original shipment, from the get-go, would be considered 1,000. The expendable factor would always be taken into account. This approach and policy remained in place throughout America's days in the Vietnam War.

Ask Saigon Sally

For American historians worried about the direction of 1950s U.S. foreign policy, Edward Buehrig's *Wilson's Foreign Policy in Perspective* (Bloomington, Ind.: University of Indiana Press, 1957) was an instant classic. Without mentioning Vietnam, Buehrig and other contributors to this edited book warned that U.S. foreign policy was bound for a big confrontation in the Third World.

Shell Shock

Although John Kennedy is often considered America's first "television president," it was Eisenhower, as early as 1953, who first used television to win support for his foreign policy.

As Ho planned, schemed, and supplied his supporters in South Vietnam, he still hoped that the South Vietnamese would destroy their awful government. Would the Americans let that happen? As Vietnam entered the new decade of the 1960s, everything seemed uncertain.

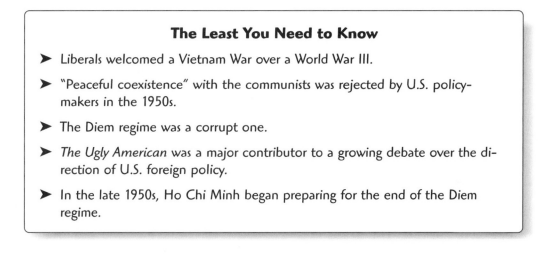

The Least You Need to Know

➤ Liberals welcomed a Vietnam War over a World War III.

➤ "Peaceful coexistence" with the communists was rejected by U.S. policymakers in the 1950s.

➤ The Diem regime was a corrupt one.

➤ *The Ugly American* was a major contributor to a growing debate over the direction of U.S. foreign policy.

➤ In the late 1950s, Ho Chi Minh began preparing for the end of the Diem regime.

Chapter 8

The Military-Industrial Complex

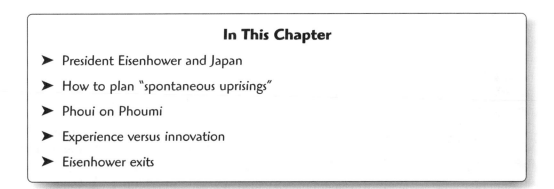

In This Chapter

➤ President Eisenhower and Japan

➤ How to plan "spontaneous uprisings"

➤ Phoui on Phoumi

➤ Experience versus innovation

➤ Eisenhower exits

The French have a knack for inventing words. One word in French can sum up a complex idea in English. *Détente* is one of those words.

In English translation, détente means to get together with people you don't necessarily like. In fact, you probably don't like them at all, wouldn't be caught dead with them in a public place, and have no regrets for your feelings. But maybe you'd be better off to talk things over with them. You don't have to change their way of thinking or even see things their way. But if an argument has been going on long enough, it might just make sense to try to get along and move ahead before things get worse. That's détente.

In 1959, America was ready for détente with the communist world. Nikita Khrushchev's American tour that year had been an amazing public relations success. He proved to be charming, funny, even grandfatherly. This was not the faceless portrait of evil depicted by John Foster Dulles. More than ever, it seemed that commies had mommies, too. Moving from confrontation to cooperation would never happen overnight, but the Khrushchev visit suggested that a 1960s détente was more than possible. Unfortunately, nobody did a thing about it.

Won't You Play with Me?

It had been something of the last hurrah, a 1960 presidential world tour of America's Cold War responsibilities. For Eisenhower, all the globe-trotting and state dinners symbolized the end of his days as the world's most important president. He looked exhausted during most of the trip, adding fuel to young Senator John Kennedy's charge that the "tired old men" in the White House needed a permanent holiday.

Eisenhower was welcomed most anywhere during his tour, but he had no welcome at all by the Japanese. And he had planned to be the first sitting president ever to visit Japan. The Japanese refusal put Eisenhower's entire Asian policy in focus, and it raised an interesting question. Just who were Washington's allies in the Asian/Pacific region?

To most everyone in the White House, Japan meant one thing: U.S. military bases for the possible war in Southeast Asia. John Foster Dulles referred to Japan as "the stationary aircraft carrier" of the Far East. The bases had proven their worth in the Korean War, and if a shooting war was inevitable in Vietnam and elsewhere in Southeast Asia, they would play an important staging, training, and supply role. Huge Kadena Air Base on the island of Okinawa had been especially involved in daily bombing runs to Korea, and the Defense Department planned a similar role for it in its contingency plans for a Southeast Asian war.

The Japanese resented America's callous attitude in seeing their nation merely as a potential military base. Washington envisioned U.S. bases in Japan but forgot about the Japanese people themselves. In 1959 and 1960, the Japanese were quick to label all Americans "ugly." Few Japanese considered their country merely a hunk of available real estate to be used in an upcoming war against fellow Asians.

In 1960, U.S.-Japan mutual security treaty negotiations were in full swing. The White House thought the negotiation process would be a piece of cake. Instead, the bases issue was complicated by the resurgence of Japanese pride.

Ask Saigon Sally

During 1950 and 1951, John Foster Dulles, fresh from his defeat in the New York Senate race, served as the Truman administration's senior consultant and principal negotiator of the formal peace treaty with Japan. He claimed that this experience made him an "Asian specialist."

Shell Shock

As chairman of the Rockefeller Foundation in 1960, Dean Rusk (a future secretary of state) warned President Eisenhower that the full support of Asian/Pacific allies (such as Japan) was required before marching into Vietnam.

For Japan, the 1960s held great promise. The postwar reconstruction period was over, the American occupation government was gone, and the nation was about to enter a new decade with a host of get-rich-quick economic policies. But the Americans still dictated terms to the Japanese and treated Japanese nationals like footnotes to their larger defense plans. "Demos," or Japanese-style anti-American political demonstrations, were popular in 1960. Snake dancing and carefully organized marches near U.S. military bases were common. It was a tricky situation for Eisenhower, but not a fatal one.

In any event, the Japanese government canceled plans for Eisenhower's tour. The president's safety, read the official statement, could not be assured, and they were right. Inejiro Asanuma, leader of Japan's anti-U.S. bases Socialist Party, was assassinated in October 1960. Saying no to the U.S. president won plenty of political brownie points for some Japanese politicians. But getting the Americans mad would not open the American market to Japanese consumer goodies. Pride had its limits, and the security treaty was signed. U.S. bases in Japan were assured a free ride for years.

Would Japan endorse America's Vietnam policy? Eisenhower was pretty sure all was well there, but he was the first president to even ask the question. Keeping Asians happy was hard work.

Getting It Together in South Vietnam

While the White House worried about Japan and the upcoming 1960 presidential election, Ngo Dinh Diem got tough in South Vietnam. His so-called *10/59 Law* was the most oppressive one yet.

Proclaiming most every non-Diem political activity in South Vietnam "subversive," the 10/59 Law granted the Diem regime full authority to create new police and secret police forces to destroy all "threats to the state." Everyone from a die-hard ex-Vietminh to a grumbling rice farmer could now be executed for

Ask Saigon Sally

President Diem often spoke personally with senior businessmen from America, Japan, and elsewhere. Sometimes his decisions were odd ones. For instance, Diem refused to allow the Chevrolet Corvette to be sold in South Vietnam. The car's name was too French.

Jarhead Jargon

The **10/59** (or October 1959) **Law** was the equivalent of a declaration of martial law over South Vietnam. President Diem conferred dictatorial authority upon himself and his family in the name of "national emergency." Even staunch American anticommunists questioned his reasoning in the matter, and the decision increased rather than lessened opposition to his regime.

his treasonous beliefs. This approach was reminiscent of the "thought police" that accompanied Japanese occupation forces during World War II. But South Vietnam was not supposed to be at war, and the Eisenhower administration worried that Diem had gone too far.

Worries, on the other hand, were not policies, and Diem stayed his course. The new law permitted the South Vietnamese military to search any home they wanted, jail any suspicious character they wanted, and throw the others in *agrovilles*. It also gave some of its officers the opportunity to loot innocent people and enrich themselves. This was an especially welcomed opportunity to those majors and colonels whom the Diem family had not personally taken under their wing.

Diem's new definition of oppression played well into Ho Chi Minh's hands, but the Vietcong were not yet ready to challenge him. The 10/59 Law had also created Diem regime loyalty tribunals that moved from village to village, investigated entire families, and put hundreds on trial. The trials were brief, and the tribunal judges preferred quick executions of defendants to long jail terms. On some occasions, curious bystanders of the village trials were arrested and executed as well. Their crime was their own interest in the proceedings, which, apparently, meant that they were sympathetic toward those on trial.

Tales from the Front

The Diem regime's first director of its strategic hamlet program was Colonel Pham Ngoc Thao. The Colonel speedily evacuated villages and resettled their inhabitants with a certain brutality that shocked the U.S. Embassy. His tactics also turned thousands of South Vietnamese against their government. But that was the point. Colonel Pham Ngoc Thao was also an early Vietcong supporter and agent.

Somehow Diem's new secret police and the wandering tribunals were expected to end all significant opposition to the Saigon government. Instead, his terror tactics won more adherents to the Vietcong. The question for Ho was what to do with this growing new version of the old Vietminh.

Spontaneous Uprisings

Adding insult to injury, Diem still insisted on holding district elections in 1960. Under Hanoi's direct orders, the Vietcong were to demonstrate against this mockery of democratic fair play. North Vietnamese political advisors in the south, along with pro-Ho South Vietnamese communists, were supposed to organize mass demonstrations against these elections.

The North Vietnamese government asked for riots, chaos, and a show of mass disapproval. The result was what Ho called "spontaneous uprisings." Apparently he saw no irony in the fact that his supporters down south spent three months in careful planning for "spontaneous" uprisings."

In the Tra Bong district, near the central highlands, Vietcong demonstrators seized 15 villages in a wild rampage that caught the Diem authorities off guard. Other temporary takeovers were accomplished in the far south of the Mekong Delta.

An aerial view of a village in Vietcong-controlled Tay Ninh province, 45 miles northwest of Saigon, in the early 1960s.

National Archives Still Pictures Unit, College Park, Maryland, and photographer Charles E. Sparrow.

However, the locations of most of the 1960 "spontaneous uprisings" did not come as a surprise to Diem. Most of them took place in areas where the Vietminh had once redistributed land to peasants following the war with the French. After Diem returned this same land to the original landowners, the locals vowed revenge. The Vietcong offered to organize all of that pent-up hostility, and succeeded.

Confusing matters were reports of Diem's own troops, in areas such as the Kien Hoa province in the Mekong Delta, joining and leading "spontaneous uprisings." Ho made a big deal about this development, publicly insisting that it symbolized the beginning of the end for the Diem regime. In reality, Vietcong troops, dressed as government soldiers, had led the way in Kien Hoa, as Ho was well aware.

Ask Saigon Sally

Diem also had big problems with organized crime. The Binh Xuyen criminal organization enjoyed a monopoly on vice for a while in Saigon, and it protected its interests with a private army of more than 2,000 men.

Ask Saigon Sally

One of the symbols of success for the North Vietnamese was the bicycle. It was a primary carrier of supplies on the Ho Chi Minh Trail. Laden with saddlebags and baskets, the bicycle was not ridden. It was led and balanced by a specially rigged tether held by a North Vietnamese trooper.

The spontaneous uprisings did not go unnoticed by America's CIA, although it was difficult for an American to move out of Saigon to find out exactly what was going on. It was unsafe for Americans to travel even 15 miles from downtown, the CIA reported.

The "spontaneous uprisings" had turned South Vietnam into the biggest orgy of bloodshed since the war with the French. This was not the way Washington wanted to begin a new decade of relations with Diem's South Vietnam. But there were also plenty of anti-Diem South Vietnamese who disagreed with this violent turn of events. Such demonstrations exposed antigovernment positions to government troops, they argued, making it difficult to plan for more effective offensive operations later.

NLF Reforms

Ho did not like being lectured by his more cautious South Vietnamese supporters, and he vowed to take better control of the anti-Diem resistance—if he could. Throughout history, revolutionaries have always been a squabbling bunch, and the Vietnamese revolutionaries were no exception.

On December 20, 1960, Ho's desire for tighter discipline and coordination of revolutionary efforts down south was formalized in the creation of the National Liberation Front (NLF). Frankly, the NLF was nothing new as far as the Ho Chi Minh approach was concerned. All resistance efforts in South Vietnam were now to be coordinated by communists who supported unification with the North and the end of Diem. But anybody who hated Diem was still welcome in the organization, and it even announced certain reforms to come.

Land redistribution remained at the top of the reform list, and a formal name for the resistance fighters in this organization would be announced early in 1961. They eventually became the People's Liberation Armed Forces (PLAF). In spite of all the organization and alphabet-soup acronyms, most noncommunists would still call antigovernment forces in South Vietnam the Vietcong.

Laos and Vietnam

As America turned its attention to the 1960 presidential race, things went from bad to worse in Southeast Asia. President Eisenhower worried that his administration had been looking at the wrong country over there. The communist threat in the country of Laos, Vietnam's neighbor, now loomed larger than anywhere in South Vietnam.

To a large degree, the Laos problem was one of America's own making. If few people were watching America's actions in mid-1950s Vietnam, even fewer were paying attention to what they were doing in Laos. Laos had welcomed the regional peace settlement announced at the 1954 Geneva Conference on Asia, but violence resumed shortly after the conference was over. The procommunist Pathet Lao and the anticommunist Royal Lao Army continued to clash. The Geneva delegates had ordered the two competing armies to get along. They were supposed to have established a coalition government, but it took a war to make it happen.

Phouma, Phoui, and Phoumi

In early 1958, everything fell apart. Encouraged and supported by the CIA, right-wing forces within the coalition government seized control of the country. Prime Minister Souvanna Phouma, a prince in the Lao royal family, had tried to maintain a neutral position before this coup, acting as chief mediator between communist and noncommunist forces. Because the Pathet Lao leader was Phouma's own half-brother, Souphanouvong, it was easier than it might have otherwise been for him to maintain a dialog. And Phouma had a decent relationship with the myriad of political factions in Laos.

Shell Shock

The Eisenhower administration's view of Laos was based on that of Ngo Dinh Luyen, Diem's younger brother. As the official spokesperson for the Diem regime, Luyen insisted that the fall of either Laos or Vietnam would mean the end of democracy in all of Asia.

Shell Shock

Shortly before John Kennedy's inaugural, the new president met with the exiting Dwight Eisenhower. Much of their discussion stressed foreign affairs issues. Laos was mentioned occasionally. Vietnam was never mentioned at all.

Given the level of respect that Phouma was generally accorded in the country, he was one of the few who could have succeeded in maintaining this political balancing act. But when he was removed from power, the violence returned. The new right-wing government arrested all pro-Pathet Lao officials and ordered their military units near the Laotian capital of Vientiane to surrender their arms. The Pathet Lao refused to comply, fled the capital area, and prepared for a great offensive against the new government.

Souphanouvong broke out of jail and raced through the jungle to lead his Pathet Lao once more. The new right-wing leader of Laos was named Phoumi, and Washington held him personally responsible for Souphanouvong's escape.

The CIA swung into action again, and a new coup leader took over Laos. A guy named Phoui replaced Phoumi. And in protest to this madness, former Prime Minister Phouma joined up with his half-brother Souphanouvong against Phoui.

The Commies Creep Closer

In 1960, the Pathet Lao continued to win most of its skirmishes against the right-wing government troops. This did not bode well for the Eisenhower administration. Another country was about to go communist, and on America's own watch to boot. That development would put the Republican presidential candidate, Vice President Nixon, in peril, for he would not be able to claim that the Eisenhower administration had held the line against advancing communism.

Jarhead Jargon

Dating back to the British Parliament of the 1760s, the term **lame duck** refers to the lapsing term of an outgoing elected official. Often a derogatory term, it implies that that official is powerless to initiate new programs or policies, as well as preoccupied with image-making and a respectful exit from office.

The Laos problem, the *lame duck* Eisenhower hoped, would linger into the next presidency. An American intervention could be determined then. In any event, during the heat of the 1960 presidential campaign, Eisenhower told the press that the "real matter of concern" in Southeast Asia was indeed Laos, and not, for the moment, South Vietnam.

At least in America, the CIA's involvement in the collapse of the Geneva-established coalition government of Laos was not an issue of public discussion or record. Ho Chi Minh complained that the United States had created the mess in Laos, but his comments had little effect on U.S. public opinion.

Both Ho and Khrushchev took advantage of the silver platter that the United States had provided them in Laos. Both men could smell blood, and the Pathet Lao received arms and economic support from both their governments. On the other side, some $300 million would be spent on Laos between 1959 and 1961. Most of it fell into corrupt hands, and the rest of it appeared to be going to a lost cause. The Pentagon labeled the anticommunist forces in Laos the worst-trained military outfit in all of Southeast Asia, and it was getting awfully late to do much about it.

A Statesman to the Rescue?

No matter how you looked at it, good ole American politics and Southeast Asia policy-making were joined at the hip. Everybody and his uncle was on record for opposing communism over there, and in the 1960 election, smart money was on whoever promised to kill commies better than the other guy.

Vice President Nixon had the hometown advantage. He pushed the right anticommunist buttons, and he was ahead in the polls going into the campaign. Born in 1913, Nixon, if he won, would be one of the youngest presidents America ever had. Unfortunately for Nixon, his Democratic opponent, John Kennedy, was born in 1917. It would be Kennedy who could say with a straight face that his opponent represented "old politics," stealing the young-and-eager image away from Nixon.

Touting anticommunist credentials that included early work with *HUAC* and even debating Nikita Khrushchev, Nixon said experience mattered. Touting both "massive retaliation" and an anti–"ugly American" Peace Corps, Kennedy said innovation mattered. Innovation beat experience by less than a 1 percent margin.

Shortly before leaving office, Eisenhower had some final words on the subject of anticommunist commitment. In his farewell address, Eisenhower complained about a "military-industrial complex" that heightened Cold War tensions and made too much money off it all. Winning the Cold War, Eisenhower admitted, was a tough job. Now it was John Kennedy's turn.

Ask Saigon Sally

Following Richard Nixon's defeat in the presidential race in 1960 and in the race for governor of California in 1962, the former vice president returned to private law practice. Most of his clients included large Japanese corporations and other Asian/Pacific-based businesses.

Jarhead Jargon

Although its roots went back to 1938, the House Un-American Affairs Committee or **HUAC** was founded on January 3, 1945. Dedicated to probing communist subversion in government, labor unions, and the press, HUAC continued its work into the 1970s.

The Least You Need to Know

➤ A thaw in the Cold War was not possible in 1960.

➤ Washington had taken Asian/Pacific allies, such as Japan, for granted.

➤ The Diem regime became more oppressive and the Vietcong better organized by 1960.

➤ CIA involvement in Laos only assisted the Pathet Lao cause there.

➤ Although President Eisenhower complained about a "military-industrial complex," the commitment to Cold War victory remained strong.

Chapter 9

Enter the New Frontier

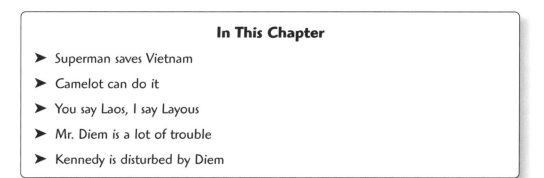

In This Chapter

➤ Superman saves Vietnam

➤ Camelot can do it

➤ You say Laos, I say Layous

➤ Mr. Diem is a lot of trouble

➤ Kennedy is disturbed by Diem

He said that he wanted to "make America great again." Great again? In hindsight, that sounds mighty strange. In 1960, when John Kennedy uttered these words, the U.S. dollar was supreme in world business, and the U.S. economy, in general, was the envy of the world. A typical family could live off Dad's salary, Mom did not have to work, two quality-constructed American-made cars were in the garage, and you did not have to be a millionaire to have that comfy summer home on the lake. All of this was protected by a U.S. military that still had an invincible reputation.

Sure, there had been stumbles in Korea, but everybody knew that artificial restraints had been put on American troops over there. World War II was a fresh memory, and the country was proud of its winning ways and heritage. America was "great!" There was no "again" about it. Or so it looks from the vantage point of the twenty-first century.

In 1960, most Americans agreed with Kennedy's concern that the country's power and might was fading. Communism was still on the march abroad, and racism suddenly seemed obvious and unacceptable at home. Maybe new policies and new leadership were required to wade through the 1960s. Time was running out for the good guys, many believed. A little house cleaning was needed.

Can't You See That Big Red "S" Under My Shirt?

Commitment, determination, and can-do policies were going to win the Cold War, said Kennedy, and the great battleground was going to be somewhere in the Pacific. The world was on the verge of becoming "the Pacific Century," he argued. Whether that "Century" was going to be a capitalist or a communist one depended on the United States, the most important Pacific country on Kennedy's list.

Kennedy's Presidential Bid

During the 1960 presidential campaign, Kennedy's campaign manager, younger brother Robert, insisted on grassroots campaigning, a rigorous, grueling, cross-country effort that had the candidate wondering what state he was in. Though he always got plenty of applause for his Peace Corps proposal, most of the cheering came from college students, and in 1960, the 26th amendment (the right to vote for 18- to 21-year-olds) was more than a decade away. It was their parents who needed to cheer the Kennedy message, and many of them thought Kennedy's Peace Corps proposal was wimpy.

Tales from the Front

Growing up in Brooklyn and southern New Jersey outside of Philadelphia, Ken Berez "escaped" his mundane life and joined the U.S. Army right out of high school. He came back from Vietnam with one leg paralyzed by a spinal wound, and still too young to vote. He became a leading advocate for the right to vote for 18–21-year-olds, and later became the associate director of the Vietnam Veterans of America Association.

Although he later regretted it, Kennedy turned the Cold War on the Eisenhower administration, accusing it of not having enough nuclear missiles in the defense arsenal. The Eisenhower folks also closed too many military bases, he said, putting fiscal conservatism ahead of adequate military protection. Real "massive retaliation," Kennedy insisted, meant more nuclear weapons, more military men, more bases, more economic warfare, and the Peace Corps. Throwing everything America has at the communists, he promised, would lead to Cold War victory by 1970. This *"pay any price, bear any burden"* commitment was dramatic stuff, and because of it, the Kennedys believed, they won the 1960 election.

For a time, President Kennedy's posh champagne lifestyle wowed the nation. It seemed that the country had elected not just a president, but royalty. The new president looked more handsome than ever, and his First Lady, Jacqueline, was beautiful, elegant, and spoke French. There was a First Kid as well, and soon to be another. No one could remember the last time anything but grandchildren had been crawling the floors of the White House. Vietnam couldn't have been further away during this time, but Kennedy still paid close attention.

Jarhead Jargon

The expression **"pay any price, bear any burden"** came out of John Kennedy's 1961 inaugural address. For years afterward, politicians, journalists, and historians said this one expression symbolized the entire Kennedy administration's commitment to the aging Truman Doctrine and to the anticommunist crusade in general.

Kennedy's Can-Do Team

In 1961, Buddhist-led protests of the Diem regime were growing in strength, and oppressive laws did not stop them. Helping Kennedy decide what to do about Vietnam was his supercabinet of superintellects with superaccomplishments. There was, for example, a new, youthful secretary of defense, Robert McNamara. When he was in his thirties, the man had turned the down-on-its-luck Ford Motor Company around. Maybe his managerial skill could marshal the Defense Department for its great tasks ahead.

There was also the economic genius Walt W. Rostow, who had written about the strong possibility of an upcoming irony of grand proportions. He predicted that the communist world would soon have the economic clout to influence world events better than the capitalist world. His work added a sense of urgency to the capitalist-versus-communist confrontation. There was even Arthur Schlesinger Jr., an accomplished historian and son of another famous historian. He was there to keep a former Harvard political science major, Kennedy, on track. The press joked that there were more Ivy League Ph.D. types in the Kennedy administration than at most colleges and universities.

Kennedy's Vietnam decision-making was made in an atmosphere of political and intellectual hardball. Although Kennedy himself had never been comfortable with the label of Harvard intellectual, he expected a combination of youthful enthusiasm and academic elitism to win out where the Eisenhower team had failed. His father, Joseph Kennedy Sr., had taught him "never to shrink in the face of adversity," and he thought most Americans viewed life in the same manner of commitment and combat.

Years before, as a Harvard University football player, Kennedy had once finished a game with a severely injured leg. When asked by the press how he could have played in such obvious pain, he did not understand the question. He had helped his team win the game, Kennedy said. The real pain would have been to quit and lose.

Although the American people loved seeing the Kennedys at play on Cape Cod or just looking pretty at a fancy concert, the new administration was proud of its work-aholic record. There were few weekends or days off at 1600 Pennsylvania Avenue. Kennedy had railed against the quiet, golf-playing Eisenhower. A cabinet meeting called for 2 A.M. on a Saturday was not unusual, and if one cabinet member decided to switch the language of discussion to French, for example, Kennedy hoped his team was able to handle it.

Shell Shock

An early supporter of extensive economic aid plans for Diem, Senator Mike Mansfield (Democrat, Montana), a close Kennedy friend, was nicknamed "the senator from Vietnam" by some of his colleagues. Ironically, one decade later, Mansfield was one of the Vietnam War's loudest critics.

Some cabinet members would swim laps in the White House pool to get toned and ready for the long, tough combat of a Kennedy cabinet discussion. Others didn't see dozens of laps in a pool as being quite good enough, and downed several martinis before the swim. That made it more challenging and truly prepared them for the meeting to come. The White House had not seen this type of policy-making before, but the Kennedy team presented its approach to the press as normal, the way it must be, and even fun. Government was not government. It was a crusade. Ho Chi Minh didn't have a chance.

Even Kennedy's version of a reformed military reflected his can-do approach. Although the American military always had elite groups in its ranks, Kennedy was especially proud of his Special Forces. The original organizational plan for this special version of the World War II Army Rangers was amazing, and it was classic Kennedy.

The president expected Special Forces volunteers to be over six feet tall, to be excellent academic students, and flawless marksmen. Some expertise in hand-to-hand fighting or the martial arts was encouraged as well. If these credentials could be filled, then a rigorous training program, combining CIA field agent skills with Marine Corps drill instruction techniques, was next. If you survived, you could wear a green beret along with your fancy new uniform.

Your Special Forces mission would be twofold. First, you were supposed to represent the most effective killer elite in the history of anybody's military, and second, you were expected to temper all this special training with acts of humanitarian kindness.

The Special Forces could be told to assault and pacify the perimeter of a South Vietnamese village in the morning, and then inoculate the children there in the afternoon. This was supposed to kill that infamous "ugly American" image as well as kill communists. And Kennedy wasted little time putting these new military units to work.

Privately, Kennedy had much more faith in the Special Forces than in his new Peace Corps. The idea that a recent graduate from the University of Iowa could make a difference in the everyday life of Vietnamese villagers was pretty far-fetched to Kennedy. But his Peace Corps was designed to do just that, and it continued to receive rave reviews from a country that wanted to help its president win the Cold War. Publicly, of course, Kennedy welcomed all the excitement, and it was easier to find a Peace Corps volunteer than a guy who could meet Kennedy's original requirements for the Special Forces. Superman, apparently, did not live in Iowa or even on Cape Cod.

Getting the Job Done

In 1961, Kennedy dispatched General Maxwell Taylor and Professor Rostow, the new national security advisor, to Saigon on a fact-finding mission. They returned to the White House with a dismal report, but Diem, they concluded, could hang on with more U.S. help. They recommended a healthy economic aid package plus 8,000 U.S. troops. The latter was supposed to be a message to the Vietcong and Ho Chi Minh that the United States still stood behind Diem.

Undersecretary of State George Ball disagreed. He compared the mess in South Vietnam to the worst phases of any social revolution. The *NVA* and *PAVN* were a rough bunch, too, and the United States, he predicted, was about to inherit all the problems that once defeated the French. If the 8,000 men went to Vietnam now, Ball warned Kennedy, it would take another 300,000 to protect them. The slow pattern of escalation would be an exact replica of France's mistakes, he said, and the Kennedy administration was supposed to be smarter than the French.

Kennedy told Ball that his analysis was way off and that the current Vietnam scene was different from the old days of the French empire. In his own way, Ball reminded President Kennedy of his Senate days when he took pride in his recognition

Jarhead Jargon

A certain alphabet soup accompanies any study of the North Vietnamese military. Both **NVA** (North Vietnamese Army) and **PAVN** (People's Army of Vietnam) refer to North Vietnamese troops.

Ask Saigon Sally

By making "anticommunist show-pieces" out of Guam and the Trust Territory of the Pacific Islands, said Kennedy advisor Anthony Solomon, America could prove that it cared about Asian/ Pacific residents. That made better sense, he said in 1962, than war in Vietnam.

Ask Saigon Sally

In confidence, John Kennedy once told his brother Robert that he worried about showing too much "profile" and not enough "courage" in Cold War matters.

of Third World arguments and concerns. Whatever happened to Senator Kennedy, the man who warmed to the hopes and dreams of Third World residents? Ball was out of bounds here, and Kennedy told him to keep his opinions to himself.

Privately, Kennedy told his brother Robert that Ball's views and reminders troubled him and that common sense suggested that the undersecretary was dead right. But what could he do? Political reality and Kennedy's own career suggested more Cold War jousting, not less.

Where Is "Layous?"

To the new Kennedy administration, South Vietnam was in trouble and Laos was further south than that. During the first news conference of his presidency, Kennedy admitted that the anticommunist cause looked weak in Laos, and that a lot of work needed to be done there. Of course, he pronounced Laos as "Layous," thanks to his part-Harvard and mostly Cape Cod accent. The press made good fun of that accent, asking Kennedy to find "Layous" on a map for them. Few journalists were ready to see gloom and doom in poor, forgettable Laos. But Kennedy saw red, and he had three reasons why.

First, the CIA told him that Laos's neighbors were watching his response closely. Was Kennedy's New Frontier of can-do determination a lot of hot air or real policy? A quick military response might be soon required, the CIA argued, if U.S. respect was to be maintained in the region. The "loss" of Laos would truly mean the end of that respect, and, perhaps, the triggering of the famous dominos across Asia.

Second, if things went from bad to worse in Laos, Kennedy's divided Congress might move solidly into the Republican camp during the 1962 congressional elections. The last thing that he needed was to be declared "soft on communism." It would be the kiss of death for his administration, the young president believed. It was irrelevant that he considered any "soft on communism" charge a stupid, below-the-belt political tactic.

Third, Laos included the main highway, in a manner of speaking, of the Ho Chi Minh Trail. If Laos went communist, it would be much easier for North Vietnamese troops to travel down the trail, build it up even more, and cause more misery in South Vietnam.

In the end, a negotiated cease-fire and a new coalition government would be arranged for Laos. After years of madness, common sense finally prevailed. Kennedy would consider himself lucky there. Meanwhile, thanks to the Ho Chi Minh Trail, the United States would become a frequent violator of Laos's integrity and independence. Luck did not follow Kennedy into Vietnam.

Who Will Rid Me of This Troublesome Man?

According to legend, lore, and even history, good King Henry II of England, tired of the political challenges and downright uppityness of his old friend Thomas Becket, the Archbishop of Canterbury, let it be known to his strongest supporters that he wished Becket was out of his hair and even dead. In 1170, four of Henry's most trusted knights murdered Becket.

Henry claimed to be shocked at what happened. He uttered a few words, and soon afterward, an important public figure was dead. Power is an amazing thing, and, although Becket's death troubled him, it was, Henry reasoned, good for the monarchy and good for the future of his country. But few Englishmen agreed, and their political pressure and concern later forced Henry to lobby for Becket's sainthood. Henry even agreed to his own public whipping for his role in the man's murder. What a mess.

John Kennedy knew the Becket tale well. It almost repeated itself over the fate of Ngo Dinh Diem.

Shell Shock

In early 1961, the U.S. ambassador to India, John Kenneth Galbraith, advised Kennedy against a U.S. military role in Laos, for the Royal Laotian Army, he said, was "inferior to a battalion of conscientious objectors from World War I."

Ask Saigon Sally

In March 1961, the Women's Liberation Association was founded in South Vietnam. A wing of the Vietcong, this association volunteered members to serve in everything from guerrilla operations to informant work.

Diem's Weaknesses

Throughout the Kennedy years, Diem's days were always numbered. Within weeks after the Kennedy team settled into the White House, Diem's Army of the Republic of Vietnam, or ARVN, was better equipped than ever before. ARVN had dozens of U.S. helicopters to transport itself along with the U.S. advisors to various trouble spots in the country. In 1962, ARVN even launched an offensive against the Vietcong and prevailed.

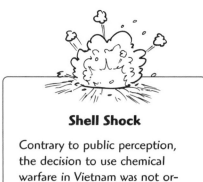

Shell Shock

Contrary to public perception, the decision to use chemical warfare in Vietnam was not ordered by President Johnson. The decision to spray herbicides across the Vietnamese countryside was made by the Kennedy administration in 1962.

Ask Saigon Sally

When Quang Duc, a Buddhist monk, set himself aflame and died protesting the Diem regime, Madame Nhu was asked for her reaction by the press. She claimed that a "barbecued" monk meant nothing to her. In fact, she offered to supply the matches and gasoline for the next "barbecue."

At first the Vietcong were temporarily taken aback by the ARVN's new technology; however, by 1963 they had automatic weapons with which to shoot down helicopters. They also trained themselves on how to counterattack the always quickly arriving ARVN and U.S. troops. During the battle of Ap Bac in early 1963, where ARVN forces outnumbered Vietcong guerrillas by 10 to 1, the Vietcong killed 61 ARVN troops, wounded 100, and shot down five U.S. helicopters.

A chief U.S. military advisor on the scene, Colonel John Paul Vann, blamed this disaster on the indifferent and terribly corrupt South Vietnamese officer corps. Some of them, he said, even believed in the inevitability of Vietcong victory. These men lived for the moment, Vann complained, and in the early 1960s, the Diem government kept them wallowing in comfort in exchange for their political support. Putting their lives in danger made little sense to them, although most realized that the clock was ticking on this dangerous lifestyle. "Live today, for tomorrow we die" was their motto. Vann preferred a dead Diem today and a retrained, reorganized ARVN tomorrow. And he wasn't alone.

Young foreign correspondents like Neil Sheehan (who later wrote a Pulitzer Prize–winning book about Vann) and David Halberstam told their readers that Diem was responsible for the impending collapse of South Vietnam to communism. But their tale of woe was countered by the U.S. Embassy in Saigon and the Diem regime itself. All was well, they proclaimed in public announcements. They urged the American people to believe them instead of the pessimistic press corps in Saigon.

Losing Diem

The best way to resolve the South Vietnam crisis was to rid the country of Diem and his awful family. In the fall of 1963, the U.S. ambassador to South Vietnam, Henry Cabot Lodge Jr., met with some ARVN officers who planned to lead a coup against the government. They wanted the White House's blessing. Kennedy offered it. Ah, shades of Henry and Becket.

During the spring of 1963, President John Kennedy poses with brothers Attorney General Robert Kennedy and Senator Edward Kennedy near the Oval Office of the White House.

John F. Kennedy Library, Boston, Massachusetts, and photographer Cecil Stoughton.

On November 1, 1963, Ngo Dinh Diem met his maker. A photograph of his crumpled, bullet-ridden body appeared on page one of newspapers around the world. Nhu was murdered as well. Kennedy was shocked. He told his brothers Robert and Ted that he had had no idea men would lose their lives over this. And in such a horrid fashion!

The Diem and Nhu murders had quite an impact on Kennedy's state of mind. For days after these killings, Kennedy rocked silently in his Oval Office rocking chair, staring at nothing. He had, in effect, ordered the deaths of foreign leaders, and it troubled him. At one point, he even told Assistant Secretary of State Roger Hilsman that it would be great if the Vietcong won their war quickly. Then America could go off to Geneva again and put together a new Geneva Accords arrangement, which would please both Ho and the American voters in 1964.

Whether the depressed Mr. Kennedy planned to chart a different Vietnam policy remains one of the great speculation points of the entire Vietnam War. Kennedy was assassinated in Dallas, Texas, exactly three weeks after the Diem coup. And, no, there was never any conspiratorial connection between the Diem and Kennedy murders (although it would make an interesting story for TV shows such as *The X-Files)*.

By supporting the Diem coup and dispatching up to 17,000 troops to South Vietnam, Kennedy had deepened his country's involvement in Vietnam. That was his real participation in the tale. Otherwise, talk was cheap.

The Least You Need to Know

➤ The Kennedy administration planned to win the Cold War.

➤ Using everything from Special Forces troops to the Peace Corps, Kennedy expected total success for U.S. policy in South Vietnam.

➤ In 1961, Laos was viewed by the Kennedy White House as a priority problem over Vietnam issues.

➤ By 1963, Kennedy's commitment to anticommunist victory in Vietnam had not wavered.

➤ The Kennedy administration was involved in the assassination of Ngo Dinh Diem.

Chapter 10

The American Lake

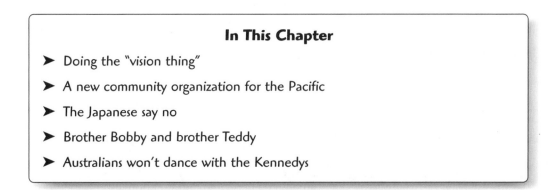

In This Chapter

➤ Doing the "vision thing"

➤ A new community organization for the Pacific

➤ The Japanese say no

➤ Brother Bobby and brother Teddy

➤ Australians won't dance with the Kennedys

In 1984, Democratic presidential candidate Jesse Jackson said President Reagan just didn't have it. Because he didn't have it, Jackson proclaimed that he'd rather have "one day of Franklin Roosevelt in a wheelchair than four more years of Ronald Reagan on a horse." Jackson was referring to what President George Bush later called "the vision thing." Franklin Roosevelt had "the vision thing." So did John Kennedy, and to Kennedy, "vision" was all-important in foreign policy-making.

Johnson's Inheritance

Lyndon Johnson inherited Kennedy's "vision," but he always thought the Kennedy White House had wasted too much time crafting their views and not enough time making law. When it came to foreign policy, Johnson believed that Kennedy's interests in the long-term destruction of communism across the Asian/Pacific region were far-fetched, unworkable, and irrelevant to the crisis in South Vietnam. Can-do

Ask Saigon Sally

In the Philippines, Claro Recto and his popular Nationalist-Citizen Party complained that Kennedy was bribing Filipinos to wage war against fellow Southeast Asians in Vietnam. The Philippines, Recto said, would never be truly independent if it took "blood money" from the Americans.

determination and planning was one thing. True success was another, and Johnson hoped to demonstrate his competence as a winning Cold Warrior.

It's not that Johnson disliked "the vision thing." Killing the appeal of communism in the land of the "ugly American" was still a logical goal to him. He just had a more straightforward approach than the Kennedys: Shoot the bastards.

To John Kennedy, his cabinet, and most foreign policy analysts of the early 1960s, Vietnam had been one piece of a larger pie. Worrying about dominoes falling in Southeast Asia had been a preoccupation of the 1950s. In 1961, Kennedy wasn't worried that much about losing dominoes. Kennedys don't lose.

Kennedy's biggest headache involved finding the right way to win all of the Asian-Pacific region to America's side in the Cold War. Communism was supposed to wither and die during his watch. Consequently, he preoccupied his administration with a number of plans and schemes to accomplish this task. Vice President Johnson, always the realist, thought the plans and schemes were silly. But what if they worked? He maintained a low profile while the Kennedy team tried to woo and win happy American allies in the Pacific region.

So You Want to Be a Millionaire?

If you walked into the State Department's main entrance during the early 1960s, you would have seen a large portrait of William Seward shining down upon you. As the secretary of state for Presidents Abraham Lincoln and Andrew Johnson, Seward had long been praised for his effective policy-making. Years before Kennedy and his New Frontier visions for the Asian/Pacific world, Seward had predicted the Pacific would be an "American lake." His policies had laid a foundation for U.S. military–basing privileges in the Pacific, region-wide economic investment, and spirited competition with other nations out there.

Kennedy liked to quote Seward when speaking to State Department officials. In short, he wanted to modernize the Seward approach of endless influence in the Asian/Pacific world. This time, Kennedy expected the United States to look more generous and less imperialist.

Dollars and Sense

Back in the late 1940s, Americans had rallied to Secretary of State George Marshall and his call to rebuild Europe with U.S. tax dollars. Just over a decade later, those same Americans saw great promise in Kennedy's Peace Corps and his clever Alliance for Progress program for Latin America. Regular folks wanted to participate in that march to Cold War victory, and he heard the loud applause during his inaugural address when he told Americans to "ask not what your country can do for you; ask what you can do for your country."

Kennedy's Alliance for Progress had been a response to Castro's Cuba, and he made billions of U.S. dollars available for Latin American infrastructure development. "Ugly American" rumblings were common across Latin America, and Castro was becoming something of the admired underdog. His poor, struggling island nation had beaten back an American-supported invasion at the Bay of Pigs. What might have been a heroic last stand became a great victory. This was legendary stuff, especially in the face of do-nothing, lackluster Latin American policies from the State Department. Washington, went the popular saying south of the border, was more interested in rocketing to the moon than helping out a neighbor who spoke Spanish.

Shell Shock

Arturo Morales-Carrion, Kennedy's own deputy assistant secretary for inter-American affairs, opposed the Alliance for Progress as too idealistic, too wasteful, and too expensive.

To Kennedy, this type of sentiment in poor Latin America helped the communist cause. America's big bucks, for noble projects ranging from hospitals to new roads, were expected to unite North and South America as one bastion of anticommunism. Castro would be left to stew on his little island, an irrelevant dictator under a palm tree. Dollars and cents were important tools for winning the Cold War, Kennedy insisted, and he had no apologies to Johnson and others who would rather spend every penny on military hardware. The Pacific was next.

Between April and November 1961, Secretary of State Dean Rusk honed his plan to "stimulate great economic progress" in various locations throughout the Asian/Pacific region. Rusk recommended against an aid plan for every single country over there, but he did have strategies for quite a few of them.

His new aid plan was like the Alliance for Progress, but the accent was on *like*. The region was too big and too diverse to expect the type of immediate results seen in Latin America. Washington needed help, Rusk argued. Rich nations such as Australia and Japan could write some checks, too, and that would be great PR as well.

Both Rusk and Kennedy hated the idea of being called economic imperialists. It was as bad as being called the "ugly American." If America had financial support to aid the Pacific Third World from several Pacific nations with money, that would be a whole different ballgame.

The New Pacific Community

With this goal in mind, Rusk planned an elaborate new international organization for Asian-Pacific relief. At first, he called it the Pacific League of Nations, but that reminded too many of the old post–World War I League of Nations. The latter had been little more than a debating society, rejected by the U.S. Senate; more than 40 years later, it still had a lousy reputation.

Renamed the New Pacific Community, the new organization was expected to assume all United Nations economic aid plans for the Asian/Pacific region. Kennedy and Rusk believed that the United Nations had not done a very good job out there. The ongoing troubles in Southeast Asia proved it. Hence the United States and a handful of allies would magnify and accelerate all existing aid plans and invent dozens more.

Given the concern over economic imperialism, the new organization would not be headquartered in the United States. Even United Nations critics had complained about the U.N.'s New York offices. The New Pacific Community would be set up in Australia, Rusk suggested.

The Australians were living their own version of the American success story. In the early 1960s, they were pointing the way to real influence throughout the Asian/ Pacific region, and it made sense to take advantage of their growing affluence. Or so Secretary Rusk insisted.

Tales from the Front

Joining the foreign service in 1962, Richard Holbroke was an old friend of the son of Secretary of State Dean Rusk, and he used every connection possible to get to Vietnam. He didn't want to miss it. His superiors suggested that military victory was only weeks away, and Holbroke feared that the "only excitement" in U.S. foreign policy at the time was going to pass him by. Once in Vietnam, he became a province advisor and later an aide to both Ambassadors Lodge and Taylor. The most frustrating moment of his life, Holbroke now says, was when he realized that Washington and even Saigon hadn't a clue what was going on in Vietnam. And that moment came as early as 1963. Holbroke went on to open normalization relations with the Vietnamese during the Carter administration, and served as President Bill Clinton's last U.N. Ambassador.

Kennedy loved Rusk's plan, and he made it his own. The negotiations to create this tower of American influence and money dragged on throughout the early 1960s. Key areas of the Pacific were earmarked for key roles in this crusade. For instance, the American possessions, namely Guam and the Trust Territory of the Pacific Islands, were to receive the first checks.

Shortly after Kennedy took office, Nikita Khrushchev had made a damning speech at the U.N. criticizing America's inability to take care of its own Pacific region inhabitants. "Free the American colonial Pacific!" he had shouted, and Kennedy heard the challenge. Frankly, Khrushchev had been right. The world's highest rate of tuberculosis could be found in the American-administered Pacific islands. Unemployment there was seven times the national average, and the only consistent policy Washington maintained for the islands was cutting their administrative budget. Kennedy changed all that, creating a Congressional seat (Delegate) for Guam, building hospitals and roads, and announcing the possibility of new political status for all those islands. America, the good, had arrived.

Please Speak Japanese, If You Please

Kennedy said that the residents of the Asian/Pacific countries were "prisoners of the Cold War." America needed to rescue them before the Soviets did. Yesterday's World War II enemy, Japan, would be especially important in the New Pacific Community organization. But selling the plan to the Japanese proved to be quite the unexpected challenge.

When it came to Kennedy's New Pacific Community plan, the Japanese continued to refuse to join. It simply was not in Japan's interest to join. Because Kennedy succeeded in getting a Trade Expansion Act (TEA) through Congress, a number of protectionist hurdles were eliminated for Japanese products. The door wasn't fully opened to Japanese imports, but it was better than nothing.

To the Japanese government of Hayato Ikeda, the New Pacific Community was a mysterious thing

Ask Saigon Sally

In 1962, the U.S. Territory of Guam's first delegate to the U.S. Congress, Antonio B. Won Pat, urged all Asian-Pacific region residents to view America as a friend.

Shell Shock

In June 1962, a special top-secret conference was held to discuss Japan's future as a happy U.S. ally. Chaired by veteran diplomat W. Avrell Harriman, this conference decided that America, Australia, and other nations must open their economies to Japanese trade immediately.

that only benefited U.S. policy. Eventually the organization would be focusing on grandiose efforts to rescue Southeast Asia, and Japan wanted no part of it. The Japanese government had set its own goals. The New Pacific Community would alter them, reroute them, and keep Japan away from big profits and even bigger dreams.

The White House didn't like to be told to jump in the lake. The Pacific was supposed to be America's lake, and others were supposed to jump. It was all very frustrating. Prime Minister Ikeda remained adamant, and Kennedy lobbied him to his dying day.

In short, Kennedy always took economic foreign policy very seriously. It would never be just bullets that won the Cold War. Dollars and cents always needed equal time. Ex-president Harry Truman even joked that John Kennedy might go down in history as the only president who knew how to write a check and spend it. The problem was convincing both Americans and Asian/Pacific residents that money was important in heading off wars in Southeast Asia. He did okay with the Alliance for Progress; why couldn't he succeed with the New Pacific Community? And American troops were already in harm's way in Vietnam.

Brother Bobby and Vietnam

Robert Kennedy, the attorney general, thought his brother's New Pacific Community was a great idea. It upset him that the Oval Office was failing in the effort to create it. He was especially upset with the people who kept saying no to his older brother. And you didn't want to get Bobby Kennedy mad.

According to his critics, Robert Kennedy was the junkyard dog of the John Kennedy administration. He never had opponents, they said. He had enemies. There was a difference, and it involved vindictive efforts to destroy all who got in his family's way.

Others said the critics confused vigor and commitment with vindictiveness. In fact, Robert Kennedy admitted that he wanted to make certain people mad. Southern white racists, organized crime bosses, and communists everywhere were on his mad list. There was nothing wrong, he thought, with an "in your face" style of governing when the cause was just.

Bobby Kennedy didn't pay much attention to Vietnam policy-making while he was attorney general. In public, he mouthed the usual anticommunist platitudes and supported his brother's efforts. Like John Kennedy, Robert Kennedy believed in the importance of economic diplomacy and regional solutions. If his brother was in trouble, he was there to help him, and the New Pacific Community was always in trouble.

In 1962, Robert Kennedy made a fast swing tour of Asian/Pacific countries. As the attorney general, his credentials for leading various diplomatic summits were weak. He talked a lot about how Asian/Pacific legal systems would be connected through the united front of the New Pacific Community. It was an awkward tactic to use. Meanwhile, most Asian/Pacific leaders simply assumed Robert Kennedy was his older brother's closest advisor. This was true.

Insisting that the New Pacific Community organization meant the difference between war and peace in Southeast Asia, Robert Kennedy's rhetoric was harsher than older brother John's. It came from the heart, but some Asian leaders thought the younger brother just had a big mouth. In fact, Robert Kennedy was impatient with the Asian/ Pacific leadership. A united front, he insisted, could avoid both major and minor wars in the region, and he denounced the "petty nationalist concerns" that prevented success. Of course, another country's national interests were never petty to that particular country.

Achmed Sukarno, the leader of Indonesia, thought Robert Kennedy was gifted in the social graces, but a little too threatening in tenor and tone. Sukarno found the younger Kennedy charming and witty when the press was watching, but the gloves were off behind closed doors. Yet Kennedy's command of the facts was clouded by the usual anticommunist fervor of the day. Whenever the attorney general figured out what was going on in the Asian/Pacific world, Sukarno once quipped, America would be blessed with a determined policy-maker. That education would take some years.

Robert Kennedy listened to his older brother's specific Vietnam troubles, too, and he discussed varying options with him. A hybrid of the old Malaya and Laos cease-fire/coalition government approach intrigued him, but that's all it did. Like brother John, he seemed to enjoy analyzing policy more than making it.

By the time of John Kennedy's assassination, Bobby's attitude toward foreign policy dilemmas from Vietnam to the *Congo Crisis* had became much more cynical. He quipped that the most workable New Frontier foreign policy involved America's relationship to the moon. The Bobby Kennedy of 1963 was not the introspective, caring soul projected in his 1968 campaign for president. It would be his opposition to the Vietnam War that defined his later campaign.

Jarhead Jargon

The Kennedy administration struggled with the **Congo Crisis** at the same time as Vietnam. From 1960 to 1963, the former Belgian Congo became a bloodbath. Kennedy authorized U.S. airlifts to assist U.N. troops in the field there. The violence ended in January 1963, and this was seen as a great example of U.N. cooperation and success.

Brother Teddy and Vietnam

Like his brothers, Teddy Kennedy stressed the importance of a regional settlement in Southeast Asia. The mess in Vietnam, he said, would soon be repeated elsewhere if there was not a larger international effort to stop the communist advance. Diem, he said, was a decent man in a troubled country. Teddy believed that a combination of Vietnamese reform, American aid, and international efforts to end poverty across the region would be the best policy. This had to be done, because the United States had a strong moral obligation to live up to its anticommunist promises.

On the Senate Judiciary Committee, Teddy expressed early concerns about Southeast Asian refugees. There were millions of victims over there, he complained, and American law was not very generous to those who sought an American home. We ask so many to fight and die for the anticommunist cause, he argued, but we do not take care of these same people should they fall on hard times.

Advocating a more generous immigration and refugee policy, Teddy saw President Lyndon Johnson sign a more open and friendly Refugee Act into law two years after he arrived in Washington. Despite all the committee hearings and legislative wrangling, few noticed Teddy Kennedy's political skill. His wild after-hours lifestyle got most of the attention.

The Copy Machine Breaks Down

From the beginning, the Kennedy administration had made it clear: The New Pacific Community plan would not work without Japan and Australia. Any capitalist offensive in the region required their happy participation. Japan's hemming and hawing was to be expected. But Australia's complaints rocked the White House.

In early 1960s Washington, the Australians were considered Americans with kangaroos, a living photocopy of U.S.-styled capitalism. A rejection of their projected role as host of the New Pacific Community headquarters was not even considered. Just as they did in the cases of Vietnam and other Pacific region countries, few American foreign policy-makers at this time studied the complexities of Australian politics. Whatever those politics were, they were irrelevant in the face of the larger struggle with communism.

Australian politics were not irrelevant to Australians. The Kennedy team found that out the hard way. Prime Minister Robert Menzies insisted that the New Pacific Community interfered with Australia's national self-interest. It was his final word. Although Kennedy went to Dallas in November 1963 still believing that the Japanese and the Australians would have a change of heart, no remained no. There would never be a New Pacific Community organization.

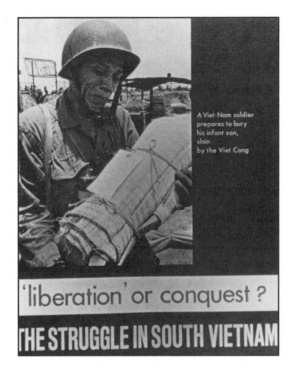

A U.S. government–issued propaganda poster shows the Vietcong as baby killers in 1963.

National Archives Still Pictures Unit, College Park, Maryland.

To fans of the New Pacific Community, it always represented a last great hope for peace. If it had worked, North Vietnam would have been isolated and surrounded by booming capitalist countries with American-supported militaries. Left poor and struggling, the North Vietnamese were supposed to rise up against their oppressors and join the cause of wealth and success.

Jarhead Jargon

A replacement for the M-113, the **APC** or Armored Personnel Carrier could carry more than 11 infantrymen plus a driver, and was constructed from aluminum armor welded over a watertight hull. It was designed to carry troops to combat, and it provided protection from small arms fire up to .50 caliber. Kennedy had authorized the creation of only two APC companies, but shortly after his assassination, and thanks to the quick transfer of former New Pacific Community funding to the military, over 2,100 APCs would soon be sent to South Vietnam.

To this day, the aging supporters of the old Kennedy plan believe that the Vietnam War would have been a short-lived affair with low casualties or no war at all had the plan worked. When the choice became clear, capitalist success or communist poverty, the average North Vietnamese would have gone with success. It was not to be, and North Vietnamese officials have always claimed that their nation never would have caved in to capitalist temptations. At least not then. Meanwhile, Kennedy administration funds already earmarked for New Pacific Community efforts were mostly transferred to the Defense Department for weapons upgrading. The APC companies in Vietnam were a direct result of this transfer.

The Least You Need to Know

➤ Through economic isolation and pressure, the Kennedy administration hoped to destroy North Vietnam and other Asian/Pacific communist states.

➤ Kennedy needed strong, wealthy allies for his New Pacific Community organization to work quickly and successfully.

➤ Japan rejected the New Pacific Community plan.

➤ Robert and Teddy Kennedy added their own twists to the John Kennedy view of Vietnam policy-making.

➤ Australia's rejection was the kiss of death to the New Pacific Community organization.

Chapter 11

The Other Vietnam?

In This Chapter

➤ Sukarno is Indonesian for communism

➤ New Frontier meets Guided Democracy

➤ Tell it to a Pope

➤ Sukarno enjoys an American Christmas

➤ Just a Vietnam War

Is the rat race getting you down? Have you had enough of endless gridlock, or that same old conversation around the water cooler? Then there's only one way out, right? You need to go to Indonesia and get shot at, beaten up, mauled, and otherwise messed around with. Of course you might find the love of your life while you're undergoing this particular midlife crisis. So don't worry, be happy. Violence in Southeast Asia can be good for your mental health.

This was the strange theme of the hit film *The Year of Living Dangerously*. One of the big blockbuster successes of the early 1980s, *The Year of Living Dangerously* starred young Mel Gibson and Sigourney Weaver. Set in Djakarta, Indonesia, during 1965, the film depicted the chaos surrounding the fall of Achmed Sukarno. Both film critics and filmgoers knew the film was about Indonesia, but most of them saw in it the madness of Vietnam. But the film was not the usual depiction of war and misery in Southeast Asia.

Ask Saigon Sally

President Achmed Sukarno gained full authority over the Indonesian government in 1957. An effective, coordinated government, Sukarno claimed, could not function with both a powerful prime minister and a powerful president. Somebody had to go, and it wasn't going to be him.

The Year of Living Dangerously reminded viewers that Indonesia could easily have been an additional Southeast Asian war for America, and it also told them that there were many of their own friends and neighbors who might have actually enjoyed it. Considered a startling revelation in its day, the film followed the lives of decent, intelligent, and even attractive-looking expatriates who didn't need booze or drugs to get high. They got high on violence or the threat of violence, and, in the 1960s, Southeast Asia was the biggest thrill around.

The film could have been set in Saigon instead of Djakarta, and that was the point. Indonesia, like Vietnam, was a powder keg ready to explode during the Kennedy and early Johnson years. But a mixture of conniving and clever diplomacy kept the United States out of a war there. The Kennedy administration was especially proud of its daring remedies to the "Indonesia problem," and President Johnson added to the Kennedy prescription. "Living Dangerously" might have been the Kennedy motto, too.

Down with Sukarno

Reflecting on his days in the Kennedy administration, the White House's "pet historian" Arthur Schlesinger Jr. once wrote that Indonesia occupied more of Kennedy's time than Laos and Vietnam combined. Vietnam and Indonesia were very different places, but Kennedy's regional outlook connected the two.

When Kennedy came to office in 1961, Achmed Sukarno, like Ho Chi Minh, was already a living legend in his country. In fact, the State Department believed that Sukarno saw himself as a living legend. As early as 1927, he had been the leader of the anti-Dutch resistance in the sternly run colony of the Dutch East Indies (or Indonesia). He had declared independence from Holland in front of his own house in August 1945. The postcolonial era in his 90 percent Muslim country, he said, would be based on "Five Principles"—nationalism, humanism, democracy, social justice, and Allah.

Sukarno and the Dutch

By 1950, Sukarno's "Five Principles" supporters had defeated the Dutch, reducing the latter's old Pacific empire to the province of West Irian in the jungles of New Guinea. The Netherlands government decided to keep West Irian because New Guinea's "primitive," loin cloth–wearing inhabitants did not oppose Dutch rule. More to the point, the Dutch dreamed of Sukarno's eventual collapse and the possible return of Dutch glory. At least in West Irian, they were positioned to come "home" after Sukarno stumbled and fell.

For a while, Sukarno opposed the communist movement in his country. The communists had been something of the backbone of the anti-Japanese resistance during the World War II Japanese occupation. Their patriotic claims rivaled Sukarno's own, and this was not good news for the ambitious anti-Dutch resistance hero. He had little use for rivals to his self-proclaimed destiny. And once he was in power, the communists proved to be a lot of trouble.

Sukarno's Indonesia was a poor, struggling country and its people were tired of violence. A communist-versus-anticommunist civil war could be the kiss of death for the new president. To keep the peace and himself in power, Sukarno welcomed communists into his cabinet. The move confused a lot of people, for he had once denounced all communists as evil fiends.

Shell Shock

In 1960, Senator Stuart Symington (Democrat, Missouri) chaired a special Democratic Party committee on efficiency and coordination in the armed forces. In his final recommendations, he claimed that America did not have the full capability to intervene and prevail in Indonesia. The next presidential administration, he warned, must prepare accordingly.

"Guided Democracy"

While Kennedy and Nixon were slugging it out during the 1960 U.S. election, Sukarno suspended all political activities and closed down most newspapers. In spite of his actions, he insisted that democracy was alive and well in Indonesia. He just defined it differently from the Americans, and that definition, he claimed, was rooted in Indonesian culture and tradition. What difference did it make that communists were part of his so-called "Guided Democracy" advisory corps? That was America's hang-up, not his.

Kennedy's "massive retaliation" and Cold War victory promises troubled the Indonesian president. Sukarno had already faced America's wrath in 1958. The Eisenhower administration had concluded that the Indonesian leader was a communist collaborator in a country that housed important U.S. oil industry interests (like Shell Oil). That made him both an ideological enemy and a threat to U.S. economic national self-interest (especially if he decided to nationalize the foreign oil industry in Indonesia). The guy was double trouble for the White House, and a CIA-led assassination team was sent to Indonesia to snuff him out.

Allen Pope, a veteran intelligence man, was in charge of the assassination mission, but his security was blown shortly after he arrived in the country. Captured, tried, and sentenced to death, even though he claimed to be an independent mercenary,

Jarhead Jargon

To Secretary of State Dean Rusk, Indonesia was a **backwater nation.** That meant it was supposed to be on the outskirts of America's major national security interests; however, Rusk still feared that Indonesia might lead to a bloody war for the United States.

Ask Saigon Sally

Although President Kennedy doubted the effectiveness of his own Peace Corps, it was needed in Indonesia. Anti-Americanism was high in that poor country, and, therefore, Kennedy sent more Peace Corps volunteers to Indonesia than to any other Asian/Pacific location. His own anti-"Ugly American" rhetoric and a watchful Congress left him no other alternative at the time.

Pope was scheduled to die sometime in 1961. Although Sukarno insisted that the execution order was irreversible, he worried about what the incoming Kennedy administration might do to avenge Mr. Pope. Would he have to spend the rest of his days fending off CIA hit squads?

Frankly, it was in the Kennedy administration's interest to keep Sukarno guessing. In public, on the other hand, the Kennedy team painted a contradictory picture. They were quick to denounce Indonesia as a *backwater nation,* but that did not match their general rhetoric about punishing communism (including governments that welcomed communists) anyplace, anytime.

The West Irian Problem

If the American government was depressed over the failure of the Pope mission, there was little reason to be. Sukarno was looking over his shoulder now, and a Sukarno who was scared was a Sukarno ready to talk with the United States. But he was a mercurial character. Sukarno advocated an early meeting with Kennedy, but not before he threatened a little "massive retaliation" of his own. Indonesia could rattle a sword, too.

Sukarno said that the Dutch must leave West Irian or face an Indonesian invasion. To make matters worse, he appealed to the Soviet Union for military aid. Holland, meanwhile, had no intention of leaving, and Dutch politicians mumbled about lobbying fellow NATO members, including the United States, Canada, and most of Western Europe, to send troops to West Irian to beat back the "procommunist Sukarno."

If NATO members wanted to prove their solidarity behind a fellow member and against advancing communism, then a West Irian military expedition, argued the Dutch, was truly in order. Things were getting out of hand, but Sukarno won plenty of applause from Indonesians for his tough talk and war preparations. Given the hopelessly struggling Indonesian economy, all Sukarno could offer was nationalist politics anyway.

American Charisma Meets Indonesian Charisma

In the spring of 1961, Sukarno met Kennedy at the White House. Kennedy thought Sukarno was a strange little man who smiled too much, talked too much, and threatened too much. Sukarno saw Kennedy as a strutting egotist, imperialist, and good buddy to the Dutch. At least Sukarno was in Washington wining and dining with the American government. Ho Chi Minh never had dinner with John Kennedy.

In spite of the clash of egos, Sukarno was left with the impression that the Americans wanted peace more than they wanted him dead. Without question, Kennedy wanted peace, but he also worried about contradicting his "pay any price, bear any burden" promises. You could not be a proper Cold Warrior and wheel-and-deal with Achmed Sukarno, too. It was a classic policy-making dilemma for American anticommunists.

Stumbling Blocks to Peace

A true stumbling block to peace was the fate of Allen Pope. The Kennedy administration maintained the stance that Pope must be freed "or else." The "or else" was never specified, prompting Sukarno to fear the worst. But this approach only heightened tensions.

Like the Vietnamese, the Indonesians could claim to have beaten both the Japanese and a European colonial power. The Pentagon maintained a healthy respect for the Indonesian guerrilla fighter. Any conflict with Indonesia was guaranteed to kill quite a few Americans. A step-by-step approach to peace would have to be taken, and each step was important. In other words, some sort of deal over Allen Pope and another deal over West Irian were required before a one-on-one peace initiative between Indonesia and the United States could be discussed. Having seen one policy struggle after another in Vietnam, the Kennedy team had little reason to be optimistic over Indonesia.

Shell Shock

Popular opinion and hindsight suggests that the Indonesians were 100 percent to blame for the war-threatening crisis over West Irian. But it took two to tango there. For months, Dutch Foreign Minister Joseph Luns insisted that there could be no compromise over Holland's full control of West Irian.

Ask Saigon Sally

Elvis Stahr, the secretary of the army in the Kennedy administration, insisted that the Kennedy White House could never champion American virtue in Vietnam, Laos, or anywhere in Southeast Asia if it left one of its own citizens and soldier-heroes (Allen Pope) to die in Indonesia.

The other charismatic guy in the White House, Robert Kennedy, would have his own dinners with Sukarno. During his 1962 Asian/Pacific tour, Robert Kennedy was ordered to pay especially close attention to Indonesian affairs. Even more specifically, John Kennedy wanted his brother to go beyond goodwill tour platitudes while in Indonesia and demand the release of Allen Pope. Or at least give it a good Harvard try. Bobby Kennedy was also supposed to offer an American mediation of the West Irian crisis to both the Indonesians and the Dutch. These were tall orders.

The younger brother followed the older brother's directives, but the Dutch government accused the Kennedys of "meddling" in their affairs. In response, Robert Kennedy advised the Dutch that they could call him all the names in the book, but the White House still wanted the West Irian matter resolved. Nothing happened. The attorney general would have better luck with the Pope case.

The Pope Case

Allen Pope had been shot down by antiaircraft fire while bombing a vessel in Ambon, Celebes. He was captured immediately. For years afterward, he blamed his Indonesian contacts for betraying his position. Pope had been tried before an Indonesian military tribunal that denounced U.S. policy whenever it had a chance to do so.

Pope was sentenced to death for aiding the enemies of Indonesia and for bearing arms against Indonesia. Nobody bought his mercenary argument. His capture came as a surprise to CIA buddies elsewhere. Pope's cover had been excellent. It even included letters sent to friends from Tanzania, East Africa, where he was supposed to have been on safari. (Pope was never in Tanzania.)

Ask Saigon Sally

Sukarno's anti-Americanism could be explained by the fact that he received a significant amount of Soviet aid. The Soviet Union gave more money to Indonesia in the early 1960s than to any other so-called noncommunist country.

Howard Jones, the American ambassador to Indonesia, stuck to his guns with regard to Pope. He consistently told Sukarno that Pope's execution would worsen U.S.-Indonesian relations to the degree that they might never recover.

Robert Kennedy offered a fresh approach. The Kennedy administration, he said, had been elected to replace the Eisenhower approach to foreign affairs. Pope's assassination mission, he stressed, was a mistake, and continued U.S.-Indonesian tensions or even a war over yesterday's mistakes would be downright stupid.

Kennedy also brought along a passionate personal appeal from Pope's wife, and Howard Jones suddenly took a compassionate stance as well. Following the attorney general's lead, Jones reminded Sukarno that both Washington and Moscow had released downed pilots in the past, and that whatever propaganda mileage the Indonesian government had won from the Pope case had already been won.

The don't-be-stupid approach worked. Sukarno released Pope, touting the innate humanitarian qualities of "Guided Democracy" versus U.S. imperialism. But there was a long way to go to keep the peace. Sukarno said the Pope release was irrelevant to West Irian, where, he vowed, Holland was destined to make its last stand in the Pacific.

To make matters worse, Sukarno insisted that as long as the United States considered "Guided Democracy" a threat to American interests, a cordial U.S.-Indonesia relationship was not to be. In any event, the Pope matter was finally out of the way. Once home, Pope offered his personal apologies to the Kennedy administration for the trouble he might have caused. Then he went back to work. For the next several years, Pope would arrange covert operations for the CIA in both Vietnam and Laos.

Shell Shock

Not everyone in the Sukarno government favored a war over West Irian. General Abdul Nasution, the longtime Indonesian military spokesman, said Sukarno should stress domestic economic recovery and stop sword rattling.

Vietnam War or Indonesia War?

There was never an either/or situation involving Vietnam and Indonesia. The Kennedy administration was ready to dispatch troops to both locations. But what a mess that would have been, and the Kennedys preferred neatness to messiness.

Tales from the Front

Sometimes U.S. military advisors learned from their students. In 1961, during Operation Typhoon, 14-man South Vietnamese intelligence teams trained in airborne and commando tactics infiltrated Laos to halt communist operations near the Ho Chi Minh Trail. Major Tran Khac Kinh served as the coordinator for most of the operation, and U.S. military advisors listened to his advice and recommendations for a successful infiltration effort.

Ask Saigon Sally

Nikita Khrushchev, the Soviet premier, visited Indonesia in February 1960. While in Djakarta, Khrushchev gave Sukarno a new Soviet navy cruiser, promised more munitions shipments pending a mutually acceptable arms deal, and spoke of Indonesia's "need" for nuclear weapons.

The Kennedys lucked out with Indonesia, and a working peace was established. It was not easily achieved. In fact, it was a very long process, and through most of it, President Kennedy doubted any solution was truly possible. He was wrong. The United States was spared an additional Southeast Asian war, and, given all the Cold War tensions of the day, only American political junkies and foreign policy experts paid attention to what happened in Indonesia.

The Kennedy administration's "Indonesia problem" had been an ominous one. And it wasn't just about Sukarno. The Indonesian Communist Party, or PKI, was the largest one outside of the Soviet Bloc. Poverty, prostitution, and the black market ruled the day throughout Indonesia. Western visitors reported being robbed by beggars moments after they got off the plane in Djakarta. Thanks to Sukarno's antiforeigner propaganda, it was largely open season on the small expatriate community gathered in Djakarta. Because of the violence and chaos, any Western investment was unlikely and the misery factor for foreigners was expected to increase. Communism thrived on misery.

U.S. Air Force C-123 transport planes drop South Vietnamese paratroopers during the March 1963 Operation Phi Hoa II, a tactical air-ground strike against the Vietcong in Tay Ninh Province, South Vietnam.

National Archives Still Pictures Unit, College Park, Maryland.

On the right side of Indonesia's political aisle, the military had reformist ideas of its own. Sukarno's army chiefs of staff favored *demobilization* of their own forces. The money saved would then be invested in jobs and infrastructure projects. A government that cared about its people, and not just chanted nationalist slogans, could kill the appeal of communism. Or so the military reasoned. Meanwhile, Sukarno stood between the PKI and his reform-minded generals, largely living off his reputation as the aging anticolonial hero. Like Diem of South Vietnam, he lived very well, and the Kennedys wondered how long the locals would tolerate it.

As long as the West Irian situation threatened war, the Indonesian military needed more and more Soviet weapons to prepare for the fight. If Sukarno fell and the PKI took over, the Indonesian communists would inherit a huge Soviet-supplied army.

By the summer of 1962, the Kennedy administration had made its move, but President Kennedy himself remained pessimistic. To jump-start the West Irian peace initiative, Secretary of State Rusk offered the Indonesians a long laundry list of good-faith economic gifts.

The U.S. aid package included a Development Grant of $17 million, $32 million of rice (four times larger than any other U.S. aid plan in the region), $40 million in wheat, flour, cotton, and other stuff, patrol boats, T-37 jet trainers, and several multimillion dollar loans to specific Indonesian industries and construction firms. Rusk told Sukarno that America's new sugar daddy role for Indonesia was just the beginning of a new era of friendship. And it wasn't even Christmas.

Jarhead Jargon

Literally meaning to "discharge from military service," the term **demobilization** was coined by the British government in the 1880s. Most often used to describe the return of troops to civilian life after a war, it is also associated with isolationist policies and anti-war causes when the recall of troops is demanded.

Shell Shock

Most noncommunist Indonesian militarists favored a war against the Dutch in West Irian, a war against the Portuguese in Timor, and a war against the British in North Borneo all at the same time. Sukarno stressed only the West Irian matter.

A War in Vietnam *Is* Good Enough for Me

In August 1962, the West Irian problem was finally resolved. Following a series of long meetings between American, Dutch, and Indonesian officials, a United Nations interim government was arranged. Over an eight-month period, the United Nations

Ask Saigon Sally

Michael Forrestal, the senior staff member for President Kennedy's National Security Council, believed that Indonesia could easily end up like Vietnam. In 1963, he advised Kennedy to "get tough" with Sukarno and wield extravagant aid plans as a lever for more anticommunist commitments and reform politics.

would oversee the transfer of Dutch power to Indonesia, and in 1969 the local residents were supposed to decide whether they wanted to remain Indonesian.

In the end, the Diem assassination and the changing scene in South Vietnam made President Kennedy think twice about Indonesia. Hoping to be in Djakarta in February 1964, Kennedy wanted to see things for himself. For the time being, it appeared that Sukarno or some Indonesian military figure could keep the communists at bay and take advantage of America's economic generosity. Pope was home, and the West Irian trouble was over. Chaos and confusion in Indonesia did not necessarily mean the introduction of U.S. troops there.

In late 1963, it looked like Vietnam might remain America's laboratory of anticommunism in Southeast Asia. John Kennedy took this assessment to the grave; he was assassinated on November 22. Lyndon Johnson was left to sort things out. As the Vietnam War heated up during his watch, the last thing Johnson needed was U.S. troops in Indonesia, too. But Sukarno's government would fall less than two years after the Kennedy assassination, and an anticommunist regime would prevail over the PKI. Many of America's fears and worries would look exaggerated and foolish just a few years after John Kennedy was gone.

To the Kennedy administration, Indonesia had had all the elements of the Vietnam misery. It was just "down the street" from Vietnam, too, but the Kennedy team had kept matters in hand. Meanwhile, their successful peace-making and aid plans did not spread to Vietnam. Unfortunately.

The Least You Need to Know

➤ A Vietnam-like War was possible in or near Indonesia during the early 1960s.

➤ To the Kennedy administration, Indonesia's political scene shared similarities to the Vietnam political scene.

➤ Achmed Sukarno posed many problems for U.S. policy-makers.

➤ American diplomacy and generous aid packages eased U.S.-Indonesian tensions.

➤ President Kennedy had planned to visit Indonesia in early 1964.

Part 3

Escalation

Americans love a winner. Part of the American psyche is "going the distance" and "getting the job done." Lyndon Johnson wanted to go the distance and get the job done in Vietnam. Whereas John Kennedy, in his view, had gone half the way to destroy the communist challenge in South Vietnam, Johnson planned to finish, to prevail where his predecessor faltered. If lies and schemes were needed to succeed, he had no problem using them. No one would question his tactics after the great victory was achieved. Who would care?

President Johnson was well aware of the effectiveness of the enemy and the corruption of our ally in Saigon. But he went ahead with an escalation of the war anyway, and hoped for the best. Certainly the North Vietnamese would sue for peace sooner rather than later, he believed. There was always light at the end of the tunnel, and America needed to be patient. He was wrong about the North Vietnamese, and the American people were not that patient.

The more U.S. troops entered the war in Vietnam, the more difficult it became to pull them out. Johnson believed he foresaw the death of his administration and the Democratic Party if he turned his back on anticommunism in a tiny Southeast Asian country. America would leave Vietnam after the victory, he concluded, but these would be famous last words.

Chapter 12

Holding the Beachhead

In This Chapter

➤ Hindsight pollutes history

➤ Ho prepares for the big game

➤ Don't rock "The Rock"

➤ Mr. McNamara takes a trip

➤ Just win it

Eureka is not a major tourist attraction. Nestled between the cornfields of central Illinois, this quaint little town holds a population of roughly 4,500. Its claim to fame is tiny Eureka College and its most famous graduate, President Ronald Reagan. In the 1980s, Reagan returned to his alma mater.

For years, Reagan had been uncomfortable speaking to student groups, and he had made few commencement speeches during his White House years. As California's candid and ultraconservative governor in the late 1960s, Reagan's hawkish views on the Vietnam War had made him less than welcome on college campuses. That fact actually enhanced his standing with conservative voters, and his castigating of student antiwar activists won him loud applause from his hard-line supporters.

Legend Sounds Better Than Fact

In Eureka, the just-reelected Reagan could be assured of cheering crowds no matter what he said. He was the hottest thing there since Dairy Queen came to town. During his speech, he praised Midwest values as the rock of Americana. Patriotism and love of family lived on in Eureka, he said, and he thanked them for their hospitality.

Reagan was also in a reflective mood during this trip down memory lane. He told the Illinois press that he was amazed at how the college scene had changed since the Vietnam days. Conservatism was "in" again, and the Young Republicans often represented the biggest student group on campus.

Times had truly changed, and so had America's perception of the Vietnam War. Popular movies and TV shows depicted the Vietnam veteran as the hero, and the politician as the villain. It was the latter, most believed, who had really "lost" the Vietnam War. Reagan had something to say about that development as well.

According to Reagan, John F. Kennedy had played a key role in the failure of America's mission in Vietnam. Reagan admired Kennedy's stirring rhetoric and dogged determination to win the Cold War, but believed that he had messed up in Vietnam. One of the reasons for that failure, Reagan said, was Kennedy's inability to prepare adequately for the war that was sure to come. The slow introduction of troops, the Diem assassination, and the callous way of dealing with Asian allies added up to too many problems to overcome, Reagan argued.

The dashing Mr. Kennedy had left a nightmare for Lyndon Johnson, and the latter could not be blamed, Reagan insisted, for a lot of the problems that followed. The war was lost even before Lyndon Johnson escalated it. Reagan concluded that through it all, the American military was exempt from the White House's stupid decisions, and it was too bad that so many screwups were made during the early 1960s.

Reagan denied that he was maligning the names of a martyred president and his successor. He just wanted to speak his mind on behalf of the military and against the political bumbling that, in his view, had ensured defeat in Vietnam.

Myths and Reality

To a large degree, Reagan bought into a grand myth and furthered it a bit, too. The myth was that the military was something of the innocent bystander in Vietnam, and that Washington was guilty of horrible sins. In reality, nobody was a bystander in Vietnam, and Washington did its best to prepare the military for war in Vietnam.

Once again, hindsight was polluting history. Reagan's reputation as the *Great Communicator* for the good soldier/bad politician thesis did not help matters. Hindsight, if given an attractive spin, can be easier to remember than history.

Jarhead Jargon

During the early years of his presidency, Ronald Reagan, nick-named the **Great Communicator** in the press, often praised another great communicator, John Kennedy. Generally, Reagan had no problem connecting his administration's foreign policies to the popular Kennedy agenda of 20 years earlier.

If Vietnam was part of the larger communist threat throughout the Asian/Pacific world, then the U.S. government had some challenging work to do—not just winning in Vietnam, but preparing for opposition throughout the region afterward. If Vietnam was part of the larger communist agenda of anti-Western liberation and Marxist dreams, then Ho Chi Minh had plenty of organizational nightmares, too—not just beating back the Americans and the South Vietnamese, but positioning himself as a leader in the continuing communist expansion. In short, the 1980s, or Reagan, view of heroes and villains remains an overly simplistic way to view the Vietnam War.

Complexity and Contradiction

If you've read every chapter so far, you know that the Vietnam War was the product of complexity and contradiction. There was nothing simple about it—the particulars of Ho's own brand of communism prove the case themselves. Preparing the way for victory was tough for both Washington and Hanoi. Quite a complicated groundwork had to be laid, and much of that groundwork took place in the early 1960s.

Ask Saigon Sally

It has been said that during the early and mid-1960s, a cautious Ho Chi Minh never said a critical word against the Chinese and Soviet governments. His independent communism had its limits, and he did not want to alienate major military benefactors.

Ho Gets Ready

In late 1963, both Moscow and Beijing needed to know what Ho Chi Minh had in mind for the next year or two. The Diem and Kennedy assassinations raised a lot of questions about the future, and Ho wasn't providing too many answers. He tried to assure the major communist powers that stepping up anti-Saigon guerrilla activity would not provoke a major military response from the Americans.

If Washington did nothing to intervene in China during the late 1940s, Ho reasoned, it wouldn't intervene in Vietnam either. The Chinese were especially worried that a U.S. victory in Vietnam would continue into China. Ho had little concern about such a possibility. He had been dealing with China's fatalistic attitude toward his country for years, and enough was enough.

Ho told the Chinese government to stop worrying. The Americans would be contained and beaten back in Vietnam if they dared to attack on a large scale. But Ho's own colleagues questioned this thesis as well as his efforts to please both Moscow and Beijing. It was easy, some of them said, for the Soviets to talk about "peaceful coexistence" with the West, and it was easy for the Chinese to stay isolationist: Nobody was shooting at them at the time! Vietnam was in a war of liberation whether Moscow or Beijing accepted it or not.

Tales from the Front

Enlisting in the Marines early in World War II, William Corson survived some of the toughest island campaigns of the war. Recruited into the OSS immediately after the war, Corson spent the next thirty years as an intelligence agent and analyst. As early as 1962, while serving in Vietnam, he complained that key South Vietnamese intelligence agents were also enemy agents at the same time. By 1965, he reported that the North Vietnamese had a stronger and more successful intelligence operation than the U.S. and ARVN combined. His complaints and warnings were ignored.

Bickering among fellow North Vietnamese "freedom fighters" could not have been too surprising to Ho. The man had encouraged independent communist thinking for years. But in those dark days following the end of Diem and Kennedy, Ho preferred to keep a warm dialogue going with powerful foreign friends, and he alienated many North Vietnamese because of it.

Jarhead Jargon

Known as the **Sino-Soviet rift,** pro-Chinese Maoist communists and pro-Soviet communists argued over ideological purity for years. The most difficult time was during the late 1950s and early 1960s when both Khrushchev and Mao threatened a major conflict over this debate.

In 1963, Ho still had his favorites. In fact, he tried to play one interested communist state off another. Official statements from his Hanoi regime praised Mao Tse-tung as the only true communist out there these days. Of course, this also meant that the Soviets had abandoned decent communist principle at the same time. Ho was testing the waters. Just who was his strongest communist ally?

The Chinese had been much more involved in Vietnamese affairs than the Soviets, and with the Vietnam War about to take an even more violent turn, Ho wanted to remind the Soviets of that fact. Of course, such reminders angered the Soviet government. The North Vietnamese leader was playing a dangerous game. Ho had to be told by his friends that caution was still the best policy. Getting caught up in what was known as the *Sino-Soviet rift* promised no good for North Vietnam.

Tales from the Front

Tran Van Bo did not fit the communist propaganda label of the poor, struggling Vietcong peasant. Born and raised in Ba Xuyen province in the Mekong Delta, Tran was the son of a successful farmer who went to work for his uncle, a wealthy rice wholesaler. If it hadn't been for the Vietnam War, Tran would have become a wealthy man himself. But he joined the Vietcong after local and corrupt Diem government officials took away his business and jailed most of his relatives and friends. Tran worked his way up through the Vietcong ranks, eventually becoming something of the paymaster for several Vietcong units. He was captured by U.S. advisors and ARVN troops in 1963. *Time/Life* Reporter Stanley Karnow made Tran famous after a series of interviews from his jail cell, providing Western audiences one of the first portraits ever of a Vietcong operative.

One of Ho's gentler critics was the great General Giap himself. Giap didn't like the idea of starting offensives in South Vietnam until a full assessment of the new governments in Saigon and Washington was completed. This was considered a little too cautious and a little too pro-"peaceful coexistence" by Ho. Giap's stature in public memory made it difficult for Ho or anyone to challenge him directly, so they went after his friends instead. Giap's closest supporters in government service were fired from their jobs.

Meanwhile, General Nguyen Chi Thanh, and not Giap, would emerge as Ho's senior military advisor during the many months of planning. And there would be more planning than fighting, at least for the time being.

Ask Saigon Sally

Whereas Ho and his North Vietnam regime believed that the new Lyndon Johnson administration spent night and day planning Vietnam War strategies, the truth was something very different. Johnson's top priority in late 1963 and early 1964 was passing John Kennedy's lingering civil rights legislation.

President Ngo Dinh Diem greets South Vietnamese Air Force personnel shortly before his assassination.

National Archives Still Pictures Unit, College Park, Maryland.

America Tries to Get Ready

The United States enjoyed military basing privileges across the Asian/Pacific region. When it came to a war in Vietnam, some were more important than others. For instance, Clark Air Base, near Angeles City in the Philippines, would soon become America's largest air force installation on the planet. Given its Southeast Asian location, this sprawling base's role in the Vietnam War was assured. Kadena Air Base on the American-occupied island of Okinawa was important, too. Its role in the Korean War had been essential, and its role in the upcoming Vietnam War was guaranteed as well.

Anderson Air Base on the U.S. Territory of Guam had also demonstrated its worthiness during the Korean War, and would soon be synonymous with President Johnson's Operation ROLLING THUNDER B-52 raids over North Vietnam. But all these bases, so vital to air operations to come, were living on borrowed time. Or so it seemed during the days of the Kennedy-Johnson transition.

Shell Shock

Chamorro (Guamanian) rights advocates insisted that Anderson Air Base, Naval Station, and Naval Air Station on their small island made them prisoners in their own land.

Murmurs in the Pacific

In 1963, the growing Nationalist-Citizen Party in the Philippines insisted that the presence of the U.S. bases robbed the country of its independence. Its leader, Claro Recto, was a strong challenger to President Carlos Garcia, and even the latter was good at making anti-American threats.

In Tokyo, the movement to end American rule over the Japanese island of Okinawa and all neighboring Ryukyu Islands was quickly becoming part of respectable, mainstream politics. Both the Japanese left and the right seemed to agree that Japan could never be truly independent and move forward if part of its sovereignty was still under the command of the Americans.

On Guam, the Territorial Legislature insisted that Anderson Air Base, which occupied much of the northern section of the 32-mile-long island, was located on ancestral land. More to the point, residents of northern Guam had been evacuated from it during and after World War II. They wanted to return home, and the U.S. Navy and Interior Department governments there ignored them. It was becoming quite a mess.

One of John Kennedy's worst nightmares was to get involved in a Southeast Asian war and then lose the regional peace at the same time. Whereas the cerebral Mr. Kennedy always worried over the larger diplomatic and geopolitical significance of developments in the region, Vice President Johnson was more concerned about solid agreements to keep U.S. bases up and running.

Ask Saigon Sally

As vice president, Lyndon Johnson chaired the Executive Branch Council on National Aeronautics and Space and another on the Peace Corps. He undertook official visits to more than 30 countries before being sworn in as president on November 22, 1963.

Johnson Visits the Pacific

With Kennedy's permission, Johnson went out to the Pacific to put a lid on all the anti-American, anti-bases politics. Putting lids on things was hard work, but Johnson was good at it.

One decade before Johnson's mission to the Philippines, the "Huk" rebellion had been put down there. Supported by communists everywhere, the Huk revolt had involved a coalition of religious, ethnic, and political activists that later reminded some people of the Vietcong. The United States had offered limited assistance to put down the violence, and the rebellion had been short-lived. To Johnson, the same quick action could be accomplished in South Vietnam.

Johnson offered a fancy economic package to the Philippines government, promising not to complain about Manila's usual corruption and graft involving American aid.

Shell Shock

Following the Kennedy assassination, National Security Council Advisor Walt Rostow recommended to the new president, Lyndon Johnson, that the Vietnam situation must be watched very, very carefully. If it even appeared that the Vietcong were gaining the upper hand, Rostow advised a "massive retaliation" response.

In return for America's generosity, he expected the Philippines' full cooperation over military basing privileges throughout the length of any Vietnam War. Manila's own role in that war, Johnson suggested, might be in the interest of the Philippines, too. It could demonstrate Manila's anticommunist solidarity with Washington.

Known for no-nonsense wheeling and dealing with foreign leaders, Johnson pulled few punches. He could understand corruption and confusion in the Philippines, but he would not tolerate anti-Americanism in Japan. He told the Ikeda government to stop making noise over Okinawa. "Reversion," as far as he was concerned, would disturb America's huge military presence on the island, and there must be no rocking of "The Rock" (Okinawa's military nickname) during the Vietnam War.

As for Guam, Johnson was even more indignant. The Guamanians could complain about things through their new delegate in Congress, Johnson believed.

In the meantime, any talk about usurping Anderson base property was good old-fashioned treason as far as he was concerned.

The Pacific trip was fresh in mind when Johnson became president, and he was pretty sure that all was well with his Asian/Pacific military infrastructure. Although Johnson would be a bit more diplomatic and gentleman-like during his presidency, he always thought Kennedy had been too polite to the uppity Pacific allies. He also assumed that America was already at war in Vietnam, while Kennedy preferred to believe that somehow, some way, his policies were preventing that war.

Vacation in Vietnam

Like Ho Chi Minh, Secretary of Defense Robert McNamara worried about the impact of the Diem and Kennedy assassinations on Vietnam. Less than one month after Kennedy was buried, McNamara headed to Saigon. He had to see things for himself.

Publicly, McNamara painted a rosy picture. The recent assassinations meant nothing to the larger scheme of things, he told the press, and the Vietcong still didn't have a prayer. Privately, all was gloom and doom. McNamara had just been to Vietnam in October 1963. He said then that everything was under control. But now, in December 1963, he feared that he had been spoon-fed lies and propaganda by both Vietnamese and American officials.

The South Vietnamese army, McNamara reported, lost more weapons than it captured, and the Vietcong were systematically gaining control of the countryside. This wasn't just a Vietnamese problem, he stressed. The American Embassy and military there were commanded by dreamers and fools; a lot of Americans were to blame for this mess. He told President Johnson to expect a communist victory in the next few months. Obviously, the secretary of defense did not have a pleasant visit.

McNamara found himself in the middle of a feud between the U.S. ambassador, Henry Cabot Lodge Jr., and the American military commander, General Paul Harkins. Even their support staff and aides did not get along. For a while, Harkins and Lodge did not permit McNamara to use embassy communications during his trip. They worried that the secretary was sending negative reports back to Washington. They were right. America should fear the worst over there, McNamara concluded.

Back in the White House, the always straight-shooting General Curtis LeMay said the time was right for a large-scale strike. LeMay was the commander of the Air Force, and he worried that the military advantage in Vietnam was slipping to the enemy. Later criticized for being an early extremist and even a "mad bomber," LeMay was just doing his job as Air Force commander. He recommended a large-scale bombing campaign over North Vietnam, an outrageous suggestion at the time, and he drew cold, blank stares from Johnson and the leftover Kennedy cabinet.

LeMay and the Joint Chiefs of Staff would respond to the McNamara assessment with their own bureaucratic and political-sounding recommendation to the president. McNamara's depressing views were used to justify a stepping-up of military operations in Vietnam.

Ask Saigon Sally

Lyndon Johnson once referred to Senator Richard Russell (Democrat, Georgia) as one of his great political mentors and teachers. As early as December 1963, Russell warned Johnson to stay out of Vietnam.

Ask Saigon Sally

From the beginning, Johnson was uncomfortable with the leftover Kennedy cabinet. He said that they were all a bunch of Harvard elitists who liked "white socks" and sailing around a "female island" (Martha's Vineyard).

Specifically, LeMay and his colleagues resurrected the old domino theory. Southeast Asia was about to go, they said, and it would be the new Johnson administration's fault. This communist success would lead to daring communist go-for-broke offensives in Latin America and Africa as well. Vietnam was just the beginning, they warned. A combination of air strikes, commando raids, and joint American–South Vietnamese military offensives could save the day. There could be no turning back.

133

War Can Ruin a Good Night's Sleep

Within days after he became the world's most powerful president, Lyndon Johnson was referring to Vietnam as "my war." A so-called Situation Room was built in the White House basement to monitor the latest Vietnam War events, and it was not unusual for Johnson to appear down there at 2 A.M. or 3 A.M. Wearing bedclothes and toting a flashlight, just in case, he would read the latest battle reports coming in from faraway Vietnam. It was usually depressing stuff, but he was proud of "his" heroes in Vietnam.

There is an old expression that suggests that war remains too important to be left to the generals and admirals. Lyndon Johnson certainly agreed with it, and he expected to be fully informed about every aspect and development of the Vietnam War. Unfortunately, most of his staff was aware of this personal interest and usually told him only what he wanted to hear.

Shell Shock

Years after the Vietnam War, President Johnson's press secretary, Bill Moyers, once commented that the weeks following the Kennedy assassination were pivotal ones in the U.S.–South Vietnam relationship. No one in the Johnson administration, he said, including Johnson, knew exactly what to do.

Just two days after he became president, Johnson offered his assessment of the Vietnam scene. He told Ambassador Lodge in Saigon that he considered the whole Vietnam problem a pretty easy one to solve. You didn't need a Harvard Ph.D. for this one. In short, the war in Vietnam was about the international communist conspiracy. The violence in South Vietnam, he said, was due to "external forces" in the communist world, and that one of the major reasons for the stumbling and bumbling of the Saigon regime was because America's commitment to defeating communism in South Vietnam needed to be reaffirmed and strengthened. Further Kennedyesque analysis was not required. Highbrow, middle-of-the-night cabinet discussions in English or French were no longer necessary either.

Although some of the early Johnson rhetoric about Vietnam was the same as the Kennedy rhetoric, it usually meant something different. Kennedy had spoken often about "holding the beachhead" over there. To Kennedy, this meant shoring up diplomatic and economic relationships with a variety of Asian/Pacific countries. By doing so, you assured your national security priorities at the same time and, it was hoped, kept other countries from turning into Vietnams.

To Johnson, "holding the beachhead" had more military significance. It meant beating back opponents to the Saigon regime and making a tough anticommunist statement in South Vietnam. There would be nothing like a decisive military victory to influence events in all those other Asian/Pacific countries.

134

"Holding the beachhead" in South Vietnam, said Johnson, meant winning a war. Throughout his presidency, Johnson would struggle over the right method to achieve it.

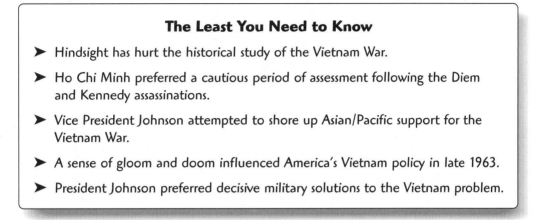

The Least You Need to Know

➤ Hindsight has hurt the historical study of the Vietnam War.

➤ Ho Chi Minh preferred a cautious period of assessment following the Diem and Kennedy assassinations.

➤ Vice President Johnson attempted to shore up Asian/Pacific support for the Vietnam War.

➤ A sense of gloom and doom influenced America's Vietnam policy in late 1963.

➤ President Johnson preferred decisive military solutions to the Vietnam problem.

All the Way with LBJ

They were two different people. One was strictly Dom Perignon, Pierre Cardin, and a Gulf Star sloop. The other was Schlitz, JC Penney, and a borrowed fishing boat. John Kennedy and Lyndon Johnson, many believed, were the Mutt and Jeff of early 1960s American politics. And first impressions died hard.

Following the Kennedy assassination, there were plenty of Americans who were concerned that an uncouth country bumpkin had replaced their beloved patrician president. For a while, Johnson appeared to prove them right.

America Goes to the Dogs?

Shortly after his presidency began, Johnson held a news conference on the White House lawn. Having brought his champion beagles with him from the impressive LBJ Ranch in central Texas, Johnson cautioned reporters to watch where they stepped on that lawn. The Kennedys had had dogs also—usually immaculately groomed springer spaniels—but the reporters had never had to watch where they stepped. At one point during the Johnson news conference, the president interrupted the play of two energetic beagles and held both of them up by their ears for all the world to see. Dog lovers were outraged for months. A Kennedy would never dangle dogs by their ears.

Ask Saigon Sally

Throughout the Vietnam War, Johnson made references to his own military service days during World War II. His references gave the impression of a long, distinguished military career. In reality, he had served seven months in the U.S. Navy.

Throughout his presidency, Johnson would prove that he was quite a character. Although he usually appeared stilted and formal with the press, in private he was a boisterous, back-slapping, jolly joker. But he was a bright and focused jolly joker. According to his former colleagues in the Congress, the former Senate majority leader was an engaging and brilliant man, whereas Kennedy had been a pretty suit.

Although the press was quick to denounce Johnson's lack of charisma, what they were really trying to say was that they missed John Kennedy's kind of charisma. For instance, the conventional wisdom of the day suggested that Kennedy had had a sophisticated wit; Johnson had off-color jokes.

Charisma or not, Johnson planned to pass the Kennedy promises into legislative record. He also vowed to succeed in Vietnam where Kennedy had hesitated or stumbled. Accepting Kennedy's challenge to win the Cold War by 1970, the Johnson team set out to prove that where the Kennedys dreamed and schemed, the Johnsons planned and succeeded. It was a matter of tactics. Kennedy always analyzed and analyzed again. Johnson intended to act. Victory in Vietnam was a matter of action.

LBJ, Texas Populist

Born in 1908, Lyndon Baines Johnson grew up in the rugged hill country near Austin, Texas. Forever touting the Democratic Party as his "home" or "family," Johnson served his country as representative, senator, vice president, and thirty-sixth president. Franklin Roosevelt, he liked to say in the 1960s, had been his "political papa," but Texas politics shaped his views as well.

Texas Politics

Georgia's Tom Watson and Nebraska's William Jennings Bryan had influenced Texas profoundly near the turn of the century. Tom Watson had been a founding father of the *Populist Party,* and after his unsuccessful 1892 White House bid, Bryan wedded the Populists and the Democrats into one mad-as-hell bunch. To a good Populist, government was an endless well of reform, action, and dedication to the common man. Trying to do the right thing was honorable. Doing the right thing—and succeeding with it politically—was much better.

In the struggling Texas farm country, this message was especially welcome, and it taught the political junkies of the region that one man could truly make a difference. All the country needed, the old Populist doctrine suggested, was one tough, no-nonsense frontiersman who was not afraid to act, challenge the status quo, and uplift the downtrodden.

This kind of philosophy was tailor-made for Vietnam War leadership. To Johnson, inaction had been a legacy of Kennedy's Vietnam policy. A combination of strong U.S. military commitment in South Vietnam, massive economic aid, and political strong-arming of South Vietnam's rich and powerful would get the job done. And Johnson even brought plenty of skills to the task that Kennedy hadn't had.

For example, as a former director of the National Youth Administration in Texas, Johnson had had experience in innovative policy-making. The National Youth Administration was a *New Deal* agency largely defined, organized, and administered by Johnson himself. His reputation as a mover-and-shaker got him into the U.S. Congress in 1937. Running against Establishment politicians, Johnson won his district by only a few votes. Because of this election, the sarcastic nickname of "Landslide Lyndon" would haunt him for years.

Jarhead Jargon

Beginning in the rural U.S. South in the 1880s and spreading nationwide by 1892, the **Populist Party** favored government action to rescue the failing family farm, an activist economic foreign policy abroad, and anti–Big Business legislation at home. A powerful, unassailable president was supposed to initiate these reforms, but the Populists never won the White House.

Jarhead Jargon

The **New Deal** was President Franklin Roosevelt's frenetic legislative agenda to end the Great Depression of the 1930s. Consisting of dozens of new government agencies under the headings of Relief, Recovery, and Reform, the New Deal represented the height of government interventionism in the economy, elevated the powers of the presidency, and rescued a wounded capitalist system.

Johnson's Rising Star

Eleven years later, Johnson would be elected to the Senate, where he demonstrated a forceful, in-your-face style of legislating. By the mid-1950s he had become majority leader. No issue was too sacred for cutting a deal. Johnson had no problems dealing on civil rights issues with former or existing members of the Ku Klux Klan in the Deep South delegations of Congress.

Shell Shock

Lyndon Johnson was not always a political animal. A 1930 graduate of Southwest Texas State Teachers College, Johnson taught high school in Houston. He later claimed that teaching was much more difficult than being president.

Jarhead Jargon

Although he was accused of borrowing his administration's title, the **Great Society,** from a socialist book, Johnson first called for this new era of government activism and New Deal–like reform during his May 1964 commencement speech at the University of Michigan.

The states of the Deep South were among the poorest of the nation. Getting highway assistance funding could connect struggling rural areas to urban economies. Of course, as both senator and president, Johnson would tell those KKK men that this new heaven on earth was only a vote away if they supported civil rights reform. To die-hard liberals and dedicated civil rights activists, such wheeling-and-dealing was the equivalent to making pacts with Satan. Johnson didn't care. A KKK member voting yes on civil rights? He enjoyed the irony.

Like Franklin Roosevelt, Johnson considered domestic legislation more important than foreign policy; however, as the heir to Kennedy's "pay any price, bear any burden" agenda, Johnson was also saddled with the march to Cold War victory by 1970. He would have few bargains for the Vietnamese in the face of this larger goal.

Johnson later noted that he entered the White House with "golden shackles." He was tied to the promise of inevitable Cold War victory, but he also had an ambitious domestic agenda in civil rights, urban renewal, and medical care. If he withdrew the United States from the confrontation in Vietnam, Johnson was convinced that America would revert to a Red Scare–like mentality over expanding communism.

Pro–Joe McCarthy sentiment still seethed beneath the surface, Johnson believed. His administration would have to pay the price of endless investigations and accusations if it "lost Southeast Asia." Accused of being soft on communism remained the kiss of death for any politician at that time, and Johnson believed that he could never have a sweeping success with his domestic agenda if he neglected anticommunist crusading abroad. He had to win in Vietnam and enforce his so-called *Great Society* domestic reform measures at the same time.

The good Populist and the good Democrat could always succeed with the right dose of vigor and commitment. Franklin Roosevelt had triumphed over the Great Depression and World War II. Certainly, Johnson reasoned, his administration could further the New Deal social agenda and win a brushfire war in a tiny Southeast Asian country.

Beating Kennedys

To Johnson, the Kennedy administration had flirted dangerously with disaster in Vietnam. Disaster, to Johnson, meant hammering out some sort of convoluted deal there, and then pulling out U.S. troops. Although the Kennedys had never implemented such a deal, Johnson had always had his concerns.

A Kennedy sipping champagne with a communist aggressor, Johnson always believed, equaled the kiss of death for the Democratic party. Any deal with Ho would remind Americans of Neville Chamberlain's deal with Hitler over Czechoslovakia in 1938. Those memories were still fresh in mind, and Johnson had no intention of being a Chamberlain.

At first, Johnson was not sure where the old Kennedy cabinet truly stood on Vietnam. In the beginning, he tried to convince them that he needed as much information as possible about Vietnam. He received tons of position papers and analyses from them because of it, and, today, these thick reports fill hundreds of bulging file boxes at the Lyndon Johnson Library in Austin, Texas.

In reality, Johnson couldn't have cared less about all this paperwork. He preferred to exercise full control over national security decisions, and Vietnam was the biggest security crisis out there. In contrast to his political mentor, Franklin Roosevelt, Johnson expected to hear "yes, sir" from his cabinet and staff. Analysis was optional.

Shell Shock

In the fall of 1938 in Munich, Germany, the British and French governments agreed with Adolf Hitler that the northern section of the twenty-year-old independent nation of Czechoslovakia must be surrendered to Nazi Germany. The Czechs were not invited to the conference in which this decision was made. Meanwhile, the British government claimed that granting Hitler what he wanted prevented a major war and offered "peace in our time."

Ask Saigon Sally

Although he prided himself on his simple, quiet lifestyle, Johnson had no problem putting on a dramatic stunt or two. In 1966, for instance, he signed an education reform bill in the tiny schoolhouse of Cotulla, Texas, where he went to grade school.

Shell Shock

One of the reasons Kennedy's secretary of state, Dean Rusk, was allowed to keep his job with Lyndon Johnson was his Vietnam advice to the new president in 1964. Rusk cautioned Johnson not to be suckered by any North Vietnamese peace feelers to his fresh-on-the-job administration. Any peace effort now, he said, would be ill-intentioned and insincere.

The Wicked Truth

In December 1963, Johnson learned the wicked truth from Secretary of Defense Robert McNamara. South Vietnam was in worse shape than anyone realized. Kennedy had often relied on situation reports from Saigon, but there was more to South Vietnam than just Saigon.

Ask Saigon Sally

In early 1964, Johnson had his fair share of foreign policy problems. They included riots in the Panama Canal Zone, a tiff with Fidel Castro over the U.S. base at Guantanamo, and an impending war between Greece and Turkey over Cyprus.

In the Mekong Delta, where nearly 40 percent of the population lived, pro-Diem authorities had lost control as early as August 1963. No one in the White House even knew about it. Especially troubling were reports from Long An, south of Saigon. The Vietcong had entered the poorly guarded refugee camps and hamlets there, asking the residents to return to their homes. Most complied without question.

The contradiction between the reports in the field versus the upbeat, optimistic accounts from Saigon would be characteristic of Vietnam War information-gathering. Johnson would pick and choose what he wanted to believe. Most of the time, he welcomed the rosy reports out of Saigon. But Johnson was not one to avoid conflict by looking on the bright side. He liked to shake the trees now and then, too, and getting rid of some of the leftover Kennedy intellectuals helped in the task.

Throwing Out the Leftovers

General Paul Harkins in Vietnam was seen as one of the worst of the Kennedy holdovers. Johnson joked that Harkins was the guy who thought the snowball could survive in hell. In short, Harkins was so optimistic about inevitable American and South Vietnamese victory, and so in love with the Saigon regime, that he was useless to the military mission there. Or so Johnson concluded. The president had similar opinions of Harkins's boss, Maxwell Taylor, the chairman of the Joint Chiefs of Staff. Taylor was replaced by master planner and organizer General Earle Wheeler.

Johnson had said Taylor couldn't plan a trip to the men's room, but he was unaccountably deemed good enough to be the new U.S. ambassador to South Vietnam. The old ambassador, Henry Cabot Lodge Jr., and Taylor traveled to Saigon with a message of patience. A great escalation of men and money would soon be heading to Saigon, he told the government there. Taylor was right, but he no longer had a say in the matter.

Roger Hilsman, a doubting Thomas about the Vietnam situation and a longtime Kennedy family confidant, was just plain kicked out, and another doubter of Vietnam military solutions, veteran gentleman diplomat W. Averell Harriman, was ordered to work on matters of African policy. Johnson preferred to call this a "house cleaning" instead of a "purge." In any event, with Robert Kennedy soon to launch his own Senate career, Johnson truly took care of the "leftover" problem. No one suggested to him that the real problem wasn't Kennedy staffers, but Vietnam.

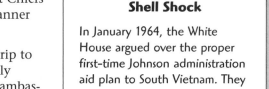

Shell Shock

In January 1964, the White House argued over the proper first-time Johnson administration aid plan to South Vietnam. They finally agreed on $125 million, but admitted that much more would be needed later.

Ask Saigon Sally

According to Senator Bourke Hickenlooper (Republican, Iowa) in 1964, William Westmoreland was destined to be the greatest general of the twentieth century, and the communist threat in Vietnam was equivalent to the nuclear war threat of the 1962 Cuban Missile Crisis.

Westmoreland to the Rescue

Paul Harkins's successor was General William C. Westmoreland. A West Point graduate from Spartanburg, South Carolina, Westmoreland was an admirer of Douglas MacArthur. MacArthur had once told him that Vietnam would be a fine command but "fraught with peril," too. This proved to be more than prophetic.

Westmoreland accepted his command, wondering if it had Eisenhower-like political possibilities after the war was over. As the handsome Southern gentleman, he always looked in command, and, from the beginning, he hoped to draw clear distinctions between himself and his struggling predecessor. In private, he was quick to denounce the ARVN as a corrupt and lousy army.

President Lyndon Johnson and General William Westmoreland confer in Honolulu (1966).

Lyndon Baines Johnson Library, Austin, Texas.

Predicting that America could beat the Vietcong before the South Vietnamese re-formed their government and adequately trained their military, Westmoreland advocated large numbers of U.S. ground troops to get the job done. Meanwhile, he cared little for air assaults against North Vietnamese targets unless a big escalation on the ground was part of the scenario.

The new general's idea of a thorough escalation involved at least 200,000 troops. He would spend a full year making sure these men were decently established and prepared to fight a sweeping campaign in Vietnam. Then, systematic *sweep-and-destroy missions* would take out the enemy everywhere in South Vietnam. As a World War II combat veteran, West Point superintendent, and former aide to General Taylor, Westmoreland was believed to know what he was talking about.

Jarhead Jargon

Sweep-and-destroy missions, also called search and destroy, involved the U.S. Army effort to eliminate Vietcong strongholds throughout South Vietnam, but the stress was placed on the Saigon area. One of the more controversial missions was Operation Abilene in April 1966. Designed to clear out Vietcong sanctuaries only 40 miles east of Saigon, Operation Abilene was only partially successful and resulted in heavy casualties for the U.S. Army's First Infantry ("Big Red One") Division.

ARVN on the Ropes

At the time Johnson became president, the Ho Chi Minh Trail was still a primitive collection of jungle paths. It remained virtually impossible to detect from the air, and was still the only North Vietnamese supply line to the south. While the new American president shuffled his cabinet and military team, the North Vietnamese assessed the worthiness of their trail.

Colonel Bui Tin, an editor for North Vietnam's army newspaper, was one of the leading investigators. Traveling down the trail was tough going, he reported, but he was optimistic that the jungle paths could soon become something of a superhighway of infiltration and military transportation.

Tales from the Front

Later complaining that he was lied to by both generals and presidents, and even fooled by his own statistics guaranteeing victory, Robert "Blowtorch Bob" Komer ran President Johnson's pacification program in Vietnam. Komer claims to have convinced himself that military victory was always possible because Americans are a "can-do people." Komer also served as the deputy defense secretary for President Jimmy Carter.

In early 1964, it could take five weeks for a North Vietnamese trooper to reach a South Vietnamese destination. Malaria and other tropical diseases were as much an enemy to them as the ARVN and the Americans. Wearing dark clothes to mask detection, the North Vietnamese spent their nights in clearings away from the jungle paths. They often relied on Vietcong or Laotian allies to reach their destinations. Bui Tin complained to Ho that this was an awfully tenuous way to supply troops.

Ask Saigon Sally

One of the first top-secret U.S. battle plans to bomb North Vietnam was submitted to President Johnson in March 1964. It was written by William Bundy, the assistant secretary of state for Far Eastern affairs.

Meanwhile, Hanoi's version of the U.S. Army Corps of Engineers would be sent south to reconstruct the Ho Chi Minh Trail. A long war seemed to be in the cards, and North Vietnam could succeed, but only as long as it had the supplies to keep up the fight down south.

Westmoreland planned to win the war before any grand reconstruction of the Ho Chi Minh Trail was completed. Then, after the U.S. victory, the ARVN was supposed to make sure that the North Vietnamese and Vietcong didn't come back for seconds. If America won too quickly, however, the ARVN role would be a real problem.

The ARVN, in a way, were North Vietnam's best ally. More than 5,500 ARVN troopers deserted their posts per month in 1964. Nearly 45 percent of the countryside and some 50 percent of the South Vietnamese population were under Vietcong rule by the middle of that year. Although his speeches continued to praise the ARVN to the heavens, Westmoreland's battle plans divorced the U.S. military from them.

At best, Westmoreland told his staff privately, the ARVN could be used as reserve forces in the great battles to come. As the American victory neared, he planned to "motivate" the ARVN to take on the *mop-up operations*. But he couldn't do it alone.

Jarhead Jargon

Mop-up operations were designed to follow major offensives on the part of the U.S. military. For instance, Operation Ala Moana was launched to destroy the Vietcong presence in the major rice-producing region near Saigon. Ala Moana went on for five months in 1967, resulting in a Vietcong retreat. This permitted the U.S. Army's 25th Division the opportunity to occupy or mop-up a region (Hau Nghia province) that had otherwise been a Vietcong stronghold.

Jarhead Jargon

In February 1964, Johnson began to talk about his **"big tent."** This was a reference to resurrecting the 1930s Grand Coalition of Franklin Roosevelt on the domestic scene. Abroad, the new Grand Coalition would include all noncommunist Third World nations. Under Johnson's "big tent" leadership, the downtrodden at home and overseas could be assured endless U.S. government support.

While the U.S. military launched its offensives in South Vietnam (according to the plan), Westmoreland expected Washington to be especially generous to the Saigon regime and the ARVN. Massive economic aid programs, massive shipments of military hardware, as well as Stateside administrative and specialized military training for the best and brightest in South Vietnam, would all assist in the "motivation" effort. Like Johnson, Westmoreland insisted that the taxpayer bill for it was irrelevant for the time being. Fiscal matters could be argued over later. The price of victory was always high, and few Americans would tolerate defeat in an even more forgettable place than Korea.

Uncle Lyndon, Your Good Buddy

The year 1964 was an American general election year. Whereas Presidents George Bush and Bill Clinton would tear up on national television when describing the burdens of power, Johnson, like Franklin Roosevelt, loved power. He had no apologies for liking his job, and he saw few obstacles to government influence.

During the early Democratic party primaries, Johnson began to talk about America's *"big tent."* No one would be left out of the U.S. government's generosity, he said. Be it unemployed African Americans in a Detroit ghetto or a bombed-out family in a refugee camp near Saigon, the Johnson administration promised to make a difference. It was humanism on steroids, and it was classic Johnson electioneering.

When presenting his early "big tent" message, Johnson offered certain contradictions. On the one hand, his was a "Don't mess with Texas" message. Big, tough Lyndon Johnson was going to get those bigots at home and all those Vietcong and North Vietnamese guys, too. On the other hand, his message of compassion for all turned off those who thought the government had done enough in race relations and that the Vietnamese should fight their own war. As the 1964 campaign went into high gear, Johnson would have to walk a fine line between ambition and the truth. He would wander off it quite a few times.

The Least You Need to Know

➤ Lyndon Johnson's policies were guided by his Texas and Democratic party experiences.

➤ Johnson preferred his own Vietnam advisory team.

➤ General Westmoreland believed in a quick Vietnam victory.

➤ ARVN troops were in disarray during 1964.

➤ Johnson's "big tent" promises linked domestic and foreign policy ambitions.

Chapter 14

Thirty Years War, Act Three

"Are you some sort of prevert [sic] or something?" He meant "pervert," but actor Keenan Wynn's character (Colonel "Bat" Guano) in Stanley Kubrick's film *Dr. Strangelove* made his point loud and clear. Released in early 1964, Kubrick's slam dunk of Cold War politics and nuclear war threats was the "in" movie for enlightened liberals, academic types, and film freaks throughout the 1964 presidential election.

Wynn's famous line was uttered while halting a British military officer, Colonel Lionel Mandrake (played by Peter Sellers), who was trying to break into an uncooperative Coca-Cola machine. All around them a bloody battle raged, but Wynn was more concerned about Sellers's attack on a symbol of American capitalism.

To filmgoers and critics alike, this one scene in the film also symbolized the stupidity of the capitalism-versus-communism confrontation. Too many people were ready to go to war over symbols, and maybe there were just too many symbols out there.

To Lyndon Johnson, 1964 was a symbolic year, too, but he did not share Stanley Kubrick's complaints. In November 1964, Johnson would win one of the greatest landslides in the history of the U.S. presidency, and he did it as one of the most powerful presidents of all time.

Johnson's Tonkin Gulf Resolution, passed by Congress in August 1964, gave the presidency special executive privileges to conduct the Vietnam War. Again, this was a symbolic gesture, supposed to scare the living daylights out of the North Vietnamese and Vietcong.

Why? Because the tough guy from Texas was now personally in charge of the war, and he was not going to rest until victory was achieved. Frankly, this symbol was better understood in Houston than in Hanoi.

World War II Commitment?

Spring 1964 was a time for planning and scheming. In Hanoi, Ho Chi Minh launched a massive training program for his North Vietnamese troops. He wanted his boys to be at their best before heading south. In Washington, even grander plans were underway.

The first plan was the top, top secret NSAM 288 (National Security Advisor Memorandum, Number 288). In this long document, Johnson's National Security Council called for a World War II–style commitment against advancing communism in South Vietnam. That meant great numbers of U.S. ground troops and day-by-day escalations of air assaults against North Vietnam.

During this great step-up of American involvement in the war, NSAM 288 predicted a South Vietnam that would eventually be transformed into a worthy ally. Details on why and how were not present in NSAM 288, but apparently there was an underlying assumption that the Saigon regime would want to follow America's organized, disciplined lead in the fight against communism once their own region was secured.

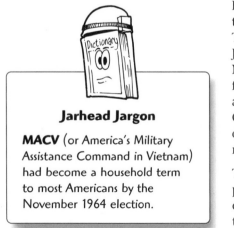

Jarhead Jargon

MACV (or America's Military Assistance Command in Vietnam) had become a household term to most Americans by the November 1964 election.

By late spring 1964, Operations Plan 37-64 was added to NSAM 288 thanks to input by *MACV* in Saigon. This, too, was a very hush-hush advisory report to Johnson, and it addressed specific matters within the NSAM 288 agenda. More than 90 targets were selected for bombing in North Vietnam. Plans were drawn to attack so-called Vietcong safe havens in Laos and Cambodia, and specific North Vietnamese ports and oceanfront villages were targeted for special bombing raids.

These elaborate and expensive plans created certain political problems for Johnson. Given the new level of U.S. involvement proposed by his security policy team, the president feared that Congress would question and analyze his Vietnam policy. Vietnam did not present the same evils and security threats as did World War II, and the president feared that the comparative lack of urgency would promote endless Congressional scrutiny over his Vietnam budget and escalation decisions.

Ask Saigon Sally

Throughout American history, presidents have sought more and more power. In the 1830s, President Andrew Jackson even violated a Supreme Court decision. Ordered to halt his policy of Indian Removal (pushing potentially hostile Indian nations beyond the Mississippi River), Jackson insisted that the Supreme Court had no right to interfere with his powers as commander in chief. He continued the Indian Removal, and Congress and public opinion backed him. Although the press labeled him King Andrew I for his action, Jackson became the first and last president to defy the Supreme Court.

To Johnson, the worst-case scenario involved congressional hearings and investigations into his support for the still corrupt and forever faltering Saigon regime. Money could be withheld or at least questioned, and troop strength issues debated endlessly. Swift military action hinged on noninterference from Congress, Johnson concluded.

The best thing going for Johnson was the fact that many congressmen, as well as many newspaper editors, had never followed day-to-day developments in Vietnam. It was still a faraway, alien place that only the White House seemed to know much about. This alleged cult of knowledge and expertise would be the best hand for the Johnson administration to play. The presidency, Johnson argued, needed special powers to conduct the war without having to play teacher and Vietnam coach for Congress.

Controversy in the Tonkin Gulf

The focus of numerous pretty paintings, the Tonkin Gulf of North Vietnam presented an image of peaceful tranquility. History did not match the image. The gulf had been something of the primary invasion route to Vietnam for years, and in August 1964 North Vietnam saw the United States taking that route.

What took place in the Tonkin Gulf would serve as President Johnson's constitutional justification for escalating the Vietnam War. It would also provide the opportunity for broadening his powers. Yet, to this day, many mysteries remain over exactly what

Jarhead Jargon

For both appearance and security reasons, President Johnson preferred to keep any South Vietnamese commando operation into North Vietnam separate from American military/espionage activities there. Any American role in a South Vietnamese–led covert operation or vice versa would be labeled **"mutual interference."**

Ask Saigon Sally

Captain John J. Herrick was the commander of *Maddox*. The destroyer was named after the U.S. Marine Corps hero from the Mexican War, Captain William Maddox.

happened, and minute-by-minute accounts in both books and films still disagree on how the story unfolded.

The "Facts"

We know that on August 2, 1964, the U.S. destroyer *Maddox* was on patrol in international waters in the Tonkin Gulf. For all effective purposes, *Maddox* was on an eavesdropping spy mission that day. Some miles further south from *Maddox's* mission, but still in North Vietnam, U.S.–backed South Vietnamese commandos, trying to put their secret American training to good use, were attempting to assault the small enemy island of Hon Me.

Training or no training, the commandos found the resistance there overwhelming, and they were forced to retreat. North Vietnamese versions of America's old World War II PT boats pursued them, and apparently concluded that the *Maddox* was part of the Hon Me mission. This was not the case, for Johnson opposed what he called *"mutual interference"* between American and South Vietnamese operations in the Tonkin Gulf. But, of course, the North Vietnamese didn't know that at the time.

Maddox beat back the North Vietnamese torpedo boat attack, and several of the North Vietnamese gunships were destroyed or damaged. Two nights later, *Maddox* was joined by *Turner Joy,* and another torpedo boat attack was reported. Neither American ship was harmed, but two North Vietnamese boats were reported sunk in the follow-up U.S. Navy report. That report remains a controversial one. There are many who claim that a second attack never took place.

On the night of the second attack, *Maddox's* sonar gear was not working properly. A late-night thunderstorm had churned up already high seas, and officially, no one on board *Maddox* was really sure what happened during the entire night. No visual sightings of enemy craft could be confirmed. The official report, therefore, differed from what apparently happened.

Tales From the Front

The U.S. Navy's Tonkin Gulf mission technically fell under the jurisdiction of Operation Plan 34-A. The latter usually employed several U.S. Navy Patrol Torpedo Boats (PT), U.S.–built light craft called "Swifts," and Norwegian-built aluminum craft called "Nasties." Throughout late 1963 and early 1964, these vessels transported ARVN commandos from Da Nang, South Vietnam to locations above the 17th parallel. Once ashore, the commando missions ranged from intelligence-gathering to sabotage and kidnapping.

Stepping Carefully

Johnson was especially concerned about the details. Any retaliation against the North Vietnamese required full justification. Yet Johnson soon realized that the basic fact of U.S. versus North Vietnamese vessels in the Tonkin Gulf was good enough to rally most anticommunists at home. The so-called picky points soon became irrelevant. Few Americans, Johnson concluded, would be interested in the ugly specifics. He was right, at least for the time being.

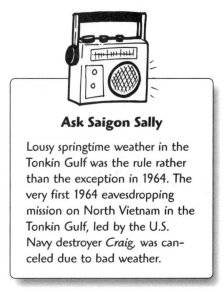

Of course, it was always possible that any major U.S. military response to an attack in the Tonkin Gulf could stimulate Soviet and/or Chinese efforts to aid North Vietnam. World War III was possible if the incident were not handled carefully, Johnson believed. He telephoned Premier Khrushchev in an effort to assure him that a widening U.S. war in Vietnam meant no hostile action against the Soviet Union. He also cabled Ho Chi Minh, warning him that his regime might face serious consequences due to the torpedo boat attack in the Tonkin Gulf. Through it all, Johnson portrayed the U.S. Navy near Vietnam as an innocent bystander attacked in international waters.

Ask Saigon Sally

Lousy springtime weather in the Tonkin Gulf was the rule rather than the exception in 1964. The very first 1964 eavesdropping mission on North Vietnam in the Tonkin Gulf, led by the U.S. Navy destroyer *Craig*, was canceled due to bad weather.

But even that fact raises questions. The North Vietnamese, the United States, and even the U.N. all disagreed over the definition of "international waters." Be it three miles, seven miles, or even twelve miles from the North Vietnam coastline, nobody could agree in 1964.

153

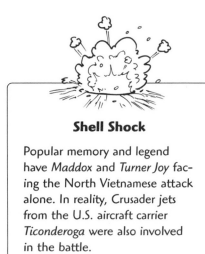

Shell Shock

Popular memory and legend have *Maddox* and *Turner Joy* facing the North Vietnamese attack alone. In reality, Crusader jets from the U.S. aircraft carrier *Ticonderoga* were also involved in the battle.

Shell Shock

While on the Senate Defense Appropriations Committee, Senator William Proxmire (Democrat, Wisconsin) opposed "wild" Vietnam expenditures as early as 1964, but, like most Americans, he rallied behind the president's call for support following the battle of Tonkin Gulf.

The navy's official painting of the battle of Tonkin Gulf shows *Maddox* and *Turner Joy* surrounded by an ocean full of North Vietnamese torpedo boats. Depicting a battle that took place on a pleasant sunny afternoon instead of in the dead of night, the painting also portrayed a horrible World War II–like naval engagement in which American seamen are blown off the decks of their ships, enemy torpedoes fill the water, and, as the old song says, bombs are "bursting in air." Reality suggested a very different scene; one of the major casualties in the Tonkin Gulf tale was the truth.

The Tonkin Gulf Resolution

If "all politics is local," then at least some of it is also "timing." Lyndon Johnson always had great timing. Although he was the first to criticize the U.S. Navy for giving him sketchy, interpretive reports over what kind of battle took place in the Tonkin Gulf, the bottom line for Johnson remained motivating the Congress and the country to accept a larger U.S. military role in Vietnam. Johnson would use the timing of the Tonkin Gulf exchange to his advantage.

In early August 1964, much of working America was on vacation, and that included members of Johnson's cabinet. Congressmen were back in their districts, and more people were thinking about the beach than Vietnam. The presidential election was a few months away, and Johnson had had enough of being in the shadow of the dead Mr. Kennedy.

Being tough on communism was always a big vote-getter in the United States, and quickly defeating the communists in Vietnam would establish a certain Johnson Doctrine. Few people would continue to mourn John Kennedy when being led by the soon-to-be victor of the Cold War. There was so much to do at home and abroad, and Johnson was ready to prove that he was the FDR-like activist that the Democratic Party always dreamed about.

Sending a Tonkin Gulf Resolution to Congress on August 5, 1964, Johnson asked for special powers to conduct the Vietnam War. He implied that few outside the White House knew what was going on in Vietnam, and he suggested that it was a situation Congress should let the experts handle.

Implying that the mysterious attack in the Tonkin Gulf was similar to the Japanese attack on Pearl Harbor, Johnson's Resolution reminded many of those dark days only 23 years earlier. TV news broadcasts showed big, black limousines pulling up to the White House. Somber Congressmen emerged, usually offering "no comment" to a concerned press, as they went on to be briefed on Vietnam by Johnson administration officials. It wasn't quite December 1941, but it had the look of "national emergency." That's exactly what the White House preferred.

At the same time that his Congress debated the future of the war, Johnson offered a secret deal to the North Vietnamese. A grand economic aid package was promised if they ended their war in South Vietnam. If not, "dire consequences" would be Hanoi's fate. To Johnson's disbelief, Ho Chi Minh opted for "dire consequences."

"Grandma's Nightshirt"

In one of the most famous quotes of his presidency, Johnson compared the contents of his Tonkin Gulf Resolution to "grandma's nightshirt. It covered everything." He won Congress's support to spend money and ship troops overseas without their input or interference. Only two senators dared to suggest that the emperor had no clothes. One was a Republican, Wayne Morse from Oregon, and the other was a Democrat, Ernest Gruening from Alaska.

Shell Shock

Pham Van Dong of the North Vietnamese government countered Johnson's Tonkin Gulf Resolution by threatening a "great war" across all of Southeast Asia. He later backtracked on that statement, noting that it was an overreaction to the latest turn of events.

The Two Dissenters

Both Morse and Gruening were aging political warhorses and throwbacks to an earlier Congress more concerned about good policy-making than killing commies. Today their questioning of the Tonkin Gulf Resolution would make matter-of-fact common sense. In 1964, those same questions equaled political suicide for these old men.

Morse was the first doubting Thomas of the two dissenters. Proud to call himself an old Teddy Roosevelt Republican, Morse, said many fellow Republicans, was simply out of touch with the modern 1960s. In reality, Morse was especially concerned about the Constitutional law aspects of the Tonkin Gulf Resolution. His questions were simple ones.

If winning the Vietnam War was going to be so easy, why, Morse asked, did the commander in chief need special powers to prosecute it? From the War of 1812 through the Korean War, U.S. presidents had never asked the Congress to shut up and put up. Why now? What was really going on in Vietnam?

Tales from the Front

On the stormy night of August 4, 1964, Navy pilot James Stockdale took off from the carrier *Ticonderoga* to provide air support for U.S. Navy vessels in the Tonkin Gulf. He never saw a North Vietnamese attack on those vessels, and said so to his superiors in Washington. But Washington ordered him to begin bombing runs against the North Vietnamese in "retaliation" for their assault. Shot down thirteen months later, Stockdale spent over seven years in a Hanoi prison. The experience left him with shock white hair and a permanent limp. After the Vietnam War, Stockdale finished his Navy career, retiring as an Admiral. In 1992, he ran as the Vice Presidential nominee for Ross Perot's Reform Party.

Morse would be hounded by his own colleagues for daring to question the president and the progress of anticommunism. To some, his questioning bordered on treason. To others, Morse was just an old fool who needed to retire, and soon.

Ask Saigon Sally

In 1972, a coalition of student-led antiwar groups at the University of Wisconsin–Milwaukee, urged their school's administration to grant Ernest Gruening an honorary degree for his "antiwar activities" in the 1964 Congress. Gruening halted their efforts and declined the honor.

Gruening's protest was more emotional than legal, although he had similar constitutional worries. Like Morse, he was a bit over the hill for most members of Congress. As the former governor of the Territory of Alaska, Gruening had fought tooth and nail for statehood much of his life, a battle he had won. Now he was considered Alaska's first senior senator, and obviously, some fellow Democrats said, the guy had worn himself out.

Gruening complained that defending South Vietnam was not in America's vital interest, its government was hated, its army was a joke, and, therefore, the place was not worth the life of one American trooper. There was much to do at home, he stressed, and Johnson's ambitious domestic agenda would soon be hurt by wasteful spending in Vietnam. The White House put him down fast.

Gruening was told that the Johnson administration could walk and chew gum at the same time. In other words, the anticommunist crusade was relevant anywhere the president said it was, and economic policies at home would always be in good shape.

Johnson never had to worry about Gruening or Morse. The two old men were shouted down by the entire Congress. Meanwhile, a fast passage of the Tonkin Gulf Resolution was requested, and the president got what he wanted. Gruening and Morse faded away, but not for long. Praised as clairvoyant heroes who could have prevented an American tragedy, Gruening and Morse were adored by student radicals, New Leftists, and hippies. As proud and traditional politicians, Gruening and Morse hated every minute of it.

President Lyndon Johnson signs the Tonkin Gulf Resolution, August 1964.

Lyndon Baines Johnson Library, Austin, Texas, and photographer Cecil Stoughton.

Mr. Right Meets Landslide Lyndon

Joking that he wouldn't mind "lobbing one" (a nuclear bomb) into the Kremlin men's room, Sen. Barry Goldwater was the 1964 Republican party nominee for president. An Air Force reservist and heir to a department store fortune, Goldwater said Johnson was dragging his feet on Vietnam. If elected president, Goldwater proclaimed that he would not hesitate a moment to nuke North Vietnam.

Emerging from a crowded field in the 1964 presidential primaries, Goldwater maintained a consistent vote count of conservatives and right-wingers. "Extremism in the defense of liberty is no vice," he shouted at the Republican party convention, "and moderation in the pursuit of justice is no virtue."

At home, Goldwater had little use for government "interference" in the economy, and he called for the end of most existing government-funded social programs. Overseas, he called for swift action to win the Cold War before America was surrounded by "creeping communism."

Goldwater's campaign slogan, "In your heart you know he's right," was countered by the Democrats' "In your guts you know he's nuts." Presenting himself as a caring soul who was finishing off the Kennedy agenda, Johnson said Vietnam would remain an "Asian boys'" war fought by "Asian boys." He said nothing about his administration's escalation plans and distrust of Saigon.

Jarhead Jargon

Political scientists, journalists, and historians continue to disagree over a universal figure for a presidential **landslide** election. Many consider 20 percent over an opponent an acceptable number, but others peg it as low as 12 percent.

Painting Goldwater as an extremist was easy for the skilled campaigner Johnson. Goldwater, the challenger, should have had Johnson on the run. Instead he was on the defensive throughout the general election. Some people didn't even understand many of Goldwater's bumper stickers and banners. For example, one simply read "Au H₂O," the chemical symbols for gold and water. It was clever, but there would be no cigar for Goldwater.

Of course, Johnson was lying. He had no intention of keeping Vietnam an "Asian boys'" war. Many voters trusted him on that point, and voted against the "extremist" Goldwater. Johnson's *landslide* success made him the number-two landslide king of the twentieth century, and just tenths of a percent behind his mentor, Franklin Roosevelt. Nobody joked about Landslide Lyndon anymore. But in a few short years, Goldwater would emerge in the public mind as the honest man who had been abused by the lying Johnson campaign.

To political pundits and historians, the 1964 election was the last great display of American liberalism. Johnson promised a government-led end to poverty and racism at home, as well as a soon-to-come victory in the Cold War. He was about to learn that it was impossible to achieve both goals at the same time, and the American people would never forget it.

The Least You Need to Know

➤ President Johnson spent early 1964 preparing for an escalation of the Vietnam War.

➤ The battle of Tonkin Gulf served the political purposes of the Johnson administration.

➤ The Tonkin Gulf Resolution granted special executive privilege to conduct the Vietnam War.

➤ Senators Morse and Gruening opposed the Tonkin Gulf Resolution on both constitutional and moral grounds.

➤ President Johnson said Vietnam was a war for "Asian boys" to fight.

Chapter 15

Death in Pleiku

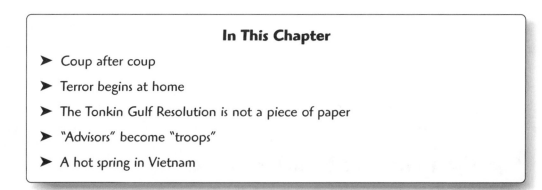

In This Chapter

➤ Coup after coup

➤ Terror begins at home

➤ The Tonkin Gulf Resolution is not a piece of paper

➤ "Advisors" become "troops"

➤ A hot spring in Vietnam

Before 1965, Vietnam was fun. At least that was the impression you got from Walter Cronkite, anchorman for the *CBS Evening News*. During the 1960s and '70s, Americans did not watch television news. They watched Walter Cronkite. Just as a *Xerox* meant a photocopy and a *Kleenex* meant a tissue, *Walter Cronkite* meant network television news. His NBC and ABC competitors were out there, but few Americans noticed.

In 1964, Cronkite went along on a bombing mission over an alleged Vietcong stronghold. Amazed at the technology, Cronkite reported the mission as though he were enjoying a thrill ride at Six Flags Magic Mountain. Cocky, confident, and enthralled by American firepower, Cronkite, like most Americans, believed in inevitable victory over our primitive enemies in Vietnam. One year later, all of that had changed.

CBS reporters used to report on the boredom of U.S. troops in "exile" in Vietnam, but in 1965 the reports were about World War II–like patrols into the bush, the determination of the enemy, and the horror of combat. Following "Charlie Company" into a rubber plantation near Saigon, newsman Charles Kuralt shocked America with his detailed reports on the everyday life of American troops. America got to know "Charlie Company" quite well. Given Kuralt's folksy, human interest–style of reporting, TV viewers in the United States began to feel the pain of the men of Charlie Company. Kuralt's camera team had free reign, and, for the first time, Americans saw their loved ones killed and maimed in Vietnam. It looked horrible out there—and the worst was yet to come.

Tales from the Front

From December 1965 through March 1966, the U.S. Army's First Cavalry Division (Airmobile), the ARVN 22nd Division, and the Third Marine Division's Amphibious Force were involved in Operation Double Eagle. Designed to trap communist forces in Quang Ngai province as well as take a rumored communist headquarters in the Tam Quan region, Double Eagle represented the height of U.S. military optimism and overconfidence at the time. The world press was encouraged by the U.S. military to report on the coming victory. But the slow-moving nature of this huge offensive permitted the enemy to escape and regroup later. Double Eagle was a miserable failure.

Big Minh and the Wrath of Khanh

General Duong Van Minh liked birds. In fact, he had quite an impressive collection of rare, exotic birds. A stocky six-footer, the general was something of the odd duck himself. Nicknamed "Big Minh," he was also an avid tennis player. So was Ambassador Henry Cabot Lodge. "Big Minh" liked to read the classics and listen to classical music. So did Lodge. Like Diem before him, "Big Minh" was considered South Vietnam's best hope in late 1963, and it was largely because Americans saw strong American qualities in him.

After the Diem assassination, "Big Minh," the U.S. Embassy-Saigon's top pick, became leader of South Vietnam. According to American policy-makers, he and his military advisors were supposed to clean up years of corruption and chaos in South Vietnam. From the beginning, "Big Minh" doubted his role as Saigon savior, and his colleagues dreamed of replacing him because of it. In fact, "Big Minh" assumed that his staff was plotting against him, and he had no problem tending to his birds while awaiting news of his ouster. Johnson insisted that the South Vietnam president personally attend to the affairs of state, but "Big Minh" cynically replied that he couldn't find any.

On "Big Minh's" watch, antigovernment demonstrations were hard to find, and the capital city became unusually quiet. For a time, the U.S. Embassy viewed the Saigon scene as symbolic of Big Minh's "refreshing" leadership. But as early as January 1964, it was obvious to the Americans that they had been fooling themselves. Vietcong success in the provinces was astounding. In terms of anticommunist progress, there was nothing "refreshing" about "Big Minh," and the Johnson administration was anxious for his eager opponents to do something about it.

Gen. Nguyen Khanh took over the government in another coup. In his late thirties and famous for his distinctive goatee and tall ego, Khanh said he would be America's best friend in South Vietnam. Although he had no problem being that friend, he also had no problem making off-color anti-American remarks now and then. The new president may have been Washington's man in Saigon, but he rarely sounded like it.

Through it all, the White House hated this confusing brand of politics. Despite the CIA presence in South Vietnam, American intelligence rarely knew who was who in the latest coup endeavors. Was it too much to ask for a competent government there?

Most of Khanh's own staff envied his new wealth and connections to the powerful Americans. Because of it, he spent much of his working day fending off possible coup attempts. When Khanh made a move against his real and imagined opponents, the Johnson administration reacted with relief that at least the guy was taking charge of something.

Khanh's biggest anticoup shakeup came after President Charles de Gaulle of France announced that his country was opening relations with Mao's China. *Neutralizing* all the wars and squabbles in Southeast Asia was supposed to be part of this dreamy China-France deal. Khanh arrested a number of generals and others for being pro–de Gaulle. It was one of the more ridiculous excuses for a political purge ever heard, even for South Vietnam. But Johnson was pleased.

The bottom line for continued U.S. support was South Vietnamese victory on the battlefield. Even though the Johnson administration had little faith in the ARVN, they were still expected to win now and then. Khanh's political opposition to a

Ask Saigon Sally

Secretary of Defense McNamara had mixed feelings about the "Big Minh" government. He found General Minh to be a sympathetic, likeable guy, but an inadequate leader for confused South Vietnam.

Jarhead Jargon

In the mid-1960s, President Charles de Gaulle of France hoped that a new China-France alliance would **neutralize,** or end, the fighting throughout France's old Indochina empire.

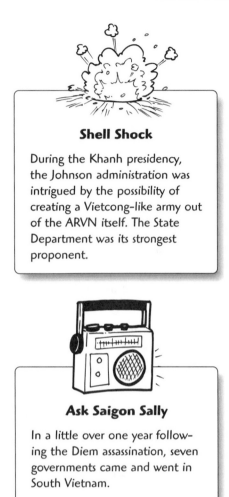

Shell Shock

During the Khanh presidency, the Johnson administration was intrigued by the possibility of creating a Vietcong-like army out of the ARVN itself. The State Department was its strongest proponent.

Ask Saigon Sally

In a little over one year following the Diem assassination, seven governments came and went in South Vietnam.

communist-noncommunist coalition government, backed by the usual anticommunist commitments, was well articulated, but his military offensive into the Mekong Delta fell flat. He then fired the division commanders in charge of the offensive, winning the hatred of the ARVN officer corps because of it.

In 1965, two of those officers, Nguyen Van Thieu, commander of the Fifth Division, and a 34-year-old air force general, Nguyen Cao Ky, led a coup against Khanh. But Khanh would not go easily. He tried to re-shuffle his government, issuing the strongest anti-communist statements yet. He also talked about putting together something of the "peoples' crusade," a combination of South Vietnamese military personnel and regular folks, to invade North Vietnam. He thought the Americans might admire his determination. In reality, they thought he was nuts.

With so much of the country occupied by the enemy, and his government facing daily coup threats, this South Vietnamese president was going to liberate North Vietnam from Ho Chi Minh? It was ridiculous to the Johnson administration. More to the point, the White House would never support such a widening of the war, even if Khanh could find somebody to join his peoples' crusade. To Johnson, an ARVN invasion of North Vietnam meant a Soviet rescue of Ho, a resulting World War III, and even nuclear confrontation. Any escalation of the war was going to be on his terms, his way, and carefully done.

Facing a massive Buddhist protest demonstration in Saigon and elsewhere, Khanh's government struggled to survive in early 1965. In the midst of the chaos, Thieu and Ky portrayed themselves as young reformers who could win the people's respect and beat back the communist challenge. It was a good tactic, or at least a better one than those championed by "Big Minh" or Khanh. Driven into exile, Khanh would claim for years that the Americans could have won their war if they had supported his early plan to attack North Vietnam. This was pure fantasy.

A Doubting Nelson

While the Johnson team moved forward with its escalation plans, there were still some annoying problems in Congress. With Gruening and Morse having been put down as crazy old fools, Johnson could claim a certain congressional solidarity as he marched into Vietnam. But another doubting Thomas appeared, and he annoyed Johnson to no end.

The freshman Democratic senator from Wisconsin, Gaylord Nelson, should have been a staunch supporter of the Tonkin Gulf Resolution. Instead, he thought that the Morse-Gruening argument had been dismissed too easily. As the tough Cold Warrior governor of Wisconsin during the Cuban Missile Crisis of October 1962, Nelson had whipped his state into an anticommunist fervor that took him all the way to the U.S. Senate. But Nelson was a complex politician. A die-hard liberal on social and economic issues, he had had little use for Joseph McCarthy's right-wing rantings. But he also combined a strong belief in Constitutional democracy with traditional anticommunism. Nelson wanted the Congress to pass a specific amendment that would strip the president of any special powers to conduct a war. And may it never happen again.

Ask Saigon Sally

In the 1970s, Senate Majority Leader Mike Mansfield claimed that many senators would have welcomed Senator Nelson's amendment opposed to the Tonkin Gulf Resolution. But few were ready to challenge Lyndon Johnson in 1964 and 1965.

On behalf of an angry President Johnson, Senator William Fulbright read Nelson the riot act. The Congress, he said, would never embarrass the presidency by discussing the Wisconsin senator's proposed amendment. Fulbright reminded Nelson of his freshman status, urging him to think about his career. It wasn't worth losing everything, he warned, in the face of a soon-to-be victorious Johnson in Vietnam. Meanwhile, the amendment was discreetly rejected and ignored. Within a few years, Fulbright would regret his dressing down of Nelson.

Terror at the Brinks Hotel

At the time, few people were paying attention to Gaylord Nelson anyway. The larger issue was their country's deepening involvement in Vietnam. As always, Johnson preferred proper timing. The Brinks Hotel incident almost provided that timing.

On Christmas Eve 1964, Vietcong terrorists struck a Bachelor Officers Quarters/military hotel complex in downtown Saigon. The attack had three goals. One was to demonstrate the incompetence of the Khanh government to protect anyone, even in the heart of Saigon. A second was to tell the Americans that there was no front or safe haven from the Vietcong. And the last was to demonstrate to fellow Vietcong just how much power they really had.

Shell Shock

In early 1965, the new Soviet premier, Aleksei Kosygin, visited Hanoi and offered more military aid to Ho Chi Minh. Ho refused the aid, for it required him to swear his complete allegiance to the Soviet view of communism first.

Only two men were involved in the bombing. Their work blew out the ground floor of the hotel, killing two Americans and injuring nearly 60 others. Both General Westmoreland and Ambassador Taylor told Johnson to bomb North Vietnam in immediate retaliation, but the president hesitated. He worried about the reaction of the American people while they sang their "peace on earth" Christmas carols. He also worried that air strikes might be an overreaction to the Brinks matter, and he wondered if the introduction of more U.S. ground troops might make better sense.

A hotel bombing did not justify the escalation that Johnson was planning. Only some sort of "spectacular action" on the part of the enemy would assure an immediate U.S. response. He hadn't a clue what that "action" might be, but it came to him in 1965.

Pleiku, My Old Country Home

Pleiku, a market town in the Central Highlands of South Vietnam, had been an important observation post and base for the French. Although it had the reputation of being a sleepy outpost, Pleiku held as much importance to the Americans as it had for the French. Although enemy activity was heavy in the area, no one messed with the Americans.

Ordered to survey the nearby routes to and from both Laos and Cambodia, the Pleiku command included both ARVN and American military units. Three miles from the ARVN base and the town, some 180 Americans lived in Camp Holloway. Most of these men were Special Forces personnel. Their home was heavily protected by bunkers and barbed wire, and their airstrip was used by both American and South Vietnamese warplanes as well as helicopters.

Pleiku Is Vietnamese for Alamo

During the early morning hours of February 7, 1965, Camp Holloway was attacked. Although well planned, the assault resembled a mad rush right through the entire facility. An American survivor remembered that there seemed to be no place safe to hide throughout the attack, and a complete massacre was feared. In reality, it was more of a hit-and-run mission. The confident Americans had been caught off guard; some were shot in their beds.

In less than 15 minutes, seven Americans had been killed and more than 100 wounded. No Vietcong prisoners were taken, but a detailed map of Camp Holloway was found on the body of one of the dead assailants. The enemy had planned his assault well, and the Americans were duly embarrassed. Westmoreland and Taylor visited the scene shortly after the battle, and both were outraged by it. They wanted

164

blood for blood, and Johnson was told to get after the North Vietnamese. Again, the president hesitated.

Just three days after the attack at Pleiku, the Vietcong helped Johnson with his decision-making. Another hotel was attacked. This one served as the headquarters for a U.S. military maintenance detachment in Qui Nhon, near the coast. The shootout that ensued was actually an enemy diversion. During the battle, Vietcong demolition experts planted charges around the hotel and blew it up. This had been their real mission. The hotel's floors collapsed, trapping dozens of its defenders. Johnson had had enough.

Jarhead Jargon

Pacification involved the effort to secure U.S. and ARVN control over South Vietnamese villages, win the locals' allegiance to the Saigon regime, and deprive the enemy of all strongholds in the countryside.

The White House Strikes Back

From the very suburbs of Saigon to the most lonely location in the entire country, *pacification* was not working. South Vietnam had been a war zone for years, but the U.S. government had never wanted to admit that to the American people. Consequently, U.S. Embassy and military personnel were allowed to bring dependents along with them to South Vietnam. Nearly 2,000 of them were still there in early 1965, and Johnson ordered them home after Pleiku. It was his first step in the escalation campaign.

The next steps involved a series of code-named air strikes. FLAMING DART I attacked enemy bases just north of the 17th parallel. FLAMING DART II was a retaliatory strike for the Qui Nhon disaster, and ROLLING THUNDER began what seemed like endless raids by USAF and Navy fighter bombers. Spearheaded by Guam's Anderson Air Base, ROLLING THUNDER would continue for nearly three years.

With Typhoon Olga bearing down on its home base of Anderson Air Base, Guam, a B-52 bomber makes an emergency landing at U-Tapao Air Base, Thailand in 1965.

National Archives Still Pictures Unit, College Park, Maryland, and photographer Richard J. Mazauskas.

Ask Saigon Sally

In February 1965, a CBS News poll indicated that 80 percent of the American people feared a communist takeover of all of Southeast Asia should the U.S. military leave South Vietnam.

On March 8, 1965, more than 3,500 U.S. Marines arrived in Vietnam, and the White House freely called them combat troops rather than *"advisors,"* a label that was finally discarded. Landing at the coastal town and base of Danang, they came ashore in amphibious landing craft. This was done largely for the U.S. press and public in the hopes of rekindling positive memories of World War II–Pacific victories. But it was a strange, awkward public relations display and it certainly had no impact on North Vietnam or the Vietcong. Danang citizenry even showed up at the beach to offer greetings. Johnson thought it looked great on TV.

Twenty thousand additional troops would soon arrive, and most of them were described as support units for the existing combat troops. Johnson wanted his boys to be comfortable in that strange land, and the new support troops would be bringing along as many Stateside goodies as they could carry.

Jarhead Jargon

The term **advisor** was misused throughout the early 1960s. Some 900 U.S. military advisors were attached to South Vietnamese forces in December 1960. In February 1962, President Kennedy began the first major buildup of U.S. forces in South Vietnam when he established the U.S. Military Command, Vietnam (MACV) in Saigon under General Paul Harkins. He also authorized those men to return fire if fired upon, formally transforming them into combat troops. By late December 1962, there were over 11,000 U.S. troops in South Vietnam, but still called advisors by their government.

Ambassador Taylor insisted that all the newly arriving troops were needed to guard existing bases and to help the ARVN hold the line. General Westmoreland wanted them on the offensive and in the field, killing Vietcong. Johnson agreed with the general, and thousands more troops were sent as well. The Vietnam War was truly on.

Springtime in Vietnam

While tens of thousands of U.S. troops poured into Vietnam, the Vietcong were unusually quiet. Ho sent four brigades south from North Vietnam to help solidify positions already won near Saigon. Otherwise, it was a time to train, watch, and wait.

In Washington, General Taylor warned that the enemy might be lulling the United States into a false sense of security. His position was backed by Undersecretary of State George Ball. But Ball was always complaining that the United States was destined to end up like the French. No one believed him, and Taylor, worried about his own neck, hated being associated with the gloom-and-doom Ball. So he wised up and started talking like the good Cold Warrior. Johnson was correct, he now said, in all Vietnam decision-making.

Shell Shock

In April 1965, Prime Minister Pham Van Dong of North Vietnam announced that peace was possible only when U.S. troops left South Vietnam and a coalition government was arranged there.

Thanks to the springtime quiet, Johnson assumed the enemy had been humbled by the very arrival of the U.S. military. He tried what would be several "peace offensives." Whereas his military efforts had macho names like ROLLING THUNDER, the Johnson "peace offensives" were usually named after pretty flowers. The most significant was Operation MAYFLOWER. Johnson temporarily halted ROLLING THUNDER in the interest of opening peace negotiations. Ho rejected it all, and that rejection was footnoted by the first Vietcong attacks of spring 1965. The ARVN was especially hard hit, forcing U.S. military officers to take personal command of some of their remnants.

Tales from the Front

South Vietnamese poet Ngoc Ky was once asked to describe the impact of the dramatic arrival of U.S. forces in 1965. He said that the destruction wrought by the American troops had "robbed his soul of his ancestors." In a country where ancestral land was very important, he had been unable to preserve and pass his own land down to his children. Vietnam would never be the same.

Ask Saigon Sally

During the spring of 1965, former President Eisenhower urged the American people to rally behind their president during these dark days in Vietnam.

May and June 1965 had become a nightmare for the South Vietnamese, and General Westmoreland now worried about a total collapse of the ARVN. It was going to be a very hot summer. The CIA even told Johnson that more U.S. troops might not make much difference.

So much for the peace and quiet. But the White House ruled out an American military withdrawal. All was not lost, and the new U.S. troop arrivals needed a chance to prove their stuff. But how many Americans would be needed?

Secretary McNamara went back to Vietnam to find out. Shocked and depressed, McNamara told Johnson that hundreds of thousands of U.S. troops might be required, and he was concerned that the American people were not ready for it. Even before McNamara left for this mission, Johnson had figured that "total war" might be necessary. That would do the trick, he believed, and the war would be over before you know it.

The Least You Need to Know

➤ Confusion ruled South Vietnamese politics.

➤ U.S. antiwar efforts were ineffective in 1964 and early 1965.

➤ The Vietcong success at Pleiku led to Johnson's escalation of the war.

➤ New U.S. military operations were accompanied by "peace offensives."

➤ Despite intelligent predictions of failure and defeat, President Johnson remained committed to U.S. military victory in Vietnam.

Chapter 16

March to Victory?

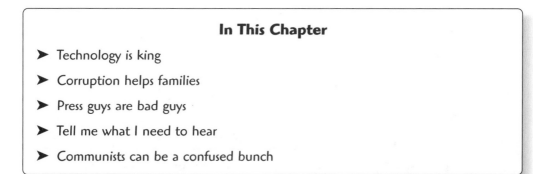

In 1965, America was in love with gear, gadgets, and stuff. On TV and in the movie theaters, the new celluloid heroes costarred with technology. James Bond, of course, led the way. In *Goldfinger,* Sean Connery's top costar was a silver Aston Martin DB-5. This limited-production sports car for the British rich was virtually unknown in the United States. It was outfitted with an ejector passenger seat, retractable front machine guns, bullet-proof spoiler, tire-shredding swept-wing spinners, and rear power hoses that could spew oil slicks, smoke screens, or Ninja stars. The bad guys never had a chance.

On NBC television's *The Man from U.N.C.L.E.*, Robert Vaughn (alias Napoleon Solo) battled evil with an array of handheld gadgets, although he appeared in a specially rigged Corvette killing machine now and then. Brilliant, handsome, and patrons of the finer things in life, superspies with good Anglo-Saxon names like James West, John Drake, Derek Flint, and Harry Palmer helped Bond and Solo dominate the screens of 1965. All had a "license to kill," and, although they suffered setbacks during their dangerous missions, they always prevailed.

Ask Saigon Sally

In Vietnam, one of the American military's most interesting gadgets was nicknamed "Puff the Magic Dragon," a specially rigged DC-3 transport plane with machine guns that could fire more than 18,000 rounds per minute.

Shell Shock

As early as 1965, economic policy expert Anthony Solomon, along with Harvard University School of Business, sponsored a special seminar on financing the Vietnam War. Their recommendations for "commonsense economics" were ignored by the White House.

To most Americans in 1965, the communist enemy in Vietnam, like the enemies of Bond and Solo, were destined to lose.

Guns and Butter

The Vietnam War was getting expensive. As thousands of American troops headed to Vietnam, Lyndon Johnson promised "guns and butter." It was an old expression, largely forgotten in American political semantics. But it meant that you "should be" able to fight a brushfire war overseas for months or even years and never see a negative impact on the economy at home. Johnson said there was no "should be" about it. America was going to win, and Wall Street did not have to worry about a thing.

The key to Johnson's financial optimism was the fact that war usually helps a domestic economy. You didn't need a Ph.D. in economics to conclude that World War II had put a swift end to what was left of the Great Depression. In the 1950s, the Cold War had led to such a boom in industrial defense contracting that Eisenhower mentioned it in his farewell address. Organized labor certainly had no problem working round-the-clock to pump out military hardware for the Vietnam War, and former Ford boss Robert McNamara told Johnson that his CEO colleagues throughout American business welcomed the new contracting boost.

But the expense of Vietnam was embarrassingly high. In 1965, U.S. Air Force operations over secondary targets in South Vietnam cost as much as the entire air war in the Pacific had cost during World War II. To make matters worse, nobody really knew how much had been spent in aerial operations over primary targets in North Vietnam.

The reason for the lax keeping of the books was the Tonkin Gulf Resolution. McNamara's Defense Department interpreted that document as a blank check for deficit spending, and the money poured into Vietnam accordingly. The irony was that McNamara had built a reputation for counting pennies. Naturally he worried that the bill was getting out of hand, and he told Johnson so. A major Vietnam casualty, he predicted, could be the value of the U.S. dollar and the worthiness of the U.S. economy itself. But McNamara was more of the enforcer of policy, and his financial views were dismissed by Johnson.

Tales from the Front

In the first 20 months of Operation Rolling Thunder, more than 300 planes were shot down. The U.S. General Accounting Office estimated that it cost the U.S. $6.60 to inflict $1.00 worth of damage in North Vietnam. Meanwhile, 200,000 North Vietnamese were pressed into antiaircraft defense work and another 500,000 were forced to repair what the Americans bombed. Unfortunately for the U.S., Rolling Thunder also forced the North Vietnamese to move more war materiel into South Vietnam and away from the bombing. This also made it more available to the Vietcong, and that was not what U.S. military planners had had in mind.

Old Kennedy financial hands still carried some weight in Johnson's Vietnam economics. Advisors such as Walt Rostow, Walter Heller, John Kenneth Galbraith, and Anthony Solomon all had interesting views on the dollars-and-cents subject for Johnson. Of course, they were all a little highbrow for the president's taste. All of them had come of age during the heyday of New Deal spending, and Johnson's Great Society was supposed to be a hybrid of the New Deal. So, their off-and-on recommendations for caution and restraint were tempered by their belief in big government and Cold War victory.

The truth is that Johnson never anticipated any economic troubles because of Vietnam. After it was all over, there might be a congressional investigation or two into wasteful spending, but who, Johnson asked, would penalize a winner because of it?

Ask Saigon Sally

Until 1965, the port of Saigon had been unable to handle major ocean traffic. The U.S. escalation of the war changed all that, and six deepwater harbor facilities were constructed by American personnel. The precise total cost of the project remains unknown.

In 1898, Johnson once reminded Rostow, Congress investigated the McKinley administration for fiscal mismanagement during the Spanish-American War, and administration figures such as Theodore Roosevelt got standing ovations and pats on the back throughout the investigation. The Spanish-American War had been a resounding, fast-moving success. End of story. To Johnson, the guns-and-butter theory was, like the old saying, "sound as a dollar." America learned quickly that neither the theory nor the saying was very "sound" at all.

171

The Early Opposition Speaks

Rising fast up the ranks of the Senate Foreign Relations Committee, Senator Frank Church (Democrat, Idaho) thought that Congress should regain its *"power of the purse."* Johnson's command of all national security policy-making was one thing. Leaving all financial power to him was another.

Jarhead Jargon

James Madison, the senior writer of both the U.S. Constitution and the rules of Congress, always assumed that Congress should have the final say in the nation's financial policy-making. He called it the **"power of the purse."**

Ask Saigon Sally

According to CBS News in 1965, the number-one traded item on the Saigon black market was U.S.-made powdered milk.

Johnson urged Church to think about his home state of Idaho before he balked any further, and, by mid-1965, Church had learned to keep his mouth shut. In these early days of the Vietnam escalation, it was hard to find any significant opposition, and Johnson was good at defusing any potential challenges.

Although his Tonkin Gulf Resolution did not compel him to consult or ask Congress for funding permission, Johnson requested $700 million in May 1965 to support the latest troop arrivals in Vietnam. Congress quickly agreed. Three years later, when many congressmen railed against "Johnson's War," the president reminded them all that they had enthusiastically agreed to his escalation measures.

The corrupt use of U.S. funding in Vietnam was a whole different ballgame. Because Johnson insisted that a lot of America must go with Americans to Vietnam, the stockpiles of American-made goodies were easy pickings for South Vietnamese black-market moguls, common thieves, and Saigon regime officials. The U.S. press and visiting U.S. dignitaries, like Senator Mike Mansfield, were appalled at the level of corruption. Their reports back home annoyed the Johnson administration, but, in the long run, the White House didn't mind if American products ended up in the hands of many South Vietnamese families. It was more than the Vietcong could give them.

With the exceptions of peace and justice, you could buy anything on the streets of Saigon, and most of it came from an American warehouse. The creation of the black-market economy in South Vietnam killed the real South Vietnamese economy. Westmoreland and Johnson tried a number of quick fixes, ranging from a special script currency for U.S. military personnel to South Vietnamese currency revaluation, but none of it worked.

While wounded and struggling ex-ARVN troops were reduced to begging and stealing to make ends meet, successful South Vietnamese black marketeers and other wartime opportunists lived the good life. In 1965, a CBS News special report on "La Dolce Vita, Saigon Style" compared the misery of Saigon street life to the jet-set lifestyle of the wives of the nouveau riche there. One film clip showed these women enjoying cigarettes laced with opium and then passing out U.S. $100 bills like candy. Its airing angered the Johnson administration. Rostow said it equaled any pro-North Vietnamese propaganda effort straight from Hanoi.

The Johnson administration might have thought the worst about the U.S. press, but they did nothing to stop the reports from Vietnam. From the beginning of the escalation and the first negative news accounts, the White House considered the press an unwitting enemy accomplice. The influence of this opinion, on the other hand, would not be truly felt until after the war was over.

Vietnam would be America's last war where the military permitted the press to roam a combat zone at will. Press movements would be tightly controlled during the 1991 Gulf War, for instance. To the Pentagon, a "television war" bred antiwar sentiment on the home front.

Shell Shock

"Let there be no doubt about it," ex-president Johnson told Walter Cronkite in 1971, the American press was contributing to the enemy's success in the Vietnam War.

Westmoreland Asks for More

Vietnam became Robert McNamara's home away from home. This time accompanying other Johnson cabinet officials to Saigon, McNamara was back in the late spring of 1965. The group was supposed to assess the latest Westmoreland request for more troops, but they wasted little time agreeing with the general. He would get 40,000 more marines and army personnel. The disagreement came over how they were to be deployed.

James Gavin crisscrossed the United States advocating an *enclave strategy* as the best way to use the more than 50,000 troops then in Vietnam. Often mistaken for impersonating a senior officer, Gavin had been America's youngest general during World War II. He went on to be John Kennedy's ambassador to France, and he learned a lot about the French misery in Vietnam from his Parisian hosts.

To Gavin, America was poised to repeat the same military mistakes as the French. If Westmoreland spread around his 50,000 troops today or tens of

Jarhead Jargon

By mid-1965, the Johnson administration favored an **enclave strategy** for the thousands of fresh U.S. troops arriving in Vietnam. That meant protecting key coastal towns and existing U.S. military bases only.

thousands more tomorrow, the French had already demonstrated that big numbers were no guarantees of success: The Vietcong would, in turn, kill big numbers of Americans. Often saying these things on TV news programs, Gavin accurately predicted that the mass killings of Americans seen on the nightly news would not be good news for the Johnson administration.

Johnson did not need much persuading. He admired Gavin and respected his conclusions. Westmoreland's new troops were given enclave strategy orders. This was consistent with the president's public descriptions of Vietnam as a defensive war. The ARVN would fight it out in the countryside, and America would defend its own secured areas.

From the beginning, Westmoreland opposed the enclave strategy. The ARVN, he told Johnson, were about to be destroyed, while American troops drank beer and watched everything from a comfy base. In June 1965, the general asked for 150,000 more men. At first, the White House thought he was kidding; however, Westmoreland said that he needed every one of them to rescue the ARVN. He hedged on whether these men could truly win the war. Johnson compromised and offered 95,000. It prompted quite a debate.

Tales from the Front

One of the more intriguing military developments of the mid-1960s was the creation of the Kit Carson Scouts. These were former Vietcong who defected and agreed to serve with U.S. combat troops, mostly as scouts but also as soldiers, interpreters, and intelligence agents. The program began when General Westmoreland learned that the 9th U.S. Marines were using recently surrendered Vietcong troopers who had asked for asylum. Westmoreland encouraged all U.S. military units to follow the example of the 9th Marines, and by 1968 over 700 ex-Vietcong were serving with U.S. forces.

High Tech vs. Low Tech

From cluster bombs exploded just above the enemy's heads to eavesdropping electronics on the Ho Chi Minh Trail to *walleye* missiles, America had a technological edge over the enemy equal to many thousands of troops in the field. This was the consensus of the Johnson administration, and a strong thesis point for CIA Director John McCone.

To McCone, the arguments over how many troops were needed were all irrelevant. American technology of the 1960s made French technology of the 1950s look prehistoric, he insisted. Comparing the French scene to the American scene was also irrelevant; McCone found it insulting for anyone to compare the lousy French military to the victorious U.S. military. Walt Rostow agreed, urging Johnson to listen to his top security advisors and avoid gut decisions here.

Westmoreland even urged Johnson to wise up and welcome the McCone thesis. He was about the only guy on the planet who could get away with telling Johnson to wise up. High-tech warfare and a fanning out of American ground troops would do the trick, Westmoreland said. The other options were the usual ones. George Ball, as always, said cut and run before it was too late. Another option stressed the enclaves policy, letting the ARVN regroup, and then seeing what happened.

To Johnson, retreat would be impossible to explain to the American people, and he really wasn't a wait-and-see kind of guy. Letting Westmoreland do his thing made the best sense to him, and, as soon as he got real results on the battlefield, another "peace offensive" would be launched on Hanoi. This time, the president predicted, the enemy would be ready to deal.

Who Should We Bomb Today?

Close to 5,000 bombing runs were made over North Vietnamese targets in the early summer of 1965. That was nearly double the number from earlier in the year. Yet this escalation was considered a compromising, cautious policy at the time.

Jarhead Jargon

Another example of America's high-tech weaponry in Vietnam was a missile called a **walleye.** It was fired from a fighter plane and reached its target courtesy of a TV camera and a pilot guiding its course from the comforts of his own aircraft.

Ask Saigon Sally

The domestic political right and not the left was the Great Society's enemy, Johnson argued. Consequently, a retreat from Vietnam would be the equivalent of political suicide and the complete destruction of his new New Deal.

There was heavy pressure on the president to take advantage of American air superiority and knock out the enemy's ability to wage war. McNamara was one of the strongest proponents of rolling more thunder into ROLLING THUNDER. His list of targets for these round-the-clock air raids went beyond the usual munitions industries and oil refineries. It included all bridges, railways, power stations, and whatever else

might be left standing. Short of nuclear war, McNamara reasoned that this was the best approach.

If he went along with McNamara's plan, Johnson wondered what might happen if Soviet and Chinese citizens in Hanoi or Haiphong were killed. Would a bombing effort just short of World War III still provoke World War III? It was something to worry about, and he looked for some outside advice. Was he being too wimpy on Vietnam? McNamara's "bombs away" approach seemed a bit much.

Called the "Wise Men," foreign policy-makers like Dean Acheson and Robert Lovett were called on by Johnson. Their years of experience were supposed to make them experts on Vietnam decision-making. In reality, Johnson's outside advisors were diehard Cold Warriors who told him what he wanted to hear. It was similar to what he heard from his cabinet, but without all the discussions of options and strategies. They assured him his approach was never wimpy, and told him to hang tough with the press and congressional critics. Victory in Vietnam, they said, was only moments away.

Tales from the Front

Often considered the most bizarre U.S. military operation of 1966, Operation Lexington III was supposed to insert a large U.S. military presence in Rung Sat Special Zone. Long declared impenetrable by the ARVN and a well-defended base of operations for the Vietcong, Rung Sat Special Zone always posed a direct threat to Saigon from the south. It was a huge mangrove swamp, and the U.S. Army First Infantry Division was ordered into it. Forced to wade in hip-deep mud and suffering from a variety of tropical diseases, the First Infantry never found that large enemy force. But they were there.

Somewhere off the coast of Vietnam, two Attack Squadron 85, VA-85, A-6A intruder attack aircraft, with tail hooks extended, prepare for landing aboard USS Kitty Hawk.

National Archives Still Pictures Unit, College Park, Maryland.

What's Happened to the Bad Guys?

In Beijing, the Chinese government's reaction to the stepped-up Vietnam War was awfully confusing. During one 48-hour period, the Chinese issued two contradictory statements. The first one said that China would never enter the Vietnam War unless the Americans invaded Chinese soil. Then Mao himself told a journalist that China was ready to assist all anti-imperialist freedom fighters in South Vietnam.

Adding to the confusion, the Soviets sought a general Beijing-Moscow agreement on Vietnam. Some sort of united front action must be possible, the Soviets argued. Finally, an official Chinese communist publication suggested that North Vietnam follow the example of the Chinese communist party in the 1940s and fight its battles proudly and defiantly on its own.

Ask Saigon Sally

In reaction to the American escalation of the war, the North Vietnamese military formed a specific infiltration unit for Ho Chi Minh Trail duty alone. The 70th Transportation Group would be in charge of moving most of the men and materiel from North Vietnam to South Vietnam.

Washington needed a road map to follow these political twists and turns. Meanwhile, Ho Chi Minh preferred to avoid grand military offensives as the Americans set up shop in Vietnam. Once again, it made sense to sit back and assess the significance of the latest U.S. move. Time, as always, would be on his side.

The Least You Need to Know

➤ The Johnson administration viewed American technology as a winning weapon in the Vietnam War.

➤ Johnson paid little attention to the financial expense of the Vietnam War.

➤ The black market in South Vietnam became more significant and influential than the legitimate South Vietnamese economy.

➤ The Johnson administration argued over the level of U.S. military escalation.

➤ The communists offered a confused response to the influx of new U.S. troops in South Vietnam.

Chapter 17

The Young Turks and the Search for Victory

South Vietnam was dirt poor. Its economy was poor, and its leaders were dirt. This was the observation of George Wildman Ball, and he never changed his assessment. John Kennedy ignored him, but admired his honesty and frankness. Lyndon Johnson ignored him, but found him awfully annoying.

An Iowa native and 1930 graduate of Illinois's Northwestern University, Ball took pride in his no-nonsense Midwestern view of U.S. foreign policy. "If Vietnam doesn't work, American policy won't work," Ball once noted, and that kind of observation won him few friends in the Cold Warrior crowd.

Ball came to the Kennedy White House in 1961 as an international trade expert, working his way up to the number-two slot in the State Department as undersecretary of state. To Ball, South Vietnam was an artificial creation, always too far gone to rescue, and the worst possible place to champion an anticommunist cause. It was amazing that he held on to his job for as long as he did. Seeing the handwriting on the wall, Ball resigned in 1966 before being fired.

Ky Is the Key?

In 1964, Ball joked that if it was Tuesday, there must be a new government in South Vietnam. Indeed, there was a certain government-of-the-month quality to South Vietnamese politics at the time, but only the undersecretary of state would dare mention it during a cabinet meeting.

Ask Saigon Sally

George Ball once shared a law office with Adlai Stevenson, the 1952 and 1956 Democratic party presidential nominee. He assisted many diplomatic endeavors, including the creation of Europe's Common Market economic unification plan.

Shell Shock

Presidents Kennedy and Johnson had a corps of outside foreign policy consultants in addition to cabinet and staff members. Prof. Henry Kissinger was one of them, and he advocated U.S. military victory in Vietnam until he changed his mind in 1967.

For President Johnson in December 1964, the man of the hour was either Nguyen Cao Ky or Nguyen Van Thieu. Take your pick. In that month, these two young, up-and-coming South Vietnamese military men created an Armed Forces Council in Saigon. Within a few weeks, the Council took over most of the affairs of state; however, it was not until February 1965 that Ky and Thieu could claim to be in charge of a real working government there.

Ky would emerge as the central figure, largely because Johnson found him the more politically attractive of the two. That did not mean Thieu was down-and-out. Ky and Thieu would be at each other's throats for years, and Thieu, even while Ky was in power, often claimed that he had more influence and pull than anyone else in the country.

The American press called Ky and Thieu the "Young Turks." That had a positive ring to it. It meant that these young guys were supposed to shake the pillars of heaven, and make everything right in South Vietnam. Specifically, that meant establishing a government that could win widespread public support, reforming the ARVN into a victorious army, and eliminating corruption at all levels. Even in 1965 and 1966, many Americans were tired of the sickening tales of defeat and confusion in South Vietnam. They wanted to believe in the "Young Turks" image. Surely an American-like government was possible in a country where American boys were dying.

At first Ky fit into this image better than Thieu, and, for a while, he brightened things up for President Johnson. The brightening was a literal thing. Ky liked to wear bright green, red, and purple clothes. A colorful scarf, a favorite among fighter pilots, was usually around his neck and a pair of stylish Foster Grant sunglasses on his face. Meanwhile, *Life* magazine declared his wife the most beautiful First Lady since Jackie Kennedy, and her sexy *Vogue* wardrobe was all the rage.

Johnson even liked what Ky had to say. The U.S. Embassy reported that Ky could draw a crowd for a speech or two. Most of what he said was a rehash of Khanh's call for a South Vietnamese attack on North Vietnam, but it was more intelligently presented. He sounded more like a studied American politician than a medieval pope calling for a children's crusade against the infidel.

That didn't mean the White House liked Ky's message. Johnson still opposed widening the war to include ARVN invasions of North Vietnam. Although no one said much about it in Washington, U.S. observers in Saigon were quick to point out that the South Vietnamese capital was surrounded by the Vietcong. The idea of marching north to Hanoi was pretty ridiculous when you couldn't march beyond your backyard. Johnson simply liked Ky's speech delivery and the fact that somebody applauded when he was done talking. Maybe the average South Vietnamese family could grow to like the guy, and that was a great first step in Johnson's view.

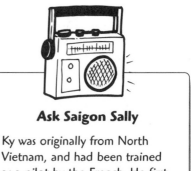

Ask Saigon Sally

Ky was originally from North Vietnam, and had been trained as a pilot by the French. He first became known to the United States as a daredevil pilot who flew CIA agents into North Vietnam.

Meanwhile, the American press's flirtation with Mr. and Mrs. Ky was a brief one. The Kys must have been distracted by all the latest fashions, for the political and military problems remained. More to the point, in person, Ky was not the charmer that the press and even Lyndon Johnson made him out to be.

Ky's relationship with the U.S. Embassy was sometimes difficult to figure out. On Monday, he could, like Diem, complain about undue U.S. interference in Saigon affairs. On Tuesday, he would act like the ultimate puppet of U.S. policy, asking American officials how he might better serve the anticommunist cause. On Wednesday, he could make snide, rude jokes about American life and culture, saying that it was the Americans who made him wear strange Western clothes. Smarmy, arrogant, sycophantic, and just plain odd, Ky was still America's best hope in South Vietnam.

While Ky talked the talk about a glorious life in South Vietnam after the American victory, Thieu concentrated on the present. Although destined to be one of the longer-lasting leaders of South Vietnam, he remained in the shadow of Ky in the mid-1960s. To those Americans concerned about nuts-and-bolts issues rather than the pomp and circumstance of Ky, Thieu made practical sense.

Thieu preferred systematic offensives against the Vietcong, working with instead of against the Buddhist community in the large cities, and cooperating in the field with the hordes of arriving American troops. On the face of it, Thieu's preferences made him the decent alternative to Ky, and, eventually, would work to his advantage.

On the other hand, Thieu was no saint. Ky charged that Thieu was one of the most corrupt officials in South Vietnam, and most of those accusations would end up being true. The White House would have to decide what it wanted. Did it want *GQ* or *Popular Mechanics*? Was corruption okay in the face of possible communist victory or not? These were never easy questions to answer.

From left to right: Nguyen Van Thieu, Lyndon Johnson, and Nguyen Cao Ky listening to the U.S. and Vietnamese National Anthems during welcoming ceremonies at Guam's International Airport, Agana, Guam, March 1967.

National Archives Still Pictures Unit, College Park, Maryland.

Shell Shock

One of the many South Vietnamese governments before the era of Ky and Thieu lasted only three months. Led by Phan Khac Suu and Tran Van Huong, this government admitted that it had no plan to win against the communists. The future, they said, was in God's hands alone.

"Many Flags"

The battlefield news during the spring and summer of 1965 remained all bad. Although the Vietcong and the Hanoi government presented a picture of unity during this period, Ho's government was deeply divided over how to attack, whom to attack, and where to concentrate the effort.

The tens of thousands of Americans who seemed to be arriving per hour should have made a difference, but instead of humbling communists into a surrender, they rallied the communists to their cause. American firepower and technology remained unable to cope with guerilla war, and there was little that was new about American strategies compared to old French strategies.

The spring of 1965 began with an act of terrorism: A Vietcong car, loaded with explosives, blew up the first three floors of the American Embassy in Saigon, killing more than 50 people. By midsummer, the battle for the Batangan Peninsula was underway. The Vietcong took heavy casualties, but still defeated the Americans there. Both the embassy attack and the battle for the Batangan Peninsula were embarrassing moments for President Johnson. But his escalation of the war remained on track, and the North Vietnamese still presented the powerful picture of solidarity, selflessness, and success.

Tales from the Front

Known as "Spookies" for their mission of close support for struggling ground troops in the "boonies," the Douglas AC-47 plane was known for its 7.62 mm Gatling-type guns, which fired thousands of rounds in minutes. It also dropped flares from 2,500 feet to light up the night sky above the enemy. Accidents did happen. In 1967, Sergeant John L. Levitow won the Congressional Medal of Honor for falling on a prematurely ignited flare that would have killed the other men on board and downed the plane. Although severely burned, Levitow survived his wounds.

If the communists could act as an organized force, why couldn't the anticommunists? It was Johnson's big question of 1965. One of his answers involved a major propaganda and practical effort known as the "Many Flags" campaign.

"Many Flags" involved a Korean War–like effort to get Asian/Pacific allies into the fight. Several nations would send troops to South Vietnam, ranging from dozens to hundreds of thousands. Johnson's wheeling-and-dealing approach to politics and diplomacy played a heavy hand here.

Tales from the Front

America's battle for the Batangan Peninsula along the southern coast of Quang Nhai province continued throughout much of 1965. Two ground operations were involved, code-named Starlight and Piranha. These were the first massive U.S. ground operations of the war. Although Starlight's U.S. military defeats won international attention, the U.S. Marines–led Piranha counted 183 Vietcong killed in action after this September 1965 operation was over, and only a few Marines were killed or wounded. But Quang Ngai remained a Vietcong sanctuary as late as 1968.

Shell Shock

Although the South Korean Defense Ministry still denies it, independent investigators claim that there were many massacres committed by South Korean troops against innocent South Vietnamese civilians. The death toll is conservatively estimated to be more than 8,000.

Jarhead Jargon

New Life Villages were hamlets run by Republic of Korea (ROK) troops, along with relocation centers, for evacuated South Vietnamese villagers. Most of these villagers were forced into refugee status by ROK troops, and sometimes brutally, in the effort to keep them away from Vietcong influences.

Like a ROK

The Australian and New Zealand governments quickly answered the call, but only in a limited support role. There were no apologies for their carefully defined participation. Because the Australians were leading the Asian/Pacific countries in the effort to break down the American-maintained wall of nonrecognition to Communist China, it was especially awkward being one of the "many flags" in America's war. Meanwhile, returning Australian veterans were considered by fellow countrymen to be the hired guns of the Americans.

The most controversial arrangement for allied troops was made with President Park Chung Hee of the Republic of Korea (ROK). A former general, Park had taken power courtesy of a coup. Dedicated to the quick modernization of his country, Park ran South Korea with an iron fist of martial law and extensive political prisons. Naturally, he owed the Americans a debt of thanks for their Korean War assistance. On the other hand, Park needed money to boost his modernization program, and the ROK housed more than 30,000 U.S. troops. Seoul and Washington needed each other, and Park played it up big.

Winning a handsome U.S. aid plan in return for shipping troops to Vietnam, Park was more of the wheeler-dealer than Johnson. Some 300,000 ROK troops would serve in South Vietnam over the years, and their actions in the field remain a source of controversy today.

ROK troops were not choirboys. Vietnam was a filthy war, and many of them did not suffer from the same moral and ethical dilemmas that troubled the "Ugly American"–conscious soldiers of General Westmoreland. There were also no TV network news reporters in their faces, and they often remained on the outskirts of larger American plans and operations.

The ROK Marines of Blue Dragon Brigade patrolled the Danang area, while the ROK Army Tiger and White Horse Divisions patrolled Qui Nhon and Nha Trang, respectively. *New Life Village* work occupied much of their time. Thousands of villagers, uncooperative or merely bothersome, were killed. Captured North Vietnamese documents indicated that the Koreans were especially feared and hated, but President

Park made sure that all returning veterans were treated to a hero's welcome. Any atrocity reports from Hanoi, or even from the Western press, were denied and denounced in Seoul.

Johnson received the news of endless Korean-inflicted atrocities as well, but anything that could assist the anticommunist cause was okay with him. Vietnam was a "bitch of a war," the president liked to tell his staff, and it took an even "bigger son of a bitch to win it."

What Are Friends For?

Whereas Kennedy saw the Asian/Pacific allies as a potential block of connected powerhouse economies that would kill the appeal of communism, Johnson saw the Asian/Pacific alliance as good news for promoting regional propaganda.

A good Asian/Pacific ally didn't even have to send troops; however, Johnson did expect enthusiastic endorsements of his Vietnam policy. Moving fast up the ladder of capitalist success, Japan was particularly important in the propaganda war. At first, all looked well in that department. Prime Minister Eisaku Sato was a passionate anticommunist. In fact, Sato's anticommunist speeches had Johnson wondering whether the Japanese Constitution could be modified to better accommodate U.S. policy.

Sato was constitutionally bound to maintain a military similar to America's National Guard, and that was it. No overseas military role was specified in that constitution, and Johnson's advisors were at odds over whether America should lobby to change it. The U.S. had no authority to dictate Constitutional reform to the Japanese, but it did have the joint U.S.–Japan treaty that governed the U.S. bases in Japan and their possible role in a Japan defense. Other than that, there was Japan's own commitment to the American-led anticommunist crusade. But bullying Japan certainly wouldn't win the respect and allegiance of Asians tired of the "Ugly American."

Predicting a *"diplomatic hailstorm"* against the United States should the Johnson administration pressure Japan on the constitution issue, the National Security Council urged the president not to rock any boats. If a good chunk of the "More Flags" effort was simply to look and act like united anticommunists in the face of the united communists, a shouting match with Japan would not help matters.

Jarhead Jargon

Johnson's National Security Council predicted a **"diplomatic hailstorm"** should the United States attempt to win Japan to the "More Flags" effort. They were referring to the potentially strong, negative, and anti-American reaction of countries formerly occupied by Japan's World War II military.

Ask Saigon Sally

The row between the United States and Japan over Okinawa intensified during the Johnson years. The Johnson team worried that angry diplomatic exchanges over Okinawa's political future and military role in the Vietnam War might resurrect "Ugly American" concerns across the Asian/Pacific region.

Shell Shock

In the Dominican Republic, the U.S. ambassador, W. Tapley Bennett, favored the right-wing government. In April 1965, Bennett told President Johnson that thousands had been massacred by leftist rebels. He lied.

Victory Under the Palms

If "More Flags" was a message of anticommunist unity, then the Dominican Republic invasion was a wake-up call for Hanoi. Or so the White House hoped. Propaganda was one thing; military victory was another. Ho Chi Minh seemed to understand little beyond determination, commitment, and violence. To Johnson, the 1965 U.S. invasion of the Dominican Republic demonstrated both American will and military savvy. Watch out Ho Chi Minh, Johnson was trying to say. The end is near.

The Dominican Republic Invasion

In 1962, Juan Bosch won the presidency of the Dominican Republic, and he had no apologies for his leftist views. Poverty in his struggling Caribbean island nation was worsening, and there had not been a free election there since the 1920s. Quickly overthrown in a right-wing coup, Bosch had little time to put his reform agenda to work. Pro-Bosch supporters took up arms against the government, and Johnson swung into action during the spring of 1965.

Vowing he would never permit another Castro-like government so close to the United States, Johnson sent in 33,000 U.S. troops (mostly marines) to put down the revolt. At first, Westmoreland worried about the level of big-time commitment to this "sideshow," especially while the war in Vietnam continued. Nevertheless, the marines quickly achieved their objective. They were assisted by 2,000 troops in a sort of "More Flags" effort from the Latin American–run Organization of American States (OAS). Johnson had pressured the latter to act, and a considerable amount of ill will resulted because of it.

The fact was that the U.S. military had prevailed in a tropical, suffering Third World country. Militarily and politically, Johnson had achieved what remained so elusive in Vietnam. Victory is a wonderful thing.

Tales from the Front

Operation Rolling Thunder ended up being one operation in five phases. Phase 1 (March–June 1965) concentrated on obvious military targets near Hanoi. Phase 2 (July 1965–June 1966) stressed the North Vietnamese steel industry, bridges, trains, and ships. Phase 3 (June–September 1966) attacked storage facilities. Phase 4 (October 1966–March 1968) included more industrial targets and other "sporadic attacks." Phase 5 began after the Tet Offensive, concentrating on targets between the 17th and the 19th parallels while the Johnson administration attempted to negotiate a peace plan with the North Vietnamese.

A Hint of Things to Come?

Without question, Johnson hoped this success would spread to Vietnam, and his administration predicted, of course, that it would. But Hanoi never got the message. In their view, whatever happened in the Dominican Republic had no relevance to the Vietnam scene. In fact, the North Vietnamese were amazed that they were expected to be influenced by such faraway events.

As always, Johnson remained a prisoner of his Cold War times. He thought globally. The Vietnamese thought locally. In a way, this master politician violated one of his own political axioms: All politics is local. America was losing the war in Vietnam, and all the local indications of that fact were being ignored.

The Least You Need to Know

➤ Nguyen Cao Ky offered a new kind of flashy South Vietnamese government.

➤ "The Young Turks" did not turn around the battlefield situation.

➤ Johnson sought Asian/Pacific allies through his "More Flags" program.

➤ ROK troops committed many civilian atrocities.

➤ President Johnson hoped that victory in the Dominican Republic would influence events in Vietnam.

Part 4

No Light in the Tunnel

In 1968, America got a wake-up call. After all the years of blood, effort, and endless economic aid packages, the U.S. role in Vietnam hadn't changed a thing. North Vietnam's horrific Tet Offensive proved the point, and dispatching more American troops was not the answer.

Assuming that the North Vietnamese now wanted peace as much as the White House did, Johnson initiated a peace process in Paris. But his career was over, and the enemy was more interested in victory than in peace. Promising a "secret plan" to end the war, a once-dedicated Cold Warrior, Richard Nixon, narrowly won the presidency. But as young people marched in the streets, all Nixon offered was a slow U.S. withdrawal and even an expansion of hostilities into Cambodia.

Like his predecessors, Nixon did not want to be the president who lost the Vietnam War. Yet his search for "peace with honor" was a difficult one. While his chief guru of foreign affairs, Henry Kissinger, planned a new post-Vietnam foreign policy, the war went on and on. More Americans would die during the "winding down" of the Vietnam War than during its escalation.

Question Authority

"If." If John Kennedy had lived, the Vietnam War would have ended early. If Johnson had invaded North Vietnam, or committed more troops to the fight in South Vietnam, victory would have been assured. If the press had been prevented from covering the Vietnam battlefield, the American people would not have turned against the war. And if the antiwar movement had led more demonstrations, a U.S. military withdrawal would have come quickly.

If is a seductive word. But it has little place in assessing the history of a war; and at any rate, in the case of Vietnam, all of the above "if" statements are probably false.

Those Good Old Days

Many believe that the antiwar movement had a profound impact on Washington's Vietnam War policy, and that various protests and public demonstrations made the difference between war and peace. In fact, this opinion enjoys a considerable amount

Shell Shock

Founded in April 1967, the Vietnam Veterans Against the War (VVAW) claimed a membership of 7,000. Especially stressing their efforts to help returning veterans with psychological problems due to the war, the VVAW was a very visible and controversial wing of the antiwar movement. Their credibility was hurt when it was discovered that most VVAW members had never served in Vietnam at all.

Jarhead Jargon

One of the smallest and most extreme antiwar protest groups was the **Weather Underground** or **Weathermen.** They took their name from singer Bob Dylan's "Subterranian Homesick Blues." According to Dylan, "you don't need a weatherman to know which way the wind blows."

of support on today's college campuses. Quite a few of yesterday's student protestors are today's college professors. To many of them, the protest years of the late 1960s and early 1970s were pivotal ones that shaped their lives. They were young, involved, and helping to end a horrible war. Today they're older, more sedentary, and fighting crabgrass instead of Washington. Ah, to be young again.

Nostalgia, as they say, ain't what it used to be. Although the aging antiwar protestors would have a hard time admitting it, they sound an awful lot like their World War II "Greatest Generation" parents nostalgic for the days of the Great Depression and the Good War. According to that particular myth, America was at its best during those troubled times. If only we could pull together and do great things like we did back then.

But the truth is, the 1930s produced massive unemployment, struggle, and misery in an era of legalized racism, few social services, and limited opportunities for higher education. The 1940s produced a war that left 50 million dead by the time it was over. These were not the good old days. Ditto for Vietnam. The Vietnam War produced plenty of protests that fascinated the press, but had a limited impact on Vietnam policy-making.

After the war, General Giap thanked the U.S. antiwar movement for confusing the White House, giving some solace to his troops, and acting as surrogate foreign agents for the North Vietnamese cause. His comments disturbed former antiwar leaders, for this implied that most of them had been unwitting traitors at worst, North Vietnamese stoolies at best. Given Giap's penchant for bombastic public statements, it remains unclear to this day if he really saw American antiwar protestors as North Vietnamese allies. whether true, it means that the only real influence the antiwar movement had was in Hanoi and not Washington.

Whatever Giap believed, his praises for the U.S. antiwar movement raises a serious question. What were the precise goals of the movement and what did its leaders truly hope to achieve?

As American as Apple Pie

America's New Left in the 1960s was a homegrown achievement. Traditional Socialist and Communist parties at home and abroad had a hard time figuring out groups like the Spartacist League, the *Weathermen,* the Students for a Democratic Society (SDS), or even the so-called counterculture. In fact, most of the old-line leftists regarded the maverick, independent-thinking New Left as a threat to their already tiny political base in the United States.

Tales from the Front

At age 17, Josh Cruz joined the U.S. Marine Corps, hoping that an enlistment would save him from the Vietnam-bound fate of most draftees at the time. He was wrong. Involved in heavy fighting near Phu Bai, Cruz was wounded and most of his buddies were killed. Suffering from endless flashback nightmares and survivor guilt, Cruz became a professional actor and has appeared in plays, television, and movies. Playing someone else, Cruz tells interviewers, has always helped him forget his own troubles.

To Gus Hall and his Communist Party, USA, the left-sounding student protestors of the 1960s were light-years away from being real leftists. Hall had run for president many times, and could never win more than 1 percent of the vote. Although a passionate anticapitalist, Hall once bought a multimillion-dollar winning New York lottery ticket, and turned it over to the party coffers to keep things going. Hall didn't see much irony in a capitalist gimmick financing a "let's kill capitalism" party, and young antiwar radicals never saw much use for him.

Jarhead Jargon

In Jean-Paul Sartre's complicated theory of **existentialism,** traditional communism was morally bankrupt. It stifled the individual's natural tendency to do good things and share his talents with others.

To what the press nicknamed the New Left, Hall and his mainline communist buddies were tools of the Soviet government. They were puppets on a long string without a soul or humanitarian bone in their bodies. Yet the *New Left* was hard to define. They were a confused conglomeration of disaffected liberals, students just wanting to be rebellious and outrageous, and followers of internationally known communist or socialist reformers and bad boys ranging from France's Jean-Paul Sartre and his *existentialism* to Germany's Herbert Marcuse and his complaints about the "one-dimensional man."

Jarhead Jargon

The **New Left** was a peculiarly American phenomenon. Denounced by socialist and communist parties overseas as too independent and experimental, the New Left welcomed the humanist and liberal side of socialist and communist philosophies. Borrowing from leftist thinkers ranging from Karl Marx to Mao Tse-tung, New Left adherents despised imperialism and capitalist excess and corruption, and preferred an isolationist U.S. foreign policy. The support for isolationism was reminiscent of conservative Republican views of the 1920s and 1930s. Hence, the New Left complicated the political scene, preferring political debate to political action. The New Left was more a state of mind than a political group.

Like hot-rod mechanics, American New Leftists welcomed any part that fit. They borrowed ideologies from Chinese Maoists, Vladimir Lenin (the early years), Leon Trotsky (any year), and any maverick reformer anywhere. After years of being in the closet, hounded by Joe McCarthy types, the American left wing came out in the open as the organizing force behind many antiwar demonstrations. Taking ideological potshots at both capitalist and communist political parties, the New Leftists were bright, angry, and passionately independent. Those qualities represented both their strengths and weaknesses.

In public speeches, New Leftists were good at mixing complicated philosophy with understandable English. Others, like the self-described "leaning-anarchist" Abbie Hoffman, just swore a lot. Naturally, the New Left phenomenon won a lot of attention from the press, and a lot of animosity from the vast majority of Americans who did not understand their complaints. For a time, Tom Hayden, a University of Michigan student government activist, represented the entire New Left movement to many outsiders. This brought plenty of attention to his "end the war now" cause.

Tom Hayden

Hayden's brand of New Left activism involved, at first, organizing mid-1960s university sit-ins against the war on university campuses, and then taking student followers to the streets in displays of "people power" outrage. To Hayden, everything would have been different in Vietnam if only John Kennedy had lived. Meanwhile, Lyndon Johnson went only "half the way" on civil rights and other New Deal–like reforms, he said, because of his obsession with a "racist war" in Vietnam. Because few recognized the evil of Vietnam in Washington, real reformers and peacemakers were still in the universities waiting to break into government and make things right. Or so Hayden told his colleagues.

Calling his followers the Students for a Democratic Society, or SDS, Hayden championed a multitude of causes. In fact, university-centered issues, such as support for coed dorms or establishing courses in African American studies, peace studies, and environmental studies, were especially important to the SDS. Those matters often occupied more of their time than their headline-grabbing antiwar protests.

By the late 1960s, the SDS was a nationwide student government movement with significant support on a number of campuses. Each SDS government tended to operate on its own agenda and timetable, rejecting the press's assumption that Hayden was their founding father and continuing leader. The SDS remained a strongly male-dominated outfit as well, alienating women who had joined it because of all the talk about new directions and new reforms. Women's rights groups would spin off on their own.

Whereas Hayden praised the independence of individual SDS organizations, a united, disciplined, national SDS might have been more effective in leading antiwar demonstrations. Otherwise, SDS-led protests had a certain spontaneous quality to them, and, sometimes, particularly in the months before the 1968 Tet Offensive, there were more reporters and police at a demonstration than demonstrators.

There were a number of reasons for the limited participation in these early demonstrations. First of all, the Vietnam War did not exactly disturb university life. Although the average age of a Vietnam soldier was only 19, he was a 19-year-old African American. Very few African Americans were enrolled in 1960s universities, and the federal government sponsored a *student deferment* program as well.

Although there were many who pointed out the social class inequities of student deferments, there were few SDS activists who were in favor of seeing it go. Lyndon Johnson even worried that the end of the deferments, and the mass drafting of white middle-class university students, would accelerate the growth of antiwar protests against his administration.

Jarhead Jargon

Any male student in an institution of higher learning could apply for **student deferment** status in the 1960s. By maintaining a B to B-plus average or above in his studies, he was spared from a military draft system that, most likely, would quickly send him to Vietnam.

Ask Saigon Sally

The first SDS-organized antiwar protest in Washington, D.C., took place in April 1965. Some 20,000 people were involved in the march, and its focus was on resistance to the draft.

But there were veteran SDS organizers, like Mark Rudd, who insisted that the SDS take a national stand on the issue. The end of the student deferments, he argued, would eventually bring white antiwar protestors closer to black civil rights activists. If they joined together, it would create a more powerful movement, he believed, especially if they also tried to link up with interested labor union locals. This kind of student organization/labor union alliance was a classic scenario for a communist-like revolution, and Rudd dreamed of the downfall of the "racist regime" in Washington.

Of Weathermen and Hippies

Because few wanted to march with Rudd on a more violent course of action, Rudd marched away from the SDS and founded his own Weathermen revolutionary group. It had little social impact, but it stimulated a grand debate in the country over whether America's best and brightest were going to continue the capitalist dream or not.

Shell Shock

The Weathermen grew out of the SDS "War Council" of March 1969 in Austin, Texas. Vowing to lead an "armed struggle" against the federal government, their 600 adherents preferred bombings and arson as a means of antiwar protest. Predominantly white and upper middle class, these radicals hoped to convince 18- to 25-year-olds to join their cause and create a new counterculture opposed to imperialism and racism. In reality, most Americans viewed them as a criminal organization, particularly after their destructive "Days of Rage" antiwar demonstration of October 1969 in downtown Chicago.

The United States had never seen so much commotion in its universities during a time of war. Thanks to the construction of statewide university systems in the 1950s, there were more people studying full time than ever before. Their concerns had never been heard until the Vietnam antiwar movement hit the streets.

Meanwhile, the antiwar movement's biggest enemy was good old-fashioned apathy. Many young people simply wanted to go to school, get a job, and raise a family. Others rejected both the family values route and the New Left lure. Known as the counterculture, or *hippies,* some white middle-class youths tried to "drop out" of the American mainstream all together.

Jarhead Jargon

Characterized by their long hair, casual drug use, love of rock music, and promiscuity, the **hippies** were a social phenomenon of the late 1960s and early 1970s. Usually born into comfortable white middle-class families, these young Americans rejected their parents' values and questioned a government and society that encouraged their support of the Vietnam War. Many so-called mainstream Americans shared the hippies' revulsion for the war, but had little use for their lifestyle.

In love with rock music, and wearing a seemingly required uniform of torn blue jeans, beads, and long hair, some sons and daughters of the comfortable preferred drugs, booze, and sex to the usual social responsibilities. This "drop out" craze was usually as temporary as it was personally destructive. Again, the press was fascinated by the counterculture, making the hippie life both reviled and romantic depending on one's point of view. It was also quite confusing. The press and public opinion assumed that a counterculture youth was also an antiwar protestor. This was rarely the case, for the last thing Hayden or Rudd needed was an incoherent, drugged-out protestor on the national news. They would have preferred a loyal activist, and he or she would never be found in a hippie commune. As the war dragged on, tired, disgusted Americans had no problem embracing a certain antiwar opinion, but they rarely endorsed the lifestyle and approach of the hippies and antiwar activists.

Shell Shock

The best-organized antiwar groups were associated with churches. The Friends Services Committee (a Quaker organization), the multifaith Clergy and Laymen Concerned About Vietnam (CALCAV), and the Catholic Peace Fellowship represented some of the well-funded and visible ones.

Fulbright vs. Johnson

You didn't have to be a 19-year-old student to be an antiwar demonstrator. Throughout the 1965–66 Christmas and New Year's holidays, congressmen heard a lot about their electorate's Vietnam concerns. None of the voters seemed satisfied with what was going on in Vietnam, and even congressmen on top security-classified committees, such as Armed Services or Foreign Relations, knew what was happening. The Tonkin Gulf Resolution had become an embarrassment for a lot of congressmen; most of the answers to Vietnam questions were in the White House. Legally, Johnson did not have to be candid with Congress, and he rarely was.

To Senator William Fulbright, the chair of the Senate Foreign Relations Committee, an old battle had raised its ugly head. What was more important in a democracy: the peoples' First Amendment right to know, or the president's definitions of executive privilege and national security priorities? Be it in the 1940s or now, in his twilight years of government service, Fulbright tried to side with the First Amendment.

Fulbright had voted "yes" on the Tonkin Gulf Resolution, and would regret it to his dying day. The presidency had gained too much power because of it, and he had helped to let it happen. But Fulbright's new anti-executive privilege position did not mean he now despised the presidency. Even though Johnson would deride him as Senator "Halfbright," Fulbright thought the office deserved a considerable degree of respect. If that office was occupied by a fellow Democrat, a certain political loyalty was due as well.

Tales from the Front

From 1967 to 1969, Lionel Rosenblatt and Craig Johnstone worked in the U.S. pacification program in South Vietnam. Their careers ended early when both men left their posts, against orders, and flew their own helicopter mission to rescue several South Vietnamese friends and colleagues who faced imminent death during a North Vietnamese offensive. Their mission was successful.

In February 1966, Fulbright organized a public Congressional hearing on the Vietnam War. All the senior cabinet members of the Johnson administration were called to testify. President Johnson was not even asked. Specific questions were raised about strategy, tactics, expense, and future planning. Every session was televised, a rare event. In these years before C-SPAN, television was regarded as an "intrusion" into the daily business of Congress. But 100 or more Americans were dying in Vietnam every week, and the people, Fulbright said, deserved to know why. Over 385,000 U.S. troops were in Vietnam by the end of 1966, and nearly 6,500 had been killed since the beginning of the war.

To counter what he considered Fulbright's public relations offensive, Johnson took off for Honolulu and a special Vietnam summit. He expected the world press to follow him there and abandon the Fulbright hearings accordingly. That didn't happen. Fulbright's hearings were newsworthy. Johnson's gabfest with Ky, Thieu, and Westmoreland, by comparison, was more of the same old stuff.

Nothing much happened in Honolulu. Johnson and Westmoreland agreed that more U.S. troops must be sent to Vietnam, but that had been expected because there had been nothing happening to suggest additional troop requests would be denied. Johnson wanted to see total victory in 1966—that had been expected as well. One thing that had not been expected was Johnson's extravagant praise of Ky as a great and wonderful leader, and that was a mistake.

Ky interpreted Johnson's praise as an endorsement of his leadership no matter what he did. Shortly after he returned home, Ky went after his political enemies. The new political purge prompted Buddhist riots and even an attempted military coup against him. As always, the coup attempt was covered extensively by the American media, and Ky managed to survive this most serious attempt ever against his government.

Fulbright's hearings looked noble to many, and it annoyed Johnson to no end. Writing a long "open letter" to *The New York Times,* Johnson had urged good, loyal Americans not to watch the televised hearings. The only people who would benefit from a free and easy discussion of Vietnam policy specifics, he argued, would be the North Vietnamese. His cabinet took its cue from there. They told Fulbright's committee very little about Vietnam policy-making or simply refused to answer any questions at all.

Ask Saigon Sally

Edward Lansdale returned to Vietnam in the mid-1960s after several years away from the action. He continued to argue for a strong counterinsurgency role on the part of the ARVN. In short, he wanted the South Vietnamese to carry the brunt of the war.

Ask Saigon Sally

Secretary of State Rusk did not follow President Johnson to the Honolulu conference. Carrying the burden of Vietnam policy-making to the Fulbright hearings, Rusk offered historical analyses and interesting personal opinions. He avoided discussing any security information.

To Americans hoping to learn some military details, the Fulbright hearings were disappointing. Of course, in some communities, viewers were lucky to see them at all. Responding to the president's call for loyalty and patriotism, some TV network affiliates, like Milwaukee's CBS station, WISN, refused to broadcast the hearings. WISN showed *I Love Lucy* reruns for hours on end. Some Milwaukeeans joked that the North Vietnamese should be shown the same thing. They'd break under the torture and surrender in a heartbeat.

The Fulbright hearings added to the Johnson administration's credibility gap problems. Average Americans wondered why the White House refused to answer simple queries about the progress of the war, and others now worried that the war might last many, many years. Still others wanted to trust the Johnson administration's promises of inevitable victory, but the unanswered questions about battlefield performance and goals were disturbing. Fulbright raised a certain "reasonable doubt" in the public mind, and it would not disappear until the boys came home.

Senator William Fulbright and President Lyndon Johnson discuss their Vietnam differences.

Lyndon Baines Johnson Library, Austin, Texas.

Endless War

In December 1965, the Twelfth Plenum met in North Vietnam to discuss 1966 strategies. U.S. troop strength had reached 200,000 in South Vietnam, and Westmoreland was bragging to the press about great offensives to come. The Plenum agreed that North Vietnamese victory was inevitable thanks to the weakness of the Saigon regime and, perhaps, because blind trust in Lyndon Johnson was on the wane in the United States. Once again, the North Vietnamese concluded that caution was important, but a well-planned attack or two should not be ruled out. Heavy communist casualties or not, the Americans needed to be taught that determination would always win over technology and sheer numbers of men.

Without question, these were patriotic words, and Westmoreland did indeed test North Vietnamese determination. During the first six months of 1966, U.S. troops virtually destroyed the area surrounding Saigon. The countryside was devastated to deprive the enemy of cover, and more villages than ever before were relocated to controlled hamlets.

Ask Saigon Sally

General Westmoreland's early 1966 strategy had two goals. Operation ATTLEBORO would build a defensive corridor around Saigon while simultaneously destroying enemy hideouts. Then, all infiltration routes from Laos to South Vietnam were to be blocked. None of this succeeded.

Throughout Westmoreland's fast-moving work in early 1966, the United States and the Saigon regime lost more support from the exhausted South Vietnamese people. Even more Americans would be fed up, too. The boys, as always, would not be home for Christmas.

The Least You Need To Know

➤ Myth and legend surround the impact of the antiwar movement.

➤ The antiwar movement was a complex and struggling one.

➤ The SDS added an element of organization to student-led demonstrations.

➤ The Fulbright hearings sought answers to Vietnam War problems.

➤ The Honolulu conference was meant to distract public attention from the Fulbright hearings.

Chapter 19

The Art of Lying

In This Chapter

➤ I love an adventure

➤ Showmanship is everything

➤ The truth is missing in action

➤ The United States goes into denial

➤ The decisive battle looms

Technology lost its luster in 1967. Even James Bond looked tired. *You Only Live Twice*, Sean Connery's fifth filmed adventure as James Bond, had plenty of new gadgets and paying viewers, but the critics said it was boring. Technology was boring. Bond was boring. And even Connery had had enough. He stunned his fans with the announcement that, for the moment, he sought more challenging film roles.

On television, *The Man From U.N.C.L.E.* cried uncle thanks to low ratings. Even *I Spy* went through a great transformation. Once filmed on location next door to the Vietnam War in Hong Kong or Japan, *I Spy* had been the "in" NBC hit of 1965 and 1966. Its young heroes, Kelly Robinson and Alexander Scott (played by Robert Culp and Bill Cosby), were optimistic, wise-cracking Cold Warriors who killed Asian commies and loved it week after week.

I Spy's Far East adventures were sponsored by Milwaukee's Schlitz beer company, which held the majority beer concession contracts for the U.S. military in South Vietnam. Their "Schlitz: Milwaukee and the World" commercials were filmed where

Tales from the Front

By the end of 1967, over 485,000 U.S. troops were in Vietnam, and 16,021 had been killed in action. In July 1967, some $20 billion dollars had been budgeted for the war, but Congress accurately estimated that it would take $6 billion simply to maintain the military effort there. The U.S. economy would soon be a casualty of the war, too.

Ask Saigon Sally

Antiwar slogans became more biting in 1967. "Hey, hey, LBJ, how many kids did you kill today?" replaced "Ho, Ho, Ho Chi Minh, the NLF is gonna win."

I Spy was filmed, and in 1965 and 1966, these 30-second spots implied that, just as most Asians wanted to be hip and cool like Kelly Robinson and Alexander Scott, most Asians lusted for Schlitz beer, too. But enough was enough in 1967. The Vietnam War just wasn't fun anymore, and TV viewers now equated the whole Asian/Pacific neighborhood with misery and death. *I Spy* abandoned its exotic Far East locales. Its heroes lost their optimism. The bad guys became crooks instead of commies, and the wisecracks were substituted now and then for serious comments about domestic U.S. troubles. The show was canceled. Canceling Vietnam was not that easy.

Hubert's "Great Adventure"

In a series of speeches that he would later very much regret, 1964 vice-presidential candidate Hubert H. Humphrey insisted that the Vietnam War was America's "greatest adventure of the twentieth century." Thanks to his incredible faith in the power of a generous government, and his own upbeat speaking style, the press called Humphrey "the Happy Warrior."

Bright, tireless, and a dedicated New Dealer, Humphrey had a photographic memory. He was able to pick a face from years ago out of a crowd, sometimes add the correct name to that face, and then connect present to past in an amazing display of ad lib politicking. A favorite at white working-class watering holes and union locals where back-slapping politics was always welcomed, Humphrey was admired by African Americans as well. In the late 1940s, Humphrey, then the mayor of Minneapolis, had called for a civil rights plank in the 1948 Democratic party convention platform. His commitment to civil rights reform split the Democratic Party, but he won the support of African Americans everywhere and, split or no split, the Democrats kept the White House that year.

Humphrey was a winner, and Johnson welcomed him to the White House because of it. Like Johnson, the vice president believed in the Franklin Roosevelt precedent of keeping domestic policy-making always ahead of foreign affairs; however, from the beginning, he also thought that too much time, money, and effort was being spent on Vietnam.

Whereas Johnson thought Vietnam and his domestic agenda were always well in hand at best, or temporarily compromised at worst, Humphrey never saw it that way. Civil rights, medical care, transportation, education, and urban renewal were all suffering because of the president's "tunnel vision" in Vietnam, he said privately. He even believed that Johnson did not give enough support to the First Lady and her interest in rescuing the environment. And the president knew he was saying these things.

Humphrey would be banned from most cabinet discussions on Vietnam. To Johnson, the Vice President was not a team player. It was a sad irony. Like Johnson, Humphrey considered the Democratic Party his second home. Private comments did not have to translate into public policy, particularly if those comments might harm the Party.

Ask Saigon Sally

Nicknamed "Lady Bird" since childhood, Claudia Johnson, the First Lady, was a tough politician in her own right who once managed her husband's congressional office while he was away during World War II.

Although shut out and ignored, Humphrey tried to prove his loyalty to the president and the Democratic Party by making rousing speeches in favor of the Vietnam War. Because Johnson sometimes felt uneasy in a press conference, Humphrey often became the point man with the press. Many Americans learned about the White House's position on Vietnam through a Humphrey statement to Walter Cronkite. Very few knew how he truly felt, and he masked those feelings well. His later admission of doubts and concerns would come too little and too late during his own 1968 bid for the White House.

The Government Has Two Faces

In 1967, the differences between U.S. public and private policy became especially glaring. General Westmoreland helped illustrate the point. During early 1967, the general returned to Washington for another round of troop requests. He won the White House's approval, but Congress was restless. In what amounted to the best speech of his career, Westmoreland addressed a joint session of Congress. All was well in Vietnam, he said. The ARVN was becoming a great military force, U.S. troops were enthusiastic and dedicated to their mission, and the enemy was on the run. The only problem involved domestic U.S. opinion, he concluded.

Westmoreland on Capitol Hill

Westmoreland cut a dashing figure, and the congressmen couldn't remember the last time a military man had made such a grand impression on Capitol Hill. But Fulbright and others couldn't have cared less about the general's speaking style and powers of

205

persuasion. They still doubted the entire Vietnam policy that he represented, and they wondered why his rosy picture differed so dramatically from the one that they saw on the evening news.

In top-secret White House discussions, Westmoreland admitted that the Ho Chi Minh Trail remained an effective highway of enemy transportation. Years of bombing had made little difference. He also said that total U.S. victory might not be achieved for several years, but more troops and bombing might help.

General William Westmoreland briefs President Johnson and his advisors in the White House Cabinet Room (1967).

Lyndon Baines Johnson Library, Austin, Texas, and photographer Franck Wolfe.

Jarhead Jargon

The term **scorched earth** has been used to describe one opponent's effort to lay waste to the territory of another. Meant to break an enemy's will to fight as well as deprive him of anything and everything in a given area, scorched earth can be employed by both an attacking army and a retreating army.

Secretary McNamara was disturbed by the news, and it only got worse. He learned that the major cities of North Vietnam had been largely evacuated, and that the enemy was keeping its war industries alive in scattered countryside locations. This made them hard to find, much less bomb. Meanwhile, the Ho Chi Minh Trail remained only one way to infiltrate into South Vietnam. The nation's borders were swollen with Vietcong. Westmoreland proposed huge, sweeping, and *scorched earth* offensives in concentrated areas near Saigon and the Laos/Cambodian borders. These piecemeal offensives, he believed, might slowly liberate the country.

A National Election

Offensives or no offensives, the battlefield situation was always connected to the fate of the South Vietnamese government. Johnson wanted some sort of democratic statement from the Saigon regime before the end of 1967. Meeting with Ky on Guam in March 1967, Johnson suggested that a national election would be a good way to celebrate his own August birthday.

Ky went home to announce a general election, and Johnson sent off nearly two dozen congressmen, businessmen, and clergy to act as official observers. America was winning the war, he said, and South Vietnam was soon to move from a corrupt, dictatorial, anticommunist regime to an American-like democracy. Again the truth remained elusive here.

For the South Vietnamese, the 1967 election was a trying time. The Vietcong insisted on a nationwide boycott, and marked for death many who did indeed vote. The Saigon regime regarded apathy or refusals to vote as tantamount to treason and Vietcong membership. South Vietnamese citizens were required to hold identity cards, and those cards would be hole-punched to indicate their participation in the vote. As always, the average South Vietnamese was caught in the middle of a power play, and their very lives seemed irrelevant to the players.

Nguyen Van Thieu, a figurehead in the Ky-run government, was expected to do well in the voting for chief of state, but did not. Behind the scenes, he attempted to put together a new military regime with Ky kept on as an important policy-maker, but none of this worked. Rigged voting was commonplace, yet a total unknown emerged as a serious challenger to the status quo.

Shell Shock

In 1967, the Johnson administration debated stationing huge numbers of U.S. troops at the seventeenth parallel to halt enemy infiltration. This was rejected on the grounds that the North Vietnamese would just go around them anyway.

Jarhead Jargon

Credibility gap refers to the disparity between official White House and Saigon regime statements about the progress of the war versus the facts reported by the news media and others in Vietnam.

Advocating a negotiated settlement with the Vietcong, lawyer Truong Dinh Dzu did quite well in the final tally. But Thieu had him arrested for corruption, and the Saigon regime went about its usual business. Johnson, on the other hand, could claim that democracy had spoken in South Vietnam. Those claims once again differed from the press accounts. The *CBS Evening News* covered the South Vietnam election from start to finish, and saw nothing but dictatorship, violence, and a *credibility gap* on display. Secretary McNamara urged Americans to discount these reports, but public opinion was not easily silenced anymore.

Winning and Losing at the Same Time

On the battlefield, 1967 began with Operations CEDAR FALLS and JUNCTION CITY. And it was an old battlefield. Westmoreland had tried to safeguard the area known as the Iron Triangle just north of Saigon only weeks before. This time, he threw everything he had into the Iron Triangle, a headquarters area for Vietcong activity. For symbolic reasons alone, Westmoreland hoped to destroy that headquarters along with the enemy's belief that there was a safe haven in South Vietnam.

As usual, the media went along for the ride, and they witnessed the devastation of a 55-square-mile area, total destruction of villages, and the end of a long-lasting underground tunnel network for the Vietcong. Nevertheless, almost immediately after his forces pulled back from their successful offensive, the enemy moved in again. Instead of going back for more, Westmoreland went after the alleged "Vietcong province" of South Vietnam—Tay Ninh, near the Cambodian border. This was the JUNCTION CITY campaign, and casualty figures were high for both sides. The U.S. and ARVN losses were 282 killed and 1,576 wounded, while the communists suffered 2,728 killed and even more wounded. Most of the Vietcong escaped into neutral Cambodia, and the results of both CEDAR FALLS and JUNCTION CITY were disappointing to Westmoreland.

"On the Run"

Publicly, Westmoreland proclaimed a smashing victory. The enemy was on the run, and the rest of the year would be a matter of relentless American pursuit. Privately, Westmoreland knew better, and he worried about the enemy's amazing ability to disperse, patiently regroup, and resume the fight on their own guerrilla warfare terms.

Jarhead Jargon

Because so many areas of South Vietnam had been evacuated of local residents, what they left behind was proclaimed **free-fire zones.** The U.S. military, sometimes offering warnings and sometimes not, would shoot at anything that moved in the free-fire zones.

Operation RANCH HAND was one way to solve the problem, and this U.S. defoliation campaign dated back to 1962. Some 20 percent of South Vietnam deemed to be existing cover for enemy action was defoliated with a variety of chemicals. As always, technology was supposed to make a critical difference here. Strategically, this type of chemical warfare was also expected to create a more familiar European-like battlefield. In short, there would be the U.S. bases versus the Vietcong living on the edge of destroyed jungles and countryside. With battle lines more clearly drawn, Westmoreland expected to prevail.

Free-fire zones were established in the effort to keep the American and Vietcong battle lines clear and distinct. But full evacuations of people off ancestral land, as well as static battle lines, were impossible to achieve. The U.S. press reported horrible atrocities committed under free-fire zone justification.

Tales from the Front

Defoliation had three major goals. One involved depriving the enemy of jungle growth for cover, a second involved destroying crops that he could use for food, and the third involved the destruction of jungle growth near the perimeter of U.S. bases. The preferred herbicides to do the job were Agent Orange and Agent White. Both dried out foliage. Leaves dropped off several weeks after the first spraying application (usually by specially equipped C–123 aircraft), and they would not reappear for four to six months. Oil-soluble Agent Orange was preferred during the rainy season, for it would not wash away and killed waxy leaves. It was also highly toxic to man and beast, and some mangrove forests, for instance, did not redevelop until the 1980s and 1990s.

Shell Shock

Free-fire zones produced over 300,000 South Vietnamese civilian casualties by 1968. Villagers, forcibly removed from their ancestral homes by U.S. and ARVN troops, often escaped their provided "secure hamlets" to their former homes. Immediately labeled enemy sympathizers, all "returnees" were killed. Due to the negative press at home, the U.S. military changed the name of this policy to "specified strike zones" in 1965, but killing civilians who entered a declared zone remained standard policy to 1968.

Meanwhile, Westmoreland's troops found it increasingly difficult to distinguish between free-fire zone guidelines in one area versus no free-fire zone killing in another. If America was in Vietnam to rescue people, it had lost its way at some point.

Seesaw Campaigns

Westmoreland's troops found themselves repeatedly returning to areas they had already "liberated." Each back-and-forth campaign had its own code name, and

Ask Saigon Sally

The free-fire zone galvanized the antiwar movement, and a specific anti–free-fire zone march of academics and students was organized and led in Washington, D.C., in April 1967.

Shell Shock

In the 1967 U.S.-U.S.S.R.-G.B. peace proposal, the Americans and the North Vietnamese, without telling the press, would begin a slow military withdrawal after their peace talks began. No one could agree when a U.S. bombing halt should be announced or how the end of North Vietnamese infiltration should be monitored.

1967 saw so many that the army almost ran out of clever labels for them. In Binh Dinh province alone, a longtime Vietcong hangout, there were Operations MASHER, WHITE WING, and PERSHING. After all these seesaw campaigns, the U.S. military could claim to have taken Binh Dinh's evacuated towns, but little else. But the U.S. flag flying from a town center could also suggest U.S. victory and success, and this was the point most often raised by Westmoreland's command and the U.S. Embassy. The enemy, they said, had been routed into the countryside. In reality, it was a countryside the enemy controlled, and no one was in a rout.

To Senator John Stennis (Democrat, Mississippi) on the Senate Armed Services Committee, strong supporters of the war like himself needed a clear picture of the battle scene. What was really going on? Stennis represented the other side of the story. If the war was going as badly as the press reported, he wanted Johnson to escalate further, bomb more, and destroy the Vietcong before the 1968 election. Johnson was more interested in accommodating him than those congressmen interested in ending the war, for he still believed that a military withdrawal would destroy his presidency and America's anticommunist credentials.

Meanwhile, a peace deal was still possible.

In 1967, Prime Minister Harold Wilson of Great Britain tried to get such a deal going, whereby the Soviets would offer a special plan to Ho Chi Minh. Ho was supposed to stop sending men and supplies south and Johnson was supposed to halt the bombing of North Vietnam. Wilson and Johnson fought over the proper wording of the proposal.

The Soviets could not guarantee anything from the feisty North Vietnamese, and their interest in it all involved their own bizarre plan to draw a Western alliance around China. The latter had embarked on a wild-eyed, bloodthirsty "Cultural Revolution" that twisted almost every communist doctrine to keep Mao Tse-tung in unassailable power.

None of this planning and scheming ever worked, and Johnson stayed his military course. But he still liked the idea of an "honorable peace" by the 1968 election. Time was running out.

Victory Nears?

Facing more than a half-million Vietcong in the field, Westmoreland needed more troops. A conservative estimate of just under 680,000 men would do the trick over the next few years, Westmoreland argued. If he agreed, Johnson would have to escalate the drafting procedure as well as mobilize all reserve units. The antiwar movement, on the eve of the 1968 presidential primaries, would have a fit and so would Congress. Johnson told Westmoreland to make do with roughly 540,000 men, although the general urged Johnson to come up with some clever way to send the troops he needed and hide it from the press and the Congress.

Things were getting uncomfortable for Johnson. Looking for backup, the president called together the "Wise Men" again, invited old and new staffers to sit in, and held a grand November 1967 summit.

Nothing had changed. If Johnson widened the war to include a massive World War II–like invasion of North Vietnam, the threat of Soviet involvement and World War III always lingered. If Johnson withdrew all U.S. forces, the communists would launch offensives around the world, and the voters, weaned on endless anticommunist rhetoric, would turn the Democrats out of office for years and years to come. So there was no choice but to send Westmoreland more troops and hope for the best.

George Ball, lucky to be invited to this gathering, offered his usual nay-saying advice. This time, he said angrily, old men were a bit too willing to send young men to their deaths. His comment was deemed unwise by the "Wise Men."

But 1967 did not go out with a bang. Combat reports and casualty figures were low. Westmoreland's command took advantage of the quiet to announce that the enemy was exhausted and that the war would soon be over. It was one of the grander public relations mistakes of the war. Westmoreland knew the enemy was up to something, and he hoped it was a grand go-for-broke attack. This time, he assured his staff, America would not be losing "any Dienbienphu."

Ask Saigon Sally

During the mid- and late 1960s, U.S. bombs dropped on North Vietnam equaled 300 pounds of explosives for every person living there. That also meant more than 50,000 killed in the bombing raids.

Ask Saigon Sally

When U.S. bombing of the Ho Chi Minh Trail intensified in 1967, the North Vietnamese tried shipping by sea. The Americans sank more than 1,400 ships, forcing Hanoi to stress the Ho Chi Minh Trail route.

The Least You Need to Know

➤ Vice President Humphrey supported the war in public but opposed it in private.

➤ The differences between government and press reports on battlefield conditions became most obvious by 1967.

➤ The South Vietnamese general election of 1967 did not usher in a new era of democracy.

➤ General Westmoreland launched a number of offensives during 1967, but the Vietcong continued to gain strength.

➤ Johnson's advisors continued to endorse his Vietnam policy.

Chapter 20

The Tet Offensive

In This Chapter

➤ Minds begin to change

➤ Khe Sanh and Dienbienphu are the same place

➤ Westmoreland wins and is sent to his room

➤ What does Tet mean anyway?

➤ Lyndon Johnson works on his retirement plan

At five feet three inches, and rather wide of girth, Congressman Clement Zablocki was lost in a land of political giants. A quiet maneuverer who represented his largely Polish American Milwaukee district well, Zablocki was the chairman of the House of Representatives Foreign Affairs Committee throughout much of the Vietnam War. Johnson called him his "little guy in the House," and there was never any doubt that Zablocki was a loyal Democrat. His district consisted of hard-working blue-collar types, and many of its young men had escaped the struggles of Milwaukee's south side only to discover the horrors of Vietnam.

Zablocki had made many a pro-Johnson, pro-Vietnam speech in the mid-1960s. He rubber-stamped the president's foreign policy legislation, and he touted the values of military life, duty, and patriotism. But he hated the Vietnam War. Because of Vietnam, Zablocki warned Johnson that the House might not always be there to approve his domestic legislation. Johnson rarely took such threats seriously until the 1968 Tet Offensive.

Ask Saigon Sally

More than 40,000 North Vietnamese troops had moved into South Vietnam's Quang Tri province during the late fall of 1967. Westmoreland launched Opera-tion NIAGRA to halt their advance, constituting, some say, the first real shots fired in the Tet Offensive.

During Tet, Zablocki faced quite a dilemma. He was appalled at the news reports, disgusted with Johnson's handling of the war, and preferred an immediate end to his nation's role in Vietnam. On the other hand, his constituency did not want America running out of Vietnam over the graves of their loved ones. After all the effort, and all the lives lost, the Vietnam War had been for nothing?

Zablocki had a hard time balancing his conscience with his duty to represent the concerns of his district. But he came up with a so-called Tet Offensive compromise. He told the White House that his powerful Committee would not interfere in Vietnam policy-making, but once the war was over, the presidency, he vowed, would never have Tonkin Gulf Resolution–like powers again.

Johnson laughed him off, and Richard Nixon would follow his example. Little Clement would never take on the White House, they concluded. But Tet had changed a lot of people's thinking. Some even called it the turning point of the Vietnam War. And Representative Zablocki kept his word. His War Powers Act, passed shortly after all U.S. troops were home from Vietnam, proclaimed the Tonkin Gulf Resolution unconstitutional.

The Big "Showdown"

To many traditional military historians, the first signs of weariness, fatigue, and frustration for one of the sides in a war can be seen in its desire for a great decisive battle. Victory in that battle is sought, of course, but there is also a strong interest in simply ending the misery, struggle, and pain. The French went through this soul-searching and wringing of hands back in 1954. It was America's turn in late 1967.

In November 1967, U.S. intelligence reports confirmed heavy travel on the Ho Chi Minh Trail. Several North Vietnamese divisions were being positioned near Khe Sanh in northern Quang Tri province. Khe Sanh suddenly took on a certain Dienbienphu significance to the Johnson team. The place had strategic significance for sure, but it was its symbolic importance that interested the White House.

Given all the reports of a huge enemy buildup going on, both Westmoreland and Johnson saw the possibility of a great breakthrough for the U.S. military. From Saratoga in the American Revolution to Midway and Normandy in World War II, there had been magnificent, earth-shattering successes in America's wars. Khe Sanh suggested the same possibility to Johnson and Westmoreland.

Tales from the Front

In 1967, U.S. Army Sergeant Bryant E. Middleton left his long-range reconnaissance unit to become an advisor to pro–U.S. Montagnard tribesmen and troops. Operating in areas where no other American troops were authorized to go, Middleton and his Montagnard troops scouted the Ia Drang Valley and Chu Pong Mountains. Middleton wore camouflage face paint and a tiger-stripe uniform without any indication of rank, and his unit saw some of the most vicious fighting of the war. Returning home a disabled veteran with the rank of Captain, Middleton is presently completing his second master's degree and hopes to work with the Veterans Administration someday.

To Johnson, it couldn't have come at a better time. The New Hampshire primary in the 1968 election was only weeks away. After a grand victory on the battlefield, the next step would be a quick peace. All of this would be fresh on the minds of New Hampshire voters and everyone else in 1968. The Great Society would be secure, and the Vietnam struggle would be over.

To Westmoreland, the enemy was finally doing what he wanted them to do. In his view, they didn't have a chance in a head-to-head confrontation with his boys in the field. The enemy's divisions would be beaten back, their reinforcements cut to pieces, and U.S. bases held secure. Khe Sanh would be the center of the drama, and Westmoreland banked that the North Vietnamese saw the U.S. Marines stationed at Khe Sanh in the same light as they had seen French troops in Dienbienphu 14 years earlier. Confident that his technology and firepower would prevail, Westmoreland was ready to inflict the kind of damage on the Vietnamese that they had inflicted on the French at the end of the Franco-Vietnamese War. He was even a little cocky about it all.

Ask Saigon Sally

During the Tet Offensive, 13 of the 16 provincial capitals of the Mekong Delta were attacked by the Vietcong, making a mockery of the United States and the ARVN's touted pacification program there.

Although he offered no hints or details to the press about an enemy buildup, Westmoreland did offer cryptic, boisterous comments about how his men were ready to defeat all comers. In fact, he said that he welcomed a "showdown," for then the boys would be home soon to celebrate their total victory.

Tales from the Front

There were a series of battles for Khe Sanh and its surrounding hills between January and March 1968. Three thousand Marines defended the base camp and another 3,000 were stationed on the four nearby hills. Fighting was especially fierce on the outlying hills, including hand-to-hand combat that left the Marine dead unburied for over a month. While the Marine casualties numbered in the hundreds, the estimates for enemy dead numbered as high as 15,000. Yet, only 1,600 enemy bodies were actually found.

Shell Shock

The best conservative estimate of noncombatants murdered in Hue is estimated at 3,000. Costing them 5,000 lives, it took three weeks for American and South Vietnamese forces to regain control of Hue.

America Is Surprised

On January 21, 1968, the North Vietnamese began to shell the marines at Khe Sanh. It was a relentless bombardment and a rerun of the opening salvos against Dienbienphu. While the White House waited for the enemy ground troops to attack, strange and confused reports flooded the Oval Office about wild, horrific Vietcong attacks on just about every town and government post in South Vietnam. Those attacks came as a complete surprise to both Washington and Saigon.

At first Westmoreland believed that the only significant attack underway was against Khe Sanh. As the days passed, that belief was shattered. The North Vietnamese attack on the old, stately imperial city of Hue was especially vicious. They took few prisoners, and house-to-house executions of innocent families were more common than not. Hanoi later insisted that these thousands of murders were justified during confused civil war conditions, but one of the major characteristics of the Tet Offensive was horror for the sake of horror.

At first, the defense of Hue was largely maintained by the ARVN, for Westmoreland still believed that Khe Sanh was the enemy's top objective. Even after he realized that the Tet Offensive was more than just Khe Sanh, he underestimated the huge enemy force in the Hue area. Detachments of the U.S. Army's First Cavalry Division was sent to rescue the struggling ARVN forces, but the 5th Marines and more ARVN troops were soon needed. Meanwhile, 116,000 of the town's 140,000 residents were now homeless.

As for the objectives of General Giap and his colleagues, the jury is still out. Offering different versions of the Tet Offensive planning process over the years, Giap is partially to blame for the problem. But the basic facts are clear. The lunar new year holiday of Tet was selected as the best time to attack. The element of surprise was guaranteed; it was Vietnamese tradition to lay low during the usual combination of holiday obligations and inclement weather. Also, Hanoi had once promised not to disrupt Tet.

Shell Shock

Tet was the most important holiday in Vietnam, and General Giap's holiday attack plan was a masterpiece of deception. Even his field commanders were not told the exact timing of the attack until the last moment, and NVA commanders in charge of bloody attacks against the Americans near the North Vietnamese border believed that they were at the center of the Tet Offensive. But the fall of Saigon was the primary goal.

It is also known that the North Vietnamese hoped to create mass confusion in the American ranks across South Vietnam; this demonstration of communist power was supposed to stimulate American desertions and even mutiny. If lucky, these fast-moving events would encourage the Johnson administration to rethink its position and then withdraw its troops from Vietnam sooner rather than later.

To these basic facts are added plenty of long-lasting myths and legends. One of the more popular myths suggests that the North Vietnamese deliberately timed the offensive to coincide with the February New Hampshire primary in the United States. Antiwar sentiment, stirred up by America's heavy casualties during Tet, was supposed to defeat Lyndon Johnson and lead directly to a change in U.S. policy. Nevertheless, the New Hampshire primary took place weeks after the Tet Offensive began, and it remains unlikely that North Vietnam's generalship spent much time studying voting trends in places like Nashua or Concord, New Hampshire.

Ask Saigon Sally

Tet Offensive planners hoped to lure most of the Americans into the northern sections of South Vietnam through a series of diversionary attacks. Just south of these diversions, a popular uprising would be encouraged against the Saigon regime.

Another tale involves a North Vietnamese plot to make sure maverick South Vietnamese communists were always the first ones to attack American positions. Encouraged by Hanoi to embrace a sort of banzai-like fanaticism, the South Vietnamese would hurl themselves at the Americans. This would decimate their ranks, putting Hanoi in full control of all the remaining anti-Saigon regime, anti-American efforts in South Vietnam. So, whether the battle was won or lost, Hanoi would be the political top dog when it was over. This is an interesting thesis, but it raises many questions. Given the immediate goal of military victory, why would you want to kill off so many of your supporters?

Tales from the Front

Once described as "size four feet stuffed into size six combat boots," French photo-journalist Catherine Leroy first arrived in Vietnam at the age of 21 in 1967. Photographing battle scenes from the Tet Offensive to the fall of Saigon, Leroy was admired for her "utter fearlessness" by both the press corps and combat veterans. Captured by the NVA in 1968, she even won the permission of her captors to photograph them during a mission. Her photographs stressed the brotherhood between troops rather than the horror of war, and they appeared in the leading news magazines of North America and Europe. She lives in Los Angeles today.

Shell Shock

U.S. casualties in the Tet Offensive numbered 1,100 killed. The ARVN lost 2,300, and some 12,500 civilian deaths were also recorded.

Westmoreland's troops rebounded from the early fake-outs and diversions. Meanwhile, Hanoi's loosely constructed plan failed. There were no mutinies in the American ranks, and the U.S. government did not give up on Vietnam. There was no South Vietnamese popular uprising, and the Saigon regime hung on as usual.

Westmoreland claimed military victory, and he was right. The Vietcong were especially hard hit, and they would never truly recover from the battle. Their killed-in-action estimates ranged from a low of 30,000 to a high of 40,000. On the other hand, this did not mean the end of Vietcong political influence. Most of the U.S./ARVN-controlled hamlets were devastated during Tet. When the survivors returned to their villages, the Vietcong were often there to welcome them. Not since 1965 had the Vietcong the power to influence village life on a national scale.

The Horror Show

Publicly proclaiming victory in late February 1968, Westmoreland said the "enemy was on the ropes." It would soon be much easier to *clear and hold,* he predicted. But

Westmoreland had cried wolf too much, and the American people were fed up. He even spoke of America's great victory in front of the war-torn U.S. Embassy in Saigon. After all these years, many Americans asked, why was the U.S. Embassy a battleground?

On the ever-popular *CBS Evening News,* camera crews recorded the daily misery and endless firefights of a U.S. Marine platoon in Hue. Most of them willingly told the CBS reporters that they had no idea why they were in Vietnam. At the U.S. Embassy, a major target in Saigon during Tet, American TV viewers saw both U.S. troops and pistol-packing embassy bureaucrats shooting it out with Vietcong infiltrators. And at Khe Sanh, those same viewers saw American troops in a hailstorm of artillery fire, unable to do much of anything but keep their heads down and hope for the best.

Memorable quotes emerged from the fray. One American officer was asked by a camera crew why he had just supervised the complete destruction of the village of Ben Tre. He responded that "it became necessary to destroy the town in order to save it."

A disgusted Walter Cronkite broke with his stoic, grandfatherly image and denounced Johnson's Vietnam policy at the end of one his broadcasts. The incident shocked the White House, for he stated plainly that "U.S. policy will not win the war." But most Americans were shocked by the actions of General Nguyen Ngoc Loan, head of the South Vietnamese police, who, in front of the cameras of Associated Press photographer Eddie Adams and an NBC News crew, summarily executed a Vietcong soldier by shooting him in the head. NBC aired an edited version of the execution, and Adams's picture eventually won the Pulitzer Prize.

Jarhead Jargon

The American military's effort to destroy a Vietcong sanctuary and make sure it never becomes one again was called **clear and hold.** It was a tactic easier said than done.

Ask Saigon Sally

In the mid-1970s, General Westmoreland attacked the press for having turned the enemy's military defeat at Tet into a "psychological victory" for them.

Turning Points

To Giap, the Tet Offensive vindicated his approach of long, protracted war. Win or lose, the Americans would be taught a lesson. But according to Johnson's joint chiefs of staff, the real lesson learned was the need for more U.S. troops in Vietnam.

A Saigon fire truck rushes to the scene of a Vietcong terrorist attack during the Tet Offensive.

National Archives Still Pictures Unit, College Park, Maryland.

Shell Shock

Following the Tet Offensive, the U.S. military evacuated Khe Sanh for a more defensible location. After having declared Khe Sanh so important to the progress of the war, the decision to evacuate seriously added to Johnson's credibility problems.

Although they disagreed on specifics, it was generally accepted that more than 200,000 more men were needed in South Vietnam by the end of 1968. U.S.-based reserve units and more draftees were also required. Nearly 486,000 U.S. troops were in Vietnam before the Tet Offensive began.

Because the enemy was capable of mounting a rerun of the Tet Offensive, the new troop arrivals would be used to thwart Tet Offensive II. Even more troops would be sent to U.S. bases elsewhere in the world, a move that was supposed to send a message to all communists everywhere. America might be hurting in Vietnam, but the commitment to anticommunism was stronger than ever.

The request for more men prompted a cabinet-level debate on the Vietnam War. An exhausted and depressed Secretary McNamara left the Johnson administration and was replaced by Clark Clifford. As a junior cabinet member in 1965, Clifford had opposed the Vietnam escalation, but then quickly changed his mind. For three years, he had been a loyal supporter of the war. Now, he insisted on an in-depth analysis of the full Vietnam situation before acting on any escalation request.

Clifford's civilian advisors concluded that more U.S. troops in Vietnam would make little difference, but they supported a modest troop increase to help maintain better security. Search-and-destroy missions should be abandoned, they said. Clifford also supported an end to the bombing of North Vietnam and favored serious peace talks with Hanoi. Secretary of State Rusk backed him up, and even the so-called "Wise Men" agreed that South Vietnam was probably a goner.

Although saddened by the turn of events, Johnson decided that Westmoreland did not need a new army in South Vietnam. Roughly 13,000 new troops were sent there, and Westmoreland was ordered home. He was dubbed the army chief of staff, and General Creighton Abrams replaced him in Saigon.

While some on the Johnson team talked more about *de-escalation* than escalation, Johnson himself advocated only a change in tactics. He disagreed with Clifford's position on a defensive posture for U.S. troops in Vietnam. The military would continue to pressure the communists as they saw fit. But he did agree to the bombing halts and negotiations with the North Vietnamese.

Johnson saw the Tet Offensive as confirmation of a stalemate situation in Vietnam. He expected the combination of communist defeat during Tet, post-Tet U.S. military stabilization, the change in American command, and the bombing halt/negotiations route to make a real difference. The National Security Council even told him that things were not that bad, and the United States would not have to make any concessions in the negotiations with Hanoi.

Ask Saigon Sally

The Wall Street Journal had once represented a solid base of conservative support for the Vietnam War. Editorializing on Tet, its editors concluded that U.S. military policy in Vietnam was now "doomed."

Jarhead Jargon

During its Tet Offensive debates, the Johnson administration disagreed on a working definition of **de-escalation.** Some said it meant pulling out U.S. troops. Others said it meant maintaining current troop strength levels.

Landslide Lyndon Retires

Suffering from heart troubles, Johnson had worried about surviving another full term in office. His bad health report combined with the bad news from Vietnam. The 1968 campaign promised to be a long, dragged-out slugfest, complete with angry antiwar protestors and an unfriendly press. The contrast to 1964 was terribly stark.

Ask Saigon Sally

In March and April 1968, General Abrams launched the largest search-and-destroy mission of the Vietnam War. More than 100,000 U.S. and ARVN troops participated in the action near Saigon.

As the Tet Offensive came to a close, Johnson had even wondered whether he was the problem standing in the way of peace. He was such a hated figure in North Vietnam. Would his willing departure from the White House open the door to a peace accord?

On March 31, 1968, Johnson asked all the television networks for special broadcast time. Having given no reason for it, most everyone assumed he was going to deliver another Vietnam situation report. Instead, he announced the end of his political career. There would be no reelection bid for Lyndon Johnson, and it was an irreversible decision. He said that he would not "seek or accept" the nomination of his Democratic Party.

Hanoi greeted the news as though it were Christmas, New Year's, and every other holiday rolled into one. They had lost on the battlefield in the Tet Offensive, but pulled ahead with a grand political coup. Victory was at hand, they shouted, and they agreed to peace talks with the U.S. government.

The White House was surprised at Hanoi's quick decision, and Johnson even hoped to see a peace before he waved goodbye in January 1969. But the North Vietnamese were far from sincere. They agreed to talk, but agreeing on a peace plan was a different matter. As always, they saw time on their side, for they interpreted the American interest in peace as weakness and defeatism. Victory might be around the corner, but the Americans would never make it easy for them.

The Least You Need to Know

➤ The Tet Offensive changed American minds about the war.

➤ Westmoreland expected victory in a great battle with the North Vietnamese.

➤ The Tet Offensive was a military victory for America and the Saigon regime.

➤ The U.S. military's request for thousands of more troops in Vietnam divided the Johnson administration.

➤ The North Vietnamese viewed both Johnson's retirement and the peace negotiations as a Tet Offensive political victory.

Chapter 21

The Battling Democrats and Campaign '68

In This Chapter

➤ Too young to vote

➤ Professor Eugene to the rescue

➤ Good Democrats, bad Democrats

➤ George Wallace can spoil things

➤ Camelot fades and Hubert gets "Unhappy"

In 1968, it seemed like no two individuals could agree on any issue at all except one. The political commentators for *Time* and *Newsweek,* academics everywhere, and the titans in both the Democratic and Republican Parties all agreed that the 18-to-21-year-old age group in the United States supported great change.

In stark contrast to all of America's previous wars, the average age of the Vietnam veteran was 19. From veterans' benefits to the war itself, the Vietnam veteran had a lot to say and deserved to be heard. The average age of the antiwar protestor was 19 as well. As they marched for peace overseas and justice at home, they shouted that "the whole world is watching." America, they implied, was tottering on the edge of revolutionary change and they were going to push it over that edge.

Too bad 19-year-olds didn't have the right to vote in 1968. It might have helped dreams turn into policies.

Getting "Clean for Gene"

As a professor of English, Eugene McCarthy had always loved poetry. As a devout Catholic, he had admired the wing of his Church that had always championed the good causes of morality and ethics. First elected to Congress in 1948, McCarthy was a master of difficult-to-understand speeches. They always sounded like Sunday sermons to some and poetry lessons to others. More at home discussing political theory than kissing babies, McCarthy was a lone-wolf Democrat in postwar U.S. politics. And Americans loved lone wolves in 1968.

The Rise of McCarthy

During the first two months of 1968, Eugene McCarthy went from obscure congressman to household name. Declaring his candidacy for the Democratic presidential nomination, McCarthy said that he dared to challenge Lyndon Johnson only because of Vietnam. That was nothing new. Exactly one year before, he had denounced the war in a rambling speech that few heard outside of Minneapolis.

Ask Saigon Sally

While both the 1968 New Hampshire primary and the Tet Offensive were in full swing, Westmoreland tabled his final request for 206,000 new troops. The top-secret request was titled Operation COMPLETE VICTORY.

Before he was an announced candidate, his speeches could be quite biting. Insisting that the White House was being run by fools, and that young Americans were dying because of that foolishness, McCarthy spoke in public what George Ball had long said in private. Westmoreland in the early McCarthy speeches was a bad propagandist, whose commander-in-chief had lost all touch with reality.

After he became an announced candidate, the biting speeches ended. Throughout 1967, McCarthy had seen his audiences flinch when he spoke what he thought was the naked truth. And most of those folks in the audience were true believers of his message. If his own supporters cringed at Vietnam straight talk, the rhetoric would have to be adjusted, toned down, and otherwise sanitized for a nationwide audience.

During the 1968 New Hampshire primary, McCarthy talked about Indochina (the old French-invented term for Vietnam, Laos, and Cambodia). Yet everyone knew he was talking about Vietnam. He talked about the American "incursion" there when everyone knew he meant "invasion." And he called for the "end of Saigon, USA," when everyone knew he meant a U.S. military withdrawal. That made him a *"dove"* (opponent to the war) versus a *"hawk"* (a supporter of the war). Politics married poetry in the McCarthy campaign.

Jarhead Jargon

The term **hawk** dates back to the Congressional "War Hawks" of 1810–1812 who favored a war with Britain in the name of honor, pride, and a deep hatred for anything English. But according to Kathleen Thompson Hill and Gerald Hill's *The Real Life Dictionary of American Politics* (Los Angeles: General Publishing Group, 1994), the term **dove** is a product of 1967–1968 Vietnam War debates, and refers to the desire for a peaceful, non-violent foreign policy. Its origin is not attributed to one person directly, such as Eugene McCarthy.

Americans had become disgusted with the endless reports of death and misery from hard-to-pronounce places in tiny Vietnam. Many didn't even want to hear the names of those places anymore, and McCarthy obliged them. Because he was challenging his party's mainstream politics and because of his oddball style, the political commentators and experts categorized McCarthy a *political stalking horse*. In the early days of the New Hampshire primary, McCarthy did not deny this categorization. He said that he wanted to be the moral conscience of the Democratic Party in the 1968 election. In short, he expected to lose big time, but wanted to make a point. Tet changed all that.

Jarhead Jargon

Eugene McCarthy was once labeled a **political stalking horse** because it was assumed he was a weak, losing candidate testing the viability of an antiwar candidacy for allegedly stronger, winning candidates such as Robert F. Kennedy or Hubert Humphrey.

New Hampshire Speaks

Anti-Establishment candidates have always done well in the nation's first presidential primary. Some say it's because of the tough, no-nonsense voters who live there. Others say it's because New Hampshire enjoys the opening salvo opportunity to speak out against the status quo or in favor of new directions. Whatever it is, McCarthy found a receptive audience amongst the Tet-stunned electorate in the March 12th New Hampshire primary. The national media quickly changed its view of McCarthy, the born loser, to McCarthy, the mover-and-shaker of the Democratic Party.

Shell Shock

Gallup and the major political polling operations in New Hampshire predicted a big loss for Eugene McCarthy. They said his popularity ranged between a low of 6 percent to a high of 20 percent. They were wrong. McCarthy took more than 40 percent of the vote there.

Even McCarthy himself began to believe in his own potential. He had been a survivor and winner in the rough-and-tumble politics of Minnesota for more than 20 years. He was no stranger to challenging elections, and the media's early dismissal of him and his campaign in New Hampshire had been unfair and premature.

University students were especially taken by McCarthy's daring run against Johnson. Although many of them had railed against the Establishment and its Vietnam War, McCarthy was something of the good guy mole within that Establishment. He also sounded a lot like one of their favorite professors. Hence, the senator confused the antiwar movement. Maybe street demonstrations were going nowhere. Maybe putting Eugene McCarthy in the White House was the way to change America for the better.

But it mattered little what university students thought. The twenty-sixth amendment (or the right for 18- to 21-year-olds to vote) was still four years away. That meant they would have to persuade their elders to do the right thing and vote McCarthy. This was easier said than done, but McCarthy's young supporters liked to be called "crusaders."

McCarthy's kids were ready to move some mountains, and that included what some called a "cultural adjustment." This meant cutting their hair, discarding the torn blue jeans, leaving the drugs at home or out of sight, keeping the rock music low, and looking the way their mainstream parents expected them to look. It was called getting "Clean for Gene," and it involved university students from across New England and elsewhere. McCarthy assembled an army of volunteers and canvass walkers in a state where contacting voters on a door-to-door basis was considered essential to victory.

The media visibility and all the enthusiastic supporters helped, but there would be no cigar for McCarthy. President Johnson won the New Hampshire primary without lifting a finger to campaign there. The final vote tally was Johnson at 48 percent and McCarthy at 42 percent. In tiny New Hampshire, that meant a difference of only 300 votes.

The pollsters and the media were nevertheless shocked. Most everyone declared McCarthy the "moral victor" there. This would confuse people for years, especially those who had not paid close attention to the race or just loved to hear the word *victor* associated with McCarthy. To these people, McCarthy was always the hands-down winner of the legendary New Hampshire primary of 1968. But they were wrong.

Ask Saigon Sally

After the Tet Offensive, Senator Fulbright called Dean Rusk to Capitol Hill to testify about what had happened. For 11 hours, and on national television, Fulbright and his Foreign Relations Committee accused the secretary of state of misleading the American people over Vietnam and the events leading to Tet. Concerned about security matters during a time of war, Rusk was less than candid with Fulbright's Committee. His evasive answers were interpreted by the Congress and many voters as another example of the Johnson administration's arrogance and mistrust of the American people.

Rough Road Ahead

Between March 12 and March 31, 1968, Johnson reminded the nation that he won New Hampshire, but few listened. His campaign advisors predicted a rough road ahead, and a potentially large defeat was possible in the critical Wisconsin primary on April 2. For decades, the Wisconsin primary meant the middle point in the primary season. Historically, the candidate who was ahead by that point or pulled ahead there got the nomination and often won the presidency.

By this time, McCarthy was doing well in the polls, and the Minnesota senator was a welcomed fixture in the upper Midwest. James Rowe, Johnson's most trusted political spin doctor, urged the president to make or make up some sort of dramatic Vietnam statement just before the Wisconsin vote. Rowe was thinking along the lines of a troop withdrawal announcement coinciding with a battle victory somewhere. He had no idea that the drama would end up being the end of Johnson's career.

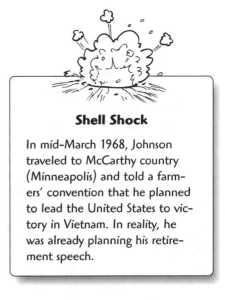

Shell Shock

In mid–March 1968, Johnson traveled to McCarthy country (Minneapolis) and told a farmers' convention that he planned to lead the United States to victory in Vietnam. In reality, he was already planning his retirement speech.

McCarthy troubled Johnson. The Minnesota senator had had objections to Great Society goals for years. McCarthy worried about public expenses, disagreed with the tenor and tone of civil rights legislation, and generally complained about Johnson's domestic agenda.

As far as the president was concerned, McCarthy was in the wrong party. Or was he? The political scene was getting so confusing. Throughout most of Johnson's career, those in favor of less government activism at home and no sword-rattling abroad were good ole conservative Republicans. But the press and the political pundits kept calling McCarthy the "liberal dove." To Johnson, today's liberal dove was yesterday's old conservative. But whatever was going on, it wasn't good news for the continuation of the New Frontier and the Great Society into the 1970s.

What About George?

If McCarthy was unacceptable to Johnson's view of the good Democrat, then George Wallace was really bad news. Wallace, Alabama's governor, was proud of his "populist" and "progressive" record as a Democrat. But he was running as the American Independent party candidate for president, and he had a long list of things that he hated. The Great Society was high on the list, although he urged so-called "dinner pail" (moderate to conservative) Democrats to join his cause.

Ask Saigon Sally

Wallace chose General Curtis Le-May, the former head of the Strategic Air Command, to be his vice-presidential running mate. LeMay advocated nuclear strikes on North Vietnam.

Having made his national reputation over opposing racial integration, Wallace was a rousing speaker. He complained about Kennedy and Johnson "big government," and how Washington, D.C., was interfering in the everyday lives of average folks. Civil rights legislation was part of that interference, he said, and the federal government had no right to supervise race relations.

In contrast to the early 1960s governor's race in Alabama, Wallace's national campaign for president avoided overtly racist remarks. His opposition to big government was often a smokescreen for working-class whites who despised African Americans and disliked the federal government's civil rights interests even more.

Wallace had little use for "pointy-headed intellectuals" like McCarthy, and all antiwar protestors were traitors and fools. Johnson, he insisted, had been pandering to the communists in the Cold War. A total commitment to military victory was needed in Vietnam, he argued, or America's suffering troops should be pulled out to safety.

When asked by the press if his either/or Vietnam statements meant he was a "hawk" or a "dove," Wallace never gave a straight answer. He always said that he was a peace advocate unless, of course, a World War II–like effort could be employed against the enemy in Vietnam and victory assured. Many of his supporters assumed that he would lay waste to Vietnam if president. Others believed that he was smart enough to know that it was all over for anticommunism in Vietnam. He'd prove his tough Cold Warrior credentials elsewhere.

Whatever Wallace meant to do in Vietnam, he continued to impress his touted "little man" in America. Of course, that "little man" coalition was white, and it was unclear what their self-proclaimed champion might accomplish as president. Because he had little use for federal government activism, he promised little in the way of government assistance to any of them.

Again, this was all quite confusing to Lyndon Johnson and longtime political observers. Both McCarthy and Wallace were protest candidates. Despite their very different styles and appeal, they were essentially arguing the same anti-Establishment message. Neither seemed to have a clue what an anti-Establishment candidate should do if he became the Establishment president.

In New Hampshire, many of Eugene McCarthy's original supporters in February would vote for George Wallace in November. The general bad-boy message of the anti-Establishment candidate was more important than anything else. As the Democrats turned to their longstanding "Happy Warrior," Hubert Humphrey, and the Republicans went back to former Vice President Richard Nixon, the anti-Establishment cause was in Wallace's hands. His popularity shot from 11 percent early in the election to over 21 percent in the fall.

Wallace was the spoiler, and given the fed-up and angry mood of the voters in 1968, even the pollsters worried about their own predictions. During the week of the election, *Time* prepared three covers, just in case, featuring Humphrey, Nixon, and Wallace. Politics as usual had gone south, and even Walter Cronkite compared the battling Democrats to the dirty fighting going on in Vietnam.

Ask Saigon Sally

Early in the Democratic primaries, Senator Edmund Muskie of Maine urged his party to stop shouting and start reasoning before it committed political suicide. His cause of party unification would win him the vice presidential nomination at the Democratic Party convention.

Shell Shock

Johnson wanted a defense of his Vietnam policy placed in the 1968 Democratic Party convention platform. At first the platform committee refused to do so, but then agreed after a compromise position on Vietnam could not be arrived at.

Good Bobby, Evil Hubert, and a November Defeat

Four days after the New Hampshire primary, Robert Kennedy joined the race for the White House. McCarthy regarded Kennedy as an opportunistic creep who stabbed him and the antiwar movement in the back. Especially to diehard McCarthy supporters, Bobby Kennedy should have announced his presidential intentions much earlier. Now, as the heir to his murdered brother's legacy, he claimed that the Democratic nomination was his. To McCarthy's strongest supporters, Kennedy came too late to both the antiwar movement and the 1968 election. The Minnesota senator agreed and vowed to fight on. Kennedys were not invincible.

His brother's assassination had changed Bobby Kennedy. After resigning from the attorney general's job, he headed to a New York Senate seat. Few New Yorkers resented the heir of Camelot and a Massachusetts guy representing their interests. He was now the "Good Bobby," dedicated to the liberal wing of his party. More eloquent than ever, he inspired a crusade of his own on behalf of poor Southern blacks, a better environment, and, in 1968, he minced few words about his opposition to the Vietnam War.

Kennedy had no problem admitting his own role in early Vietnam policy-making, and he offered very believable apologies for it. Yet his candidacy did twist and pull the antiwar movement. The good professor versus the "Good Bobby." To some, McCarthy would always have the better anti-Establishment credentials. But even Lyndon Johnson, never a friend of the Kennedys, had no problem with another Kennedy as president. The Great Society and the Democratic Party would be secure under his leadership. To Johnson, that was the bottom line.

While the Democrats battled each other, Republican Richard Nixon visited the battlefield in Vietnam.

Nixon Presidential Materials Staff, College Park, Maryland, and photographer Oliver Atkins.

Although a latecomer in the campaign, Kennedy won smashing victories in Indiana and Nebraska, and did well in the West Coast primaries, including California. His new home state of New York was next, and a knockout punch of McCarthy was

230

expected. Then it was on to the Democratic Party convention. It would have been difficult to deny Kennedy the nomination, but, of course, his party will never know what might have happened. His assassination on the night of the June 4, 1968 California primary put an end to Camelot, Part II. Kennedy had just addressed his supporters in the ballroom of the Ambassador Hotel in Los Angeles. Shot by Sirhan Sirhan moments later, he died the following morning.

The torch passed to Vice President Hubert Humphrey, although nearly all of McCarthy's "crusaders" and some of Kennedy's supporters were unhappy with a known hawk at the head of the ticket. To the antiwar movement, Chicago—the site of the Democratic Party convention—was now the symbol of evil itself. Humphrey wasn't too far behind on their list of evils. SDS organizers and *Yippies* urged their supporters to rally, and an odd coalition of young anti-Johnson activists descended on Mayor Richard J. Daley's steamy hot Chicago.

Regarding all antiwar protestors as a blight in his city, Daley turned off microphones and harassed antiwar delegates inside the convention, while outside the convention, his police clubbed, beat, and arrested demonstrators. With tear gas wafting inside the convention hall, Humphrey talked about the glories of the Great Society. Most Americans saw little that was glorious in Chicago.

Humphrey later said that he lost the election because of that bickering, bloody convention. Maybe. In any event, an Illinois government investigation into Mayor Daley's conduct at the Chicago convention concluded that it was the police who had rioted in the streets, and not the young protestors.

Jarhead Jargon

Led by Abbie Hoffman and Jerry Rubin, the Youth International Party, or **Yippies,** championed an anarchist agenda that favored an immediate end to the Vietnam War, capitalism, drug laws, work, and the police.

Shell Shock

The Saigon regime had favorites in the 1968 American election. Hoping that Republican Richard Nixon would offer better support and deals than Humphrey, they played a waiting game and refused active participation in the Paris peace negotiations until after the American electorate had spoken.

If Humphrey didn't lose because of Chicago, his "October Surprise" speech helped things along. Two months after the convention, a somber, not very "Happy Warrior"-looking Humphrey claimed that he always had a strong interest in peace. He promised to be a different president from Johnson when it came to Vietnam. The electorate was stunned by the turnaround. They thought the vice president was Johnson's greatest fan. Who was the real Hubert Humphrey? Their answer was Richard Nixon, but only by a hair.

The Least You Need to Know

➤ Eugene McCarthy represented the antiwar cause in the New Hampshire primary.

➤ Johnson viewed McCarthy as a threat to his Great Society program.

➤ George Wallace favored a World War II–like commitment in Vietnam or nothing at all.

➤ The Robert Kennedy campaign tried to combine Great Society interests and the antiwar cause.

➤ The Democratic convention in Chicago had a profound effect on the 1968 election.

Chapter 22

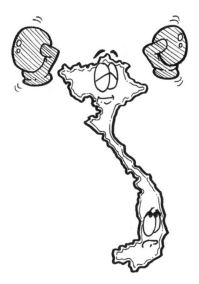

Thirty Years War, the Final Act

He said that he was "The New Nixon," and a very slim majority of Americans agreed with him. Beating Vice President Humphrey in one of the closest presidential elections of all time, Richard Nixon squeaked into the White House. He had won 43.4 percent of the vote compared to Humphrey's 42.7 percent. Nixon promised no great programs and his comments on Vietnam had been a little mysterious. But at least he wasn't cut from the same old New Frontier/Great Society cloth. Some fresh air was needed in Washington.

You Can Trust "Tricky Dicky"

Throughout his more than 20 years of public service, Nixon had dodged questions about his ethics or the lack of them. In his first run for Congress, he had made up tall tales about his World War II record, suggesting in some of his campaign brochures that he had been a combat soldier in the Pacific. Others, he later claimed, were responsible for the brochures. Meanwhile, on the campaign trail, he accused his opposition of being soft on communism. Charging one's opposition with less than patriotic behavior became a Nixon trait, and making shady deals with potential financial contributors was another.

What was a little corruption in the service of beating communism? And Nixon always wanted to be one of the leading anticommunist crusaders. Thank God for the Cold War! But this type of reasoning, combined with the gutter tactics and rhetoric, rubbed many people the wrong way. He earned the unkind label of "Tricky Dicky" early in his career, and it was a difficult label to shed. Nixon had won or lost elections by a hair for years, and that, in itself, somehow suggested a slippery character.

Proud of his humble Southern California roots, Nixon was a portrait of the hard-working, self-made man. Franklin Roosevelt's New Deal helped get him on his feet, and by all rights young Dick Nixon should have been a thankful liberal and not an anti–New Deal conservative. But he was especially proud of the fact that he worked his way up without taking too many "handouts" from anyone or any government.

Nixon resented those who relied on government help when they should have struck out on their own. And he particularly resented all those Kennedy-like rich guys who entered politics because they had nothing else to do. Once in office, they would extend government services, raising taxes on regular folks as they championed the downtrodden whom they never met. That was hypocrisy to Nixon, and he had no problem championing the interests of the white middle-class majority of Americans.

In 1968, Nixon said that he had been humbled by his 1960 defeat to John Kennedy and by his 1962 defeat in the California governor's race. Having become a trade lawyer with rich Asian/Pacific clients, citizen Nixon watched Republican Party politics from the sidelines for a while. He also watched Vietnam hound the leadership of both parties, and in 1968, Nixon claimed to be a former insider-turned-outsider with experience in Asian/Pacific politics and business. Tanned, fit, and ready to rumble, he asked the voters for a second chance.

Rabid anticommunism leads to mistakes, Nixon now admitted, implying that Vietnam was one of those mistakes. This changed man wanted to be America's new Dr. Fix It, and he favored a more cautious,

Ask Saigon Sally

Nixon admired Woodrow Wilson so much that he had Wilson's old desk put in the Oval Office. Both Wilson and Nixon regarded critics as enemies, had fragile personalities, and demanded 100 percent loyalty from the cabinet and staff.

Shell Shock

Nixon chose corporate lawyer and old friend William Rogers to be secretary of state because he was a quiet bureaucrat who had no interest in leading U.S. foreign policy. This left Nixon and his National Security Council in charge—and that was the point.

moderate path than he had advocated earlier. A war-weary America hoped "The New Nixon" was as trustworthy as advertised.

Henry the K. and Vietnamization

Nixon entered office with a weak mandate and a Democratic Party–controlled House and Senate. It bothered him. From the beginning, the Gallup Poll averred that the most popular and admired politician in America was the defeated vice presidential candidate for the Democrats, Edmund Muskie. Historically, the new, incoming president is the most admired politico. Even before Nixon was sworn into office, the political pundits were talking about a 1972 Nixon-versus-Muskie race. Conventional wisdom suggested that Muskie and the Democrats were destined to win.

The new president took all of this personally, and he was determined to prove the experts wrong. He planned to be the guy who ended the Vietnam War and the Cold War, too. His enemies would truly be silenced then, Muskie would disappear, and the historians would stop writing all those books about the wonderful Kennedys. Nixon, the great American statesman, was on his way.

At first, Nixon planned to end the Vietnam War as soon as he moved into the Oval Office. Vietnam, he told his new White House staff, was lost. We had to get out of there. During the ending days of the 1968 campaign, he had implied the end was near when he referred to a hush-hush "secret plan" to bring the boys home. Many antiwar Democrats had crossed the aisle to vote for him and his "plan." But there never had been a plan, and Nixon kept his options open.

Tales from the Front

As a U.S. navy admiral and Commander-in-Chief, Pacific Command (CINCPAC) from July 1969 to September 1972, John S. McCain, Jr. (Senator John McCain's father) was one of President Richard Nixon's staunchest defenders of "Vietnamization." A true believer in the domino theory, Admiral McCain argued that much of the Asian-Pacific region would fall to communist invaders if South Vietnam fell. In the early 1970s atmosphere of détente and Paris Peace Talks, McCain spoke his mind publicly about the need for more and not fewer anticommunist policies. In 1972, Nixon finally agreed with McCain's argument to mine North Vietnamese ports, and some historians argue that it was this action that prompted the North Vietnamese to reach an agreement with the Americans. McCain retired in 1972 and became the president of the U.S. Strategic Institute. He died in 1981.

Nixon's enthusiasm for a quick end to the war waned as he became more and more acquainted with the burdens of world power leadership. The National Security Council (NSC) was especially involved in his education there, and Nixon learned that Vietnam could not be separated from larger policy goals. For example, Kissinger and his staff insisted that an American defeat in Vietnam would trigger certain allied defections in the Pacific. It wouldn't be just a problem that the communists took advantage of. Japan, the Republic of Korea (South Korea), Thailand, and the Republic of China (Taiwan) would probably divorce themselves from any U.S. connection, kick out the U.S. military bases in their countries, and create their own, new foreign policies. Discarded by its Pacific allies and surrounded by victorious communists, the U.S. could expect a world of misery if it lost the Vietnam War. The NSC portrait was not a pretty one.

Henry Kissinger

The president's number-one teacher was a former Harvard academic and global diplomacy specialist, Henry Kissinger. Kissinger had been an on-call foreign affairs advisor during the Kennedy-Johnson years, but generally he was better known on the university circuit as a brainy, humorless guy with complicated ideas about the Cold War. Like a lot of professors, he had been attracted to Governor Nelson Rockefeller's 1968 presidential campaign. Rockefeller had touted himself as the "education candidate" and liberal Republican with "new ideas."

Defeated long before the Republican Party convention, Rockefeller offered various and gifted staffers to the Nixon campaign. The ambitious Kissinger was happy to be offered up, although he had little personal use for "Tricky Dicky." His negative impression of Nixon lived on during his White House years, but he never looked a gift horse in the mouth.

Jarhead Jargon

Shuttle diplomacy was Henry Kissinger's effort to prove that America truly cared about the concerns of its allies and potential foes. Instead of urging them to come to Washington to discuss their differences, Kissinger flew to them.

Short, a little rotund, and proud of his German accent, Kissinger had a knack for public relations that had not been seen on the National Security Council before. The council's work was top secret, but it didn't have to be unknown. If U.S. foreign policy was ready to turn over a dramatic new leaf, it needed plenty of cameras around. A single guy when he came to the White House as a National Security Council advisor, Kissinger would soon be seen in the company of Hollywood starlets, like the statuesque Jill St. John. Security policy was now officially "hip," and the press loved every minute of it.

Kissinger traveled the world with his *shuttle diplomacy* message of reconciliation and well-intentioned interests. The United States, he argued, had already learned many lessons from its long war. Concerned that

America's Cold War leadership was being rejected by its allies thanks to Vietnam, Kissinger tried to mend fences with them. Concerned that the communists might interpret that leadership as faltering also because of Vietnam, Kissinger went to them and told them otherwise. He was rarely in Washington, and the press loved this new people-to-people approach.

Vietnamization

To Kissinger, Vietnam had been a horrible mistake. But a military withdrawal would still be a bigger mistake. It meant U.S. military defeat. A quick withdrawal would accelerate Cold War tensions and challenges, and the allies, he believed, would see an unreliable America that had abandoned its friend, South Vietnam. The results would be devastating, Kissinger warned Nixon.

The alternative was a very slow-moving withdrawal. Kissinger estimated that by the early 1980s, South Vietnam would be truly able to defend itself effectively. As American troops came home in a trickle, they would leave all of their military hardware behind. The ARVN would be transformed into a powerful fighting force, and the South Vietnamese government would prevail against calls for a coalition government with the Vietcong. This withdrawal was called "Vietnamization."

The American people would be scared and outraged by the idea of a Vietnam War lingering into the '80s. Hence, withdrawal announcements of 20,000 to 30,000 men would be made at critical times, and praises sung for the reforming ARVN and Saigon regime. With well over a half-million U.S. troops in Vietnam, the withdrawal announcements wouldn't mean much anyway, but Nixon was supposed to make them with as much fanfare as possible. He had a great deal of faith in the Kissinger approach, and he complied. Always sticking to the theme that the war was ending, so why protest it, Nixon rehashed a lot of old pro-Saigon regime policies in 1969 and early 1970. They just sounded better than Johnson's or Kennedy's.

Shell Shock

During the late 1970s, Nixon was interviewed at length by BBC talk show host David Frost. Nixon admitted to Frost that, if he had to do it all over again, he would have withdrawn all U.S. forces from Vietnam immediately after taking office.

Ask Saigon Sally

For the first nine months of the Nixon administration, there were no significant antiwar demonstrations. The reasons involved lingering hopes for the "secret plan," the early "Vietnamization" announcements, and the traditional "honeymoon" American voters give new presidents on the job.

In the meantime, Kissinger promised to continue peace talks with the North Vietnamese, and in top secret cabinet meetings, Nixon promised to do outrageous things to North Vietnam now and then. That meant bombing raids over North Vietnam that were more damaging and frightening than the old Operation ROLLING THUNDER. It also meant threatening a nuclear assault whenever appropriate, but not following up on the threat. This strange combination of slow troop withdrawals, bombing escalation, massive aid for South Vietnam, and scare tactics would yield results, Kissinger predicted, sooner rather than later. But the North Vietnamese were a tough bunch. Kissinger warned his boss to be prepared for a very long haul if necessary. Throughout the Paris Peace Talks, there was the possible threat of a shift of U.S. policy toward nuclear war, but the North Vietnamese correctly interpreted it as a bluff, and the Nixon administration believed its stepped-up conventional bombing campaigns were winning results anyway.

The Protestors vs. the Great Silent Majority

By October 1969, the antiwar movement was back in the streets. The reality of a long war ahead began to sink in, and new demonstrations were organized. One in Washington included 250,000 protestors from both the civil rights movement and the antiwar movement. Another in New York featured W. Averell Harriman, once one of Lyndon Johnson's Paris Peace Talks negotiators, denouncing the war in front of a crowd of thousands. The Harriman speech indicated a growing trend. People otherwise alienated by street demonstrators were now in the streets themselves. "Vietnamization" was not a crowd pleaser.

Ask Saigon Sally

Former Wisconsin Congressman Melvyn Laird became Nixon's secretary of defense. Although never a fan of the Vietnam War, he favored retraining the ARVN as a Vietcong-like force.

But the antiwar movement had met its match with Nixon. A master of divisive politics, the president did not let angry street protestors get the best of him. In November 1969, during one of the more powerful speeches of his presidency, "The New Nixon" revisited the old Nixon and accused the antiwar movement of encouraging U.S. military defeat.

In his speech, Nixon appealed to the "great silent majority" of white middle-class moderates and conservatives, who went to work every day and never marched in any street, to rally behind "Vietnamization." Patriotism was still "in," he suggested, and the North Vietnamese were still the enemy.

Nixon's "great silent majority" speech was a hit with a Middle America ready to trust their president. The White House was flooded with congratulations and support from thousands of voters, and Nixon believed that he had just won a magnificent victory. In fact, the antiwar movement was put on the defensive, and the charge of unpatriotic behavior would haunt them like never before. Nixon had truly won an important round, as well as gained a little more time for "Vietnamization."

At Camp David, President Nixon discusses Vietnam with Henry Kissinger (left) and General Alexander Haig (right).

Nixon Presidential Materials Staff, College Park, Maryland, and photographer Oliver Atkins.

"Vietnamization" in Action

If you were a U.S. trooper in Vietnam during Nixon's first year in office, there was little evidence of a winding-down war. Troop strength reached an all-time high of 543,400 by late April 1969. No end seemed in sight. Nixon also followed the Johnson precedent of floating peace plans now and then. His May 1969 plan required the North Vietnamese to withdraw from South Vietnam and return all U.S. prisoners of war before a real peace deal was negotiated. As always, the proposition went nowhere, and the White House wondered why.

Hamburger Hill

Also like Johnson, Nixon would face bad news on the battlefield.

Operation APACHE SNOW involved one of General Abrams's first big operations as the new commander of forces in Vietnam. Invading the A Shau Valley during May 1969, Abrams hoped to dislodge a well-entrenched North Vietnamese force. An assault up Ap Bia mountain in horrible weather and a following mudslide resulted in hundreds of wounded American troops and more than 50 killed.

The Ap Bia assault took a dozen attempts, for the North Vietnamese fired down upon the marines from secure bunkers. To the Americans, Ap Bia was *Hamburger Hill*, part of General Abrams's grand sweep and "meat-grinder" objectives in the area.

Ask Saigon Sally

The North Vietnamese position on American peace plans did not change with America's change of president. They demanded the withdrawal of U.S. forces, the end of the Saigon regime, and a new coalition government.

Jarhead Jargon

The Marines called the battle of Ap Bia **"Hamburger Hill."** It was a play on General Abrams's "meat-grinder" approach against the North Vietnamese, and a recognition of their own high casualties in the effort.

Tales from the Front

Fifty-six American troops and five ARVN troops were killed at Hamburger Hill, while enemy losses were estimated at 630. Given the media criticism over Ap Bia and its immediate abandonment, the Pentagon ordered the U.S. military to avoid similar operations for the remainder of the U.S. troop withdrawal period.

The commitment to unleashing great manpower and firepower had precedent in American military lore dating back to Grant at Vicksburg in the Civil War. But Vicksburg was a long way from Ap Bia.

Immediately after the battle for Hamburger Hill, Abrams decided to abandon the area. This decision met with heavy criticism in the press, and the commander in chief caught most of the heat. Nixon's nemesis in the polls, Edmund Muskie, complained that "Vietnamization" was really escalation at worst or the same old endless war at best. The honeymoon was over, he said.

Publicizing Vietnamization

Just when the president thought he had settled the ongoing argument between the great silent majority and the antiwar movement, it heated up again. The Democrats in Congress, stung by the '68 defeat, were in an uppity mood, threatening legislation to bring the boys home and even to hold hearings on the alleged abuse of presidential power during the war. Kissinger, Laird, and Nixon agreed that a great effort to publicize Vietnamization military shipments and handovers was essential to stemming Congress's complaints. The American people needed to see that Vietnamization was a real policy, and that the war was winding down (at least for the U.S.).

America sent nearly $1 billion in military assistance to South Vietnam in 1969. A similar amount would be spent the following year. Nixon even met with President Nguyen Van Thieu, who had finally wrested power from Ky, to brief him on Vietnamization goals for his one-million-strong ARVN.

Meanwhile, General Abrams used the occasion of the Thieu-Nixon meeting to detail his battlefield successes, and then the president announced that roughly 25,000 American troops would be coming home soon. All of this was supposed to stress both America's slow withdrawal from Vietnam and its simultaneous commitment to keeping Thieu in power. It was an odd juggling act, and many voters saw it as such.

Obviously, few Americans would be patiently supporting Vietnamization into the 1980s, and so the Nixon team lied about how fast and how well that policy was going. But there was at least one accurate point made in the Nixon pitch. Abrams had won Hamburger Hill and other battles. Because of it, Hanoi was worried about the numbers game. Did they have enough troops to finish the war, and should they try to set up, like North Korea in the Korean War, a military alliance with China? These were trying times for both sides.

A Legend Is Born

Suffering from heart troubles throughout much of 1969, Ho Chi Minh's biggest concern was his health. After that, he worried about the growing ARVN, the nearly stationary U.S. forces, and Abrams's meat-grinder offensives. Any short-term victory for Hanoi was out of the question. Any effort to bully Kissinger at the continuing Paris Peace Talks would never work if North Vietnam struggled on the battlefield. Ho saw a long war ahead.

To Ho, it was the same old problem. Victory would have to come tomorrow, and more patience and caution were required today. But Ho ran out of tomorrows. He died on September 3, 1969, nearly six years before his troops declared victory over the Saigon regime.

On television, Americans saw the enemy in mourning. Even the North Vietnamese leadership wept openly. All the displays of grief seemed genuine, and that fact flew in the face of a still commonly held belief in America that most people living under communism yearned to be free from their evil rulers.

Ho was not replaced by a new dictator. A new committee now represented something of the executive branch in Hanoi, and Nixon and Kissinger hadn't a clue who might be in charge over there. In short, there was no reason to celebrate in the White House. Ho's death made North Vietnamese policy-making even more mysterious and difficult to figure out.

Ask Saigon Sally

The 1969 press might have regarded Edmund Muskie as a potential president-in-waiting, but other Democrats also had ambitions in 1972. Hubert Humphrey had not given up on the presidency, and Senators Henry Jackson and George McGovern were already contemplating a run.

Shell Shock

Having faced unacceptably high battlefield casualties in the spring and summer of 1969, the North Vietnamese government debated a number of options. Giap's call to lay low and regroup won the day.

The Least You Need to Know

➤ Richard Nixon once hoped to end the Vietnam War fast, but changed his mind soon after entering the White House.

➤ Henry Kissinger was the chief foreign policy-maker in the Nixon White House.

➤ "Vietnamization" was supposed to lead to North Vietnam's defeat.

➤ The North Vietnamese suffered heavy losses during 1969.

➤ Ho Chi Minh died in September 1969.

HEY. KNOCK IT OFF!

Cambodia

Dith Pran is lucky to be alive. As an escapee from a *Khmer Rouge* "reeducation camp" in Cambodia, Pran spent weeks making his way to safety in Thailand. Along the way, he ran into unspeakable horrors, and he offered Red Cross and United Nations authorities in Thailand a detailed glimpse of the genocide going on in Cambodia.

As a photojournalist with *The New York Times* in Cambodia, Pran had helped document the rise of the Khmer Rouge in the early 1970s. An extremist Maoist group dedicated to their odd political guru, Pol Pot, the Khmer Rouge believed in cultural and political purity. Those they decided were impure had to die, and when their purification efforts ended in the late 1970s, more than one quarter of the Cambodian population had been murdered. Some say the figure is even higher, for entire towns were wiped out. We may never know.

Jarhead Jargon

Dating to the early 1960s, the *Khmer Rouge* was founded by Saloth Sar (a French-educated communist later known as Pol Pot). Opposed to urbanization, industrialization, and all aspects of capitalism, the Khmer Rouge remained on the outskirts of Cambodian politics until the Vietnam War spread into Cambodia in 1970. Once in power, Pol Pot's government herded millions of Cambodians into slave labor camps. Although he often quoted Mao Tse-tung in his speeches, Pol Pot's communism was uniquely his own. Driven out of power by invading Vietnamese troops in 1979, the Khmer Rouge remained a force in rural Cambodian politics for years afterward.

Pran's story was the story of 1970s Cambodia, and it became the focus of a best-seller in the early 1980s and a blockbuster Academy Award–winning film in 1984, *The Killing Fields*. The term *killing fields* became synonymous with state-sponsored genocide, mass thrill murders, and radical politics gone totally insane. Today, Pran leads the Dith Pran Holocaust Awareness association, a peace and justice lobby group.

Winner of the U.N.'s Medal of Freedom Award in 1997, Pran and his group focus on the continuing plight of Cambodia and the fact that no one has been brought to justice for the Cambodian killing fields.

The full killing fields tale is a sad one in which the United States is heavily involved. Big power politics ran headlong into quiet, neutral Cambodia, and the result was war, betrayal, denial, and an era of misery and death rivaled only by Hitler's mad crusade against the Jews of Europe.

Ask Saigon Sally

Dr. Haing S. Ngor, a survivor of the Cambodian holocaust, played Dith Pran in *The Killing Fields*. Like Pran, Ngor became a political activist on behalf of Cambodian issues and donated most of his substantial earnings to the cause. In 1996, he was killed in a gangland robbery in the United States.

Things Keep Falling Apart

As 1969 came to a close, it did so with a display of power from the antiwar movement. Protests were on the rise, and they did not necessarily have to be in a New York or Washington, D.C., street. In the Senate, two of Nixon's potential Supreme Court appointees were rejected. Clement Haynsworth was labeled incompetent and G. Harold Carswell was exposed as an avowed racist. Nightly news broadcasts remained fascinated by the anti-Nixon fever in both the streets and the Congress. Once again, the president needed to take the offensive.

When asked by the press about one particularly large antiwar demonstration on Thanksgiving 1969, Nixon said he had no idea it had even taken place. He was too busy, he said, watching the Washington Redskins game on TV. This response was supposed to bond him with a middle America tired of antiwar news; however, it sounded indifferent and callous even to his supporters.

Tales from the Front

Leaving his struggling working-class diocese in Boston, Father John Ryan went to work in the refugee camps of the Thai-Cambodia border in the summer of 1970. Specializing in child care, Ryan established a "refugee city" to care for what he called "the dust of life" (war orphans and abandoned Amerasian children). He was killed during the Thai-Cambodia border clash of 1985.

The news from Vietnam remained troubling. As it had earlier in the war, CBS News attached a television crew to another Charlie Company for daily reports. This time the American people were treated to a very different U.S. military than that seen only a few years before. In one report, they saw the entire company refuse to march down a road in Tay Ninh province. The veteran foot soldiers complained that their commanding officer was too inexperienced, that the road was probably mined and booby-trapped, and that there wasn't enough cover should a firefight erupt.

Ask Saigon Sally

Agnew was famous for his catchy phrases. News reporters and editors were "nattering nabobs of negativism," and congressmen who wanted to cut funding for the Vietnam War were "pugnacious pups of parsimony."

The men of Charlie Company characterized their action as a "mutiny" in the name of self-preservation and against the "lifers" (career military officers) who made reckless decisions. Only five men followed their lieutenant down that road, and, once contacted, the company commander reversed the road decision and got his people back into the bush.

245

Jarhead Jargon

In 1970, the U.S. Army reported 2,000 cases of **fragging** in Vietnam. Fragging was a violent attack on an officer by his own men. Booby traps and grenades were the weapons of choice.

Shell Shock

Only 31 years old when he became President Nixon's personal legal counsel, John Dean was honored to be part of the White House staff. Despite the preoccupation of people his age with Vietnam issues, Dean had no opinion on Vietnam and knew little about it.

This CBS report stirred the Pentagon and angered Nixon, but things would get worse. In another CBS report, filmed just north of Saigon, young draftees were shown getting high on drugs when they were supposed to be on guard duty. The young men interviewed claimed that most everyone they knew in uniform was "drunk or stoned" some of the time, and did everything they could to stay out of harm's way the rest of the time. The war was a waste of time and lives, they insisted, and the bottom line was marking time until their "in-country" duty was over. If things threatened this status quo, there was always the last step of *fragging*, but nobody admitted to this on camera.

Spiro Agnew

As usual, Nixon implied that the controversial CBS reports were examples of unpatriotic if not treasonous behavior, but he never came out and said it. Screaming at the press, he decided, would be beneath the dignity of the presidency. But it wasn't beneath the dignity of the vice presidency. Former Maryland governor Spiro Agnew became the White House's public junkyard dog. Railing against the "conspiracy of the press" and "lefty college boys," Agnew became a darling of "hawks" and ultraconservatives across the country. If Agnew's speeches got too carried away, the president would always disassociate himself from them.

In his inaugural address, Nixon had promised that he would reason with Americans. The shouting was over, he said. Nixon kept his word, and Agnew did the shouting. But the vice president was uncomfortable with the role. During the 1968 campaign, the press asked "Spiro who?" largely because Agnew was a shy Greek American with both a lackluster record and speaking style. He used to find himself on the moderate to liberal side of issues in his party, and he struggled with his PR role for the Vietnam War. Being the pet right-winger of the administration was out of character for the man, but he remained the loyal soldier to the boss in the Oval Office.

Although his fans had no idea at the time, the tough-talking vice president drowned his sorrows with the bottle and delved into shady financial deals with sleazy defense contractors and others. The latter led to his indictment and resignation at a time that coincided with the then full-blown Watergate scandal in 1973.

Antiwar forces gather again in Washington, D.C.

Lyndon Baines Johnson Library, Austin, Texas, and photographer Frank Wolfe.

Agnew's angry speeches offered hope to conservative white middle- and working-class Americans who had seen too much change too fast. The civil rights movement, the antiwar movement, the visibility of the New Left, and the strange, endless struggle of the U.S. military in Vietnam was too much to take for Americans concerned about so-called traditional values. For many blue-collar workers, quietly supported by plenty of people stuck in office cubicles, the antiwar movement was especially annoying. Resentful of the generally well-off college kids "tearing down America" while the rest of the country worked like dogs to make ends meet, the *hard hats* had had enough in late 1969.

Organizing their own demonstrations throughout late 1969 and early 1970, dozens of union locals donned their safety hard hats, grabbed a large American flag, and paraded through the streets of large East Coast cities in a display of support for President Nixon and

Jarhead Jargon

A mixture of World War II–era unionized blue-collar workers and younger like-thinking conservatives, the **hard hats** considered the antiwar movement pro-Hanoi, anti-American, and anti-veteran.

Shell Shock

By 1970, Nixon concluded that he needed to get even bolder and more aggressive in Vietnam. The enemy needed to know that America might do just about anything to win. He called it his "madman theory."

the Vietnam War. Agnew claimed that they were the only "real patriots" in the country, and Nixon exaggerated their numbers. Noting that "millions" of hard hats had just demonstrated who truly is in charge of American public opinion, Nixon once again claimed to have gained the upper hand over the antiwar movement. Privately, Nixon knew better, and he planned a turn-the-tide offensive in Southeast Asia. His critics, he believed, were soon-to-be-forgotten footnotes in history.

The My Lai Debate

The New York Times's revelation of a U.S. military–inflicted massacre in Quang Ngai province added to the debate over Vietnam. Close to 500 men, women, and children were shot in My Lai hamlet there. The area had long been a stronghold of the Vietcong, and Lieutenant William Calley and his troops were frustrated by the effort to tell the good guys from the bad guys. The Tet Offensive had turned Vietnam into a bloodbath, and in March 1968, Calley and his men added to the horror.

Due to its reputation for high concentrations of Vietcong troops, the My Lai area had been nicknamed "Pinkville" by Calley's men. Specifically, the 1st Battalion of the 20th U.S. Army Infantry was supposed to be searching for an estimated 250 Vietcong troops there. As was so often the case in Vietnam, the enemy was very difficult to find. Calley and his men had already seen heavy fighting in the ongoing Tet Offensive, and as they neared My Lai, he lost more men to snipers, mines, and booby-traps.

Calley's war-weary unit had been nicknamed the "Butcher Brigade" by other units in the field, and they more than lived up to their reputation at My Lai. Calley found only old men, women, and children in My Lai. Theoretically, some could have been Vietcong sympathizers or even operatives. It was not unusual to see women and even children in the ranks of the Vietcong. In any event, Calley and his men began the systematic execution of the villagers. The killing stopped when an American helicopter on a scouting mission, piloted by Warrant Officer Hugh Thompson, landed his chopper in between some of Calley's men and a handful of Vietnamese villagers running for their lives.

The massacre had been covered up for two years. When the story broke, it stimulated a nationwide debate over the madness of Vietnam. To some, including Nixon, if the government jailed Calley and his men, they might as well jail thousands of Americans for atrocities in the dirty Vietnam War. To others, remembering America's prosecution of Nazi and Japanese war criminals after World War II, justice needed to be served, the victims remembered, and no crime left unpunished.

Like the Vietnam War itself, the My Lai debate was a no-win matter. The country was divided, and, by the end of his trial Calley would be sentenced to life in prison. Concluding that Calley was taking the rap for all U.S. military actions in Vietnam, the commander in chief attempted to rescue the good name of the U.S. Army and cut Calley's sentence to 20 years. It was later reduced to 10 years, and by 1974 the young lieutenant was out on parole.

When the My Lai debate began, Nixon was convinced his own administration would end up a victim of it. Even though the massacre took place under Johnson's watch, Nixon worried that his good luck in stemming the tide of antiwar opinion might soon be over. The Cambodian invasion came just in time, but it would not produce the desired result.

> **Ask Saigon Sally**
>
> It wasn't only the mainstream media that worried about the state of the U.S. military in Vietnam during 1970. *Armed Forces Journal* editorialized that America's soldiers were "dispirited" there and acting like a defeated army.

Flash Dance in Cambodia

Throughout the Johnson years, the Joint Chiefs of Staff had been frustrated by the president's opposition to invading neutral Cambodia. The Vietcong used Cambodia as a staging area for South Vietnam operations, and the government of Prince Norodom Sihanouk did little to stop them. From the Pentagon's view, Sihanouk played both sides of the street. In its opinion, heavily influenced by the Red Scare, that made him a communist ally, and American lives were lost because of it.

Nixon had authorized bombings of Vietcong sanctuaries along the Cambodian border in 1969, but had fallen short of authorizing an invasion. That changed in early 1970. An American-encouraged coup, led by General Lon Nol, forced Sihanouk out of the country. It was shocking news to many Cambodians. Sihanouk's government was similar to the non-Marxist socialist governments in Europe's Scandinavia. He had kept his country out of the war, permitting it to move its economy and institutions forward since the end of French rule in the early 1950s.

Lon Nol brought the Vietnam nightmare to Cambodia. He invited the ARVN to invade Vietcong sanctuaries, and then asked the Americans to help them out. The end of Sihanouk gave the Khmer Rouge communists stronger support than ever before, for Lon Nol was viewed as an American puppet who brought the madness of the Vietnam War to Cambodia. Lon Nol's troops had been fighting the Khmer Rouge as well, without much success. Once considered bizarre and radical, the Khmer Rouge now insisted that they were the true defenders of the nation, as well as visionaries and heroes. Now, they claimed that the new dictator who had eliminated the nation's beloved prince was leading the nation to ruin. The Khmer Rouge called for Cambodia's "liberation"

Jarhead Jargon

Learning a lesson in semantics from Eugene McCarthy's 1968 presidential campaign, Nixon did not announce that the United States was invading Cambodia. Instead, he said that the United States was involved in an **incursion,** thereby downplaying his widening of the war. McCarthy, a former English professor and poet, had softened or omitted words in his campaign that might disturb or anger his listeners.

under their leadership, and many Cambodians listened. The once civil politics of Cambodia turned increasingly violent.

On April 29, 1970, Nixon authorized the Cambodian *incursion,* giving Hanoi notice that Vietnamization did not mean America was running away from Southeast Asia. The Joint Chiefs promised a great victory, the destruction of Vietcong supplies, and endless confusion in the enemy's ranks that might benefit the American cause for months. Theoretically, those months would give Nixon some leverage to find a negotiated settlement with the North Vietnamese, and it would be an American victory that stimulated the follow-up withdrawal of all U.S. troops. The latter would be especially good news for Nixon's domestic political fortunes. And so it went.

"Patton" Blunders

Shortly before moving the war into Cambodia, Nixon viewed the hit film *Patton.* George C. Scott won an Academy Award for his portrayal of the maverick general who beat the Germans at the Battle of the Bulge and then urged his superiors to wage war against the Russians later in 1945. Considered something of the odd duck and outrageous sword-rattler in his day, Patton emerged as a misunderstood hero in the 1969 film. This no-nonsense tough guy was a winner, and if he had gotten his way, he would have taken on the commies long ago. America wouldn't be in Vietnam if it had listened to Patton. And if Patton were still around, the Vietcong wouldn't have a prayer.

Although the makers of the movie *Patton* claimed people were reading too much into their film, Nixon didn't think so. He wanted to be the new General Patton and hear the crowd roar after the Vietnam victory. Just as the World War II allies hoped to kill Hitler and his staff in their underground Berlin headquarters bunker, Nixon planned to destroy the Vietcong's headquarters in Cambodia.

Both the CIA and U.S. military intelligence experts told the president that there was no equivalent to a Berlin bunker in Cambodia. The Vietcong never consolidated their forces like that. Nevertheless, Nixon told the American people that their military was about to destroy a great headquarters and change the course of the war. It was another lie, and the incursion was a disaster.

Tales from the Front

As the son of the famous General George Patton of World War II fame, Major General George S. Patton III had a tough act to follow. The commander of the 11th Armored Cavalry Regiment in Vietnam, Patton served three tours of duty (1962–69) and proudly called his men a "splendid bunch of killers." Although he had his doubts about the war, Patton reasoned that "a soldier who does not participate in his country's wars is not a very good soldier." After the war, he retired to a quiet life of raising produce and cattle near Hamilton, Massachusetts.

Rather than destroy any imagined headquarters, the U.S. and South Vietnamese assault succeeded only in pushing the Vietcong deeper into Cambodia. Cambodian military units had done little in the past to stop Vietnamese infiltration, and they offered little assistance to the arriving American and ARVN forces. Meanwhile, the Vietcong were now in a comfortable position to aid the Khmer Rouge against Lon Nol, and Nixon announced an expensive aid plan to help Lon Nol take care of the problem. By the summer of 1970, the United States now had two corrupt and disliked Southeast Asian governments to prop up, and the Khmer Rouge continued to grow in strength. The Nixon administration claimed that the U.S. had fulfilled all of its military objectives in Cambodia. This was not the case, but it was the White House's final word on the matter.

Ask Saigon Sally

Cambodia did not help Nixon's standing in the polls. Some 71 percent now said the Vietnam War was a mistake, and only 31 percent said Nixon was doing a good job as commander in chief.

The Kent State Tragedy

Antiwar activists interpreted the Cambodian invasion as a widening of the war that might make it last the rest of the decade and beyond.

University campuses across the country saw protestors joining the cause who had not considered joining before, and the vandalism and violence associated with the anti-Cambodia protests led some university presidents to cancel classes and final exams.

251

At Kent State University, Ohio National Guardsmen shot and killed four antiwar demonstrators and wounded several others during a demonstration. The incident sparked another national debate. Nixon's only official comment in reference to the shooting was that "violence breeds violence," and 59 percent of the American people felt sorry for the predicament of the National Guardsmen.

Shell Shock

The anti-Cambodia demonstrations in Washington, D.C., were so loud and angry that the Secret Service parked buses and other vehicles in front of the White House as an extra measure of protection.

But there was much more beneath the surface of the usual pro-Vietnam versus anti-Vietnam argument here. Privately, Nixon grieved over what happened at Kent State, noting that one of his own college-age daughters could have been caught in the crossfire. He wrote sympathy notes to the victims' families. This private Nixon, of course, could not be displayed.

Meanwhile, other parents of college-age kids saw a horrible civil war–like confrontation in the wings. Most of the student protestors were 19 or 20 years old. Most of the National Guardsmen present at Kent State later claimed to have joined the guard to avoid Vietnam service. They were also 19 or 20 years old. Kids were not only killing kids in this case but antiwar people were killing antiwar people. The Vietnam tragedy kept getting more tragic.

A Warning Shot from Congress

U.S. forces withdrew from Cambodia on June 30, 1970. White House aide Charles Colson remembered years later that the failure of the Cambodia invasion created a siege mentality in the White House. Nixon felt trapped in Vietnam, and the antiwar demonstrators on Pennsylvania Avenue literally had him trapped in the White House. Congress also got on his nerves.

Senators Frank Church and John Sherman Cooper attempted to cut off all funding for the Vietnam War, short-circuit executive privilege, and restore economic foreign policy matters to Congress. In response, Nixon threatened to transfer funds from both foreign and domestic policy budgets and apply them toward the war. He then accused Church and Cooper of trying to injure the common foot soldier in Vietnam by stemming their commander in chief's money supply. Again, Nixon avoided the *T* word (treason), but Congress heard it anyway.

Senators George McGovern and Mark Hatfield even proposed legislation to bring all U.S. forces home before 1972, and the battle between the legislative and executive branches was back in high gear. Neither the McGovern-Hatfield Amendment nor the Church-Cooper Amendment passed in Congress, but Nixon had been warned. A quick peace was needed; otherwise, the powers of the presidency might soon be legislated away. This was a potential political nightmare for Nixon, but the real nightmare had just begun in Cambodia.

Ask Saigon Sally

An Oregon Republican, Mark Hatfield did his own thing. In 1970, Hatfield had called for Nixon's resignation for not living up to his end-the-war campaign promises. He continually sponsored or supported legislation to cut off Vietnam spending measures, and proposed the creation of an all-volunteer military three years before its time. Nixon wondered whether Hatfield could be somehow removed from office, but nothing ever came of the idea.

The Least You Need to Know

➤ American troops in Vietnam were dispirited and in disarray by 1970.

➤ Vice President Agnew became the angry pro–Vietnam War mouthpiece for the Nixon administration.

➤ Antiwar demonstrations were matched by pro–Vietnam War demonstrations.

➤ The U.S. and South Vietnamese invasion of Cambodia widened the war, failed in its objectives, and indirectly assisted the Khmer Rouge rise to power by bringing the war to Cambodia.

➤ The antiwar movement in the streets and in Congress was given new life by the Cambodian invasion.

Watergate

To young antiwar activists, 1972 was supposed to be a pivotal year. The political experts agreed with them. Nixon's popularity was weak, and hatred for the Vietnam War was strong. No one seemed to be minding the U.S. economy, and social issues had not been addressed in Washington since the heyday of the Great Society. There was more than a good possibility that an antiwar reformist could take the White House in 1972, and the twenty-sixth amendment truly helped things along.

Thanks to the combined efforts of Senator George McGovern and the antiwar faction in Congress, and Senator Barry Goldwater and the proveteran faction in Congress, the twenty-sixth amendment, granting the right to vote to 18- to 21-year-olds, was passed. If that age group turned its anger into votes, many predicted, the country would never be the same again.

In reality, youth voters would prove to be as apathetic as Mom and Dad. Very few 19-year-olds ran to the polls in 1972, and some joked that they were probably too stoned to show up anyway. The Democrats had a hard time picking and supporting a challenger to Nixon; the latter would fall only because of his own lifelong tendencies toward unethical and paranoid behavior.

The 1972 election ended up being the last hurrah for the antiwar movement, and some said the '60s truly ended then. In any event, Richard Nixon had certainly ended his career that year. It just took two more years to convince him of it.

Ask Saigon Sally

Codenamed LAM SON 719, the 1971 ARVN invasion of Laos was named after the village of a fifteenth-century Vietnamese freedom fighter against the Chinese.

Laos and the Uneasy Calm

After the fiasco of the Cambodian invasion, "Vietnamization" continued as planned. Nixon still worried about safe havens for the North Vietnamese in both Cambodia and Laos, and even contemplated a new, more forceful invasion of Cambodia. General Abrams opposed it, preferring more harassment of the Ho Chi Minh Trail. "Harassment" ended up being an invasion of Laos.

Nixon would not be repeating his 1970 mistakes with Cambodia. Nearly all of the Laos invading force in early 1971 would consist of ARVN troops. The United States provided air cover. But the North Vietnamese did not pull back as they did in Cambodia. The Laos sanctuaries were vital to the Ho Chi Minh Trail and the entire war in South Vietnam.

Tales from the Front

Major General Robert Molinelli served two tours of duty in Vietnam, the second of them during LAM SON 719 (the 1971 U.S. and ARVN invasion of Laos). A highly decorated helicopter commander, Molinelli lost over 60 of his 100 helicopters during LAM SON 719. At one point in the battle, he identified Soviet military advisors in action against both American and ARVN troops. He was denied permission to fire on them, and to this day insists on an official explanation from Washington on the issue.

Bad weather bogged down the ARVN advance, and the North Vietnamese refused to budge. Without the U.S. Air Force, the campaign would have been an utter disaster. Facing heavy casualties, President Thieu ordered a halt to the invasion, and in Washington, the political spinning began.

On national television, Nixon claimed the Laos invasion was a total success, and a beautiful example of Vietnamization in action. A little over 1,000 ARVN troops had been killed, the White House claimed. But the Pentagon knew better. The real estimate was closer to 8,000, and the American people had heard this kind of stuff before. If the Laos invasion had been such a success, why did the ARVN retreat? Why did they look like a defeated army? These types of questions remained as politically inappropriate as always, and, of course, were never answered by the Nixon administration.

Life magazine had sent a camera team into battle with the invading ARVN. One of their prize-winning photographers, Larry Burrows, was killed in what *Life* reported as the worst fighting of the war. Vietnamization, they said, had a long way to go, and they doubted that the South Vietnamese had much interest in it anyway.

Ask Saigon Sally

Larry Burrows was one of four American news photographers killed during the Laos invasion. He had been covering Vietnam events since the 1950s, and is considered the war's greatest combat photographer.

To Hanoi, the Laos invasion was something of a learning experience. The North Vietnamese government had been afraid of the growing ARVN with its fancy U.S.-supplied hardware. In Laos, they learned that big numbers of ARVN could be defeated as easily as small numbers. They also found it interesting that during an important invasion, the United States stayed in the air and avoided the use of ground troops. Nixon was running scared, they concluded, and Vietnamization did mean America was leaving the war behind. Too bad the pace of Vietnamization was so slow.

In the meantime, the Nixon administration, including Henry Kissinger, did its best to convince the American people that all was well in South Vietnam. President Thieu, Nixon said, was "loved" by Democrats everywhere in the country, and the ARVN was on the verge of becoming the most significant military force on the planet next to the U.S. armed forces. During the spring of 1971, this type of rhetoric was consistent and constant. It was even soothing to some Americans who wanted to believe that a certain calm was settling into South Vietnam. But nothing was calm, and privately, a deeply concerned Nixon was at a loss over what to do next.

Daniel Ellsberg Feels Your Pain

Interrupting the calm was the revelation that the Vietnam War had been the product of strange and bizarre policy-making. Nicknamed "The Pentagon Papers" by the press, the revelations were historical summaries of top-secret documents detailing the origins of America's role in Vietnam. The documents were given or "leaked" to *The New York Times* by the mysterious Daniel Ellsberg.

Ask Saigon Sally

Ellsberg once worked for the Rand Corporation "think tank." Founded in Santa Monica, California, in 1948, Rand provides policy analyses on U.S. national security and international relations issues for special government and business clients.

Jarhead Jargon

Called **"the plumbers"** because they were supposed to plug leaks, a White House team of ex-CIA and -FBI agents was created in 1971 to prevent security information from ending up in the hands of the press.

Ellsberg was a Harvard graduate who had been an aide in the Defense Department. He had served in both Washington and Saigon, and he had even been an advisor to Henry Kissinger. Throughout much of the 1960s, he had been a staunch supporter of the war. But the antiwar movement stirred his soul. A staunch moralist, Ellsberg became outraged at America's conduct in the war.

In 1967, Secretary of Defense McNamara had ordered that a secret history of the Vietnam War be put together, and Ellsberg had a final copy of the effort. Apparently this documented study was supposed to be turned over to Robert Kennedy during his 1968 campaign, and Ellsberg was proud to be connected to that campaign. Instead, the material would end up with the press three years later.

To Ellsberg, the "people's right to know" was more important than Washington's definition of national security. The Pentagon Papers contained all the sad and dirty details of the early Vietnam era, and the American people would be duly shocked after they read them. This was hot stuff.

At first Ellsberg asked *The Washington Post* to take it all, but the paper feared the Nixon administration's reaction. Nixon and Agnew often singled out the *Post* as an example of anti-Nixon, antiwar bias, more than implying that limits on free speech and the first amendment were required during times of war. To Benjamin Bradlee, the editor of *The Washington Post*, things were tough enough for his paper already.

The New York Times' publication of the Pentagon Papers angered the Nixon White House. Nixon ordered the creation of a *plumbers* group to halt what he considered treasonous activity, and if they could link Ellsberg and the entire antiwar movement to obvious acts of treason, that would be even better. Henry Kissinger gave his blessing here, agreeing that the White House faced a security crisis. He considered Ellsberg a "fanatic."

More to the point, both Nixon and Kissinger were embarrassed by Ellsberg. Nixon's efforts to paint rosy pictures of Vietnam read like all the lies Washington had fed the American people when the war began. To Nixon, the Pentagon Papers injured his own Vietnam policy, and people like Ellsberg had to be stopped. Meanwhile, Kissinger felt awful over the fact that he had once trusted Ellsberg, and he also worried that the revelations of older diplomatic efforts vis-à-vis Vietnam would harm his present-day efforts, too.

Dedicated to rescuing their boss from his latest Vietnam dilemma, the plumbers had no problem violating the law in the name of national security. They broke into the office of Ellsberg's psychiatrist, looking for smoking-gun evidence that would expose Ellsberg's treason and, it was hoped, that of his friends and colleagues as well. Names of possible accomplices, any links between communist agents and the antiwar movement, or any other inflammatory information was sought.

John Mitchell, the U.S. attorney general, believed that the heart of the 1970s communist conspiracy was the antiwar movement. With that in mind, the Nixon White House had no problem justifying its underground actions. The details of the plumbers' activities and their national security crusade would be revealed during the Watergate investigation. Shedding light on Nixon's distrust of anyone not in his inner circle, the later Watergate investigations would confirm the illegal mission of the plumbers.

Shell Shock

One of the Pentagon Papers' revelations involved U.S.-supported rigged elections in Vietnam. Partially in response to these revelations, the North Vietnamese said that they might be interested in a peace deal if President Thieu was freely and honestly elected.

In the meantime, an enemies list of public figures, ranging from entertainers such as Gregory Peck to veteran politicos such as Senator Fulbright, was put together by the Nixon staff. Some 200 names were on the list, and all were considered enemy sympathizers or worse. Facing growing opposition and the still no-win war in Vietnam, Nixon became terribly moody and bitter. He wanted to get the goods on the antiwar activists, even if it meant planting false stories in *Life* magazine about Ellsberg's treason and treasonous friends. The magazine temporarily went out of business before any false stories could be planted.

I'm the President, and You're Not

The Ellsberg matter indicated how far the Nixon team was ready to run with the security protection issue. It laid the foundation for the Watergate scandal, and it illustrated the paranoia of the entire Nixon White House. There could be no Watergate without Vietnam.

The frustration over the war, and the inability to accept criticism or opposition, led Nixon to make some strange decisions from 1972 to 1974. On top of it all was Nixon's interpretation of executive privilege. During times of war, the president must be especially powerful, he believed, and opposition to that power was treason. Few shared this view outside of the White House, but the country would learn a lot more about it after June 1972.

Shell Shock

Americans became less concerned about Vietnam as more American troops came home. Although the war waged on for the Vietnamese, some 400,000 U.S. troops were withdrawn by early 1972.

Tales from the Front

The March and April 1972 Battle of Quang Tri (or Easter Offensive) was not just a victory for American air power. The province was eventually liberated by ARVN troops, suggesting to some Washington policy-makers that "Vietnamization might be finally working." On the other hand, both the South Vietnamese and North Vietnamese learned here that the U.S. now preferred air support over ground support for ARVN.

An especially large problem for Nixon was America's growing disgust with the Saigon regime. After all these years and so many lives lost, the South Vietnamese government made little effort to look democratic, caring, or humane. The Pentagon Papers offered a dark portrait of American policy in that regard, and both Nixon and Kissinger saw political and diplomatic liabilities. Most likely, the 1972 voters would be demanding a cleaner, better government in Saigon, and the North Vietnamese dared the United States to make it happen.

Two blasts from the past, the now virtually powerless vice president of South Vietnam, Nguyen Cao Ky, and "Big Minh," offered challenges to Thieu's presidency. The White House made a big deal out of this first, great Vietnamization election, but Thieu embarrassed them all. He disqualified Ky from running, bullied Big Minh into withdrawing his candidacy, and stuffed ballot boxes to win 94 percent of the vote.

This time, the Nixon team had nothing to say to the press. There would be no more talk about a possible democratic government in Saigon someday. When speaking about Vietnam the stress would be on the U.S. troop withdrawals, and America's expectation that Thieu's government remained noncommunist. Hoping for a democratic South Vietnam was one thing, but U.S. policy was another. The still-being-enforced Truman Doctrine accentuated U.S. support for anticommunist regimes. Thieu never had to demonstrate his pro-democratic credentials, just his anticommunist ones. But the Nixon administration was reluctant to talk about its relationship with Thieu in public. Few Americans supported him. Nixon's White House news conferences about Vietnam always stressed U.S. troop withdrawals, and little else. This proved to be good politics, but not good enough to prevent all the questions about the Vietnam-related issue of Watergate.

From Quang Tri to Watergate

During the early 1972 presidential campaign, the U.S. Air Force dropped more bombs on Quang Tri province than at any other time in the war. Reminding many of their ferocity in the Tet Offensive, the North Vietnamese attacked in strength in Quang Tri. As it had in the Laos invasion, the United States stayed in the sky rather than on the ground, and the

North Vietnamese attack produced nothing but the *"Road of Horrors"* refugee crisis and a destroyed South Vietnamese province.

For Americans, it was more of the same old carnage in Vietnam. Many TV viewers switched channels to movies and game shows rather than watch more death in Southeast Asia. The news media got the message, and they highlighted presidential campaign coverage over battle coverage. This was bad news for Senator George McGovern. Opposing the horror of Vietnam was his reason for being, and hiding that horror did not help his political plans.

McGovern

Running in a crowded field of Democratic presidential hopefuls early in the primary season, McGovern was always able to win, thanks to his strong antiwar message. Even the front-runner, Ed Muskie, who tried to talk about a variety of issues, was run over by the McGovern antiwar steamroller.

McGovern appealed to the Democratic Party left as much as Goldwater had appealed to the Republican Party right. Like Goldwater, he survived the primaries thanks to consistent support from die-hards who rejected the several moderate candidates in the race. As they had with Goldwater, the party faithful would find it hard to deny McGovern the nomination, and because of this decision, they were on their way to a major defeat.

Throughout the 1972 general election, McGovern never got closer than 10 percent behind the president in the polls. To everyone's amazement, it looked like a Nixon cakewalk was ahead, and the political experts would never have predicted such a thing a few months before. McGovern's left-wing credentials, and not "Mr. Nixon's War," became the issue in the campaign.

Jarhead Jargon

In the 1972 Easter Offensive, the North Vietnamese crossed the 17th parallel into Quang Tri province with T–54 and PT–76 tanks. Remembering the Tet Offensive massacres of four years earlier, the South Vietnamese fled south on Highway 1. Parts of the road were shelled by the advancing North Vietnamese and hundreds were killed. The Quang Tri section of the highway was known as **"The Road of Horrors"** for years afterward.

Ask Saigon Sally

Ed Muskie's presidential campaign died in New Hampshire after he angrily criticized a Manchester newspaper editor for slandering his French Canadian wife. Muskie appeared to be crying, and a Nixon reelection campaign operative later falsely claimed to have drugged Muskie's coffee.

Ask Saigon Sally

McGovern's vice presidential pick, Senator Thomas Eagleton, was found to have spent time in a mental hospital for a nervous breakdown. McGovern cut Eagleton from the ticket after once proclaiming that he "stood behind Eagleton 1,000 percent."

But Nixon threatened his own good fortune when several "plumbers" and reelection operatives were arrested while breaking into the executive committee office of the Democratic Party at the new Watergate building in Washington, D.C. This failed burglary soon became a symbol of Nixon paranoia and corruption. Arraigned by a judge the following morning, the arrested burglars all claimed that their profession was "anticommunist." This bizarre answer got *The Washington Post* on their tail, and the White House decided to cover up its involvement in authorizing the break-in.

It was a deadly decision. Hiding from an inquisitive press was easier said than done, and it remains unclear what the burglars were supposed to have found at Watergate. Some of them believed that there were files there that linked the McGovern campaign to North Vietnam. This treason would be the smoking gun to kill off the antiwar movement and even the Democratic Party. If true, this smacks of the type of frustration, disgust, and anger that dominated White House decision-making at the time.

During the Watergate scandal, President Nixon meets with senior staff members in the Oval Office.

Nixon Presidential Materials Staff, College Park, Maryland.

In any event, the denials and counteraccusations hurled at the press were good enough to stall things until after the easy Nixon reelection. But the investigations didn't go away. What started in the press became a Senate investigation in the summer of 1973, and by that time, the coverup itself was an obstruction of justice issue.

"Tricky Dicky" Takes a Hike

Watergate was more than a botched burglary. Wrapped up in the misery of Vietnam, grandiose interpretations of executive privilege, and the sad personality of Richard

Nixon, Watergate symbolizes what had happened to the home front during a long, disastrous war. America's faith in government was a big casualty here. Without question, most Americans knew by the early 1970s that their government had lied about Vietnam developments. In Watergate, the government lied to protect careers and its own lame decisions. This stunned some Americans and angered the rest.

Nixon used wartime executive privilege to keep congressional and even Justice Department investigators away from White House evidence that might convict him. Loyal staff members sacrificed their careers to protect the man, believing that they had all fallen victim to their leftist, unpatriotic enemies. The American people continued to be amazed at this bizarre behavior, and couldn't have cared less about the president's love of executive privilege. The House of Representatives voted for impeachment in 1974 and a tough Senate trial was about to begin when Nixon resigned in August of that year. A *U.S. v. Nixon* court case loomed as well.

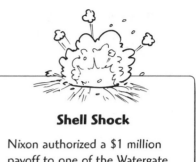

Shell Shock

Nixon authorized a $1 million payoff to one of the Watergate burglars. This order was recorded on audiotape, making it damning evidence against him in the congressional investigations of the break-in.

To his dying day 20 years later, Nixon believed his resignation had been an act of heroism. His successor, Gerald Ford, granted him a full pardon from any further prosecution. He said that it was issued in honor of Nixon's years of service, and in the name of avoiding further political polarization over Watergate.

The presidency, Nixon argued, had been under heavy attack throughout the scandal. Even Howard K. Smith, the anchorman of the *ABC Evening News* and a conservative supporter of the Nixon administration, called for a new parliamentary system where a British-like prime minister would replace the powerful president. He wasn't alone. Given the "no confidence" vote in the Parliamentary governments, a prime minister could be eliminated from office in a day. The Watergate scandal lingered for two years, while both domestic and foreign policy took a backseat. A big change was needed, many believed.

Ex-president Nixon always explained that if he had been put through a trial, the nation's anti-presidency opinion would have won out. He could have become the last U.S. president, and,

Shell Shock

Nixon's defense of executive privilege and the powerful presidency would have been at the heart of his own defense had the *U.S. v. Nixon* trial been held. In the late 1970s and 1980s, *U.S. v. Nixon* was one of the most popular mock trial cases in law schools across the United States.

therefore, his resignation saved the U.S. presidency and the Constitution. Corruption and paranoia became a grand patriotic act. It was an interesting argument, but that's all.

Tales from the Front

In Vietnam between 1970 and 1971, nurse Jacqueline Navarra Rhoads spent most of her tour with the 18th Surgical Hospital in Quang Tri. It was a so-called mass casualty care unit, and Rhoads was only 21 when she arrived there. During and after the war, few Americans knew about the horror that the Army nurses faced at Quang Tri and elsewhere in Vietnam. Her well-received 1987 book (co-authored by Dan Freedman), *Nurses in Vietnam: The Forgotten Veterans* (Austin: Texas Monthly Press), finally brought her and her fellow nurses international recognition.

Watergate or no Watergate, the Vietnam War continued. The American people might have gone into denial, turned off the TVs, and hid all the newspapers, but the war was still there. Of course, the boys filtered home during the Watergate scandal. There would be no parades or fanfare. The Vietnam War was finally a problem for the Vietnamese alone. Or was it?

The Least You Need to Know

➤ Vietnamization and the ARVN invasion of Laos were unsuccessful.

➤ President Nixon lied to the American people about the Laos failure.

➤ Frustrated by the lack of success in Vietnam, the Nixon White House viewed its critics as enemies and traitors.

➤ The Ellsberg matter was a preview of the larger Watergate scandal to come.

➤ There would have been no Watergate without the Vietnam War.

Part 5
Defeat and Renewal

In 1973 the boys came home, and Congress made sure that they stayed there. The War Powers Act made it difficult for the White House to contemplate Vietnam War, Part Three, and it ended up being a lasting legal legacy of the ugly Vietnam experience. Vietnam policy-making had involved some bizarre decisions, the American people had learned, and few trusted the Watergate-era presidency with any new life-or-death tasks. Saigon fell, and some said good riddance. America had truly changed, but this meant different things to different folks.

Movies about Vietnam reflected America's confusion over what took place there, and any diplomatic kissing and making up with Vietnam was out of the question for years. Everybody talked about what Vietnam had done to America, but few talked about what America had done to Vietnam. Time eased things. In 1997, a new era of reconciliation began with the reopening of the U.S. Embassy in Vietnam.

Chapter 25

Coming Home

In This Chapter

➤ Kissinger sends Nixon to China

➤ A checkerboard for South Vietnam

➤ Christmas is a time for bombing

➤ An almost peace for Vietnam

➤ Washington is a long way from Grand Rapids

Ronald Reagan trusted Richard Nixon, and it wasn't easy. As a die-hard supporter of Barry Goldwater, the California governor regarded Nixon as a political chameleon, a wishy-washy moderate who read too many polls. By the early 1970s, Goldwater's ill-fated run against Landslide Lyndon had been elevated to legend by many Republican conservatives. Reagan liked to speak on behalf of that legend, touting Goldwater Republicans as misunderstood patriots, victims of Democratic party lies, and the true champions of honest, no-nonsense conservatism and anticommunism.

In early 1972, when Nixon announced he was breaking America's nonrecognition of Red China and even going to Beijing himself, many Americans were shocked. But not Reagan. Ignoring the world's largest nation had been stupid, he said, but he worried about a sellout of American values and interests during a diplomatic visit over there. Given America's exhaustion over Vietnam, and the "in" ideas of the New Left, Reagan distrusted the entire Democratic Party and many Republicans with any China policy. Nixon had lifelong anticommunist credentials. He was one of the few American policy-makers, Reagan proclaimed, that the American people could trust in China.

American policy would stay on course, he predicted, and the war in Vietnam would not be compromised. Anticommunism was still in good hands with Richard Nixon.

Let's Go to China

Getting the nod from America's political right was important to Nixon. They were the financial and ideological heart and soul of the Republican Party, and the last thing he needed was both the antiwar movement and the Goldwater Republicans protesting his administration. Henry Kissinger helped him get this nod, and the trip to China was his idea.

Ask Jarhead Jargon

The Chinese premier and foreign minister, Chou En-lai, had sought a **rapprochement** with the Americans for years. Rapprochement refers to the first steps in reestablishing a relationship with a former enemy and ideological foe.

Ask Saigon Sally

American and Chinese ping-pong teams played against each other one year before the Nixon trip to China. Ping-pong is the national game of China, and the China vs. America tournaments prepared the people of both countries for the new relationship between their governments.

Since before the 1954 Geneva Conference on Asia, the Beijing regime had sought a *rapprochement* with the Americans, but nothing had come of it. The American presidents insisted that the Chinese represented the most evil of all communist governments on earth. There could be no recognition of evil. America's allies stopped ignoring China during the Vietnam War, and Henry Kissinger had no real problem with recognizing China. He thought that a new relationship with Beijing might bring some quick benefits to the United States.

First, Nixon's 1972 trip to China was wrapped up in Kissinger's academic thesis of proper U.S. diplomacy. Vietnam was always on the sidelines of Kissinger's big picture. Preventing nuclear war or World War III was that big picture, and getting along with China lessened the chances of that war.

Second, Kissinger wanted to scare the Soviets. What took place in a Nixon-Mao meeting was going to be kept secret, although hints of a very huggy-kissy relationship would be leaked to the press. If the Soviets interpreted the relationship as a budding U.S.-China military and diplomatic alliance, then they would be thinking what Kissinger wanted them to think. If the lousy China–Soviet Union relationship got even lousier, then that was good news for the United States, too.

As always, Kissinger thought a shouting match between the two big commie powers was great news for Washington. A divided communist world was supposed to be a good thing for the capitalist world. Given the many allies shouting at America for its "racist war" in Vietnam, it would be wonderful to see the communists at each other's throats for once.

Third, a new U.S.-China relationship would further isolate North Vietnam. The Soviets, now concerned about their own national security, would sever their connections to the North Vietnamese. Or so Kissinger hoped. This was a very roundabout way to influence Vietnam events, but Kissinger loved geopolitics. It was also quite a gamble.

Tales from the Front

In 1972, President Richard Nixon offered special recognition and press attention to the heroism of the guided missile frigate U.S.S. *Biddle*. Its mission was to patrol the Tonkin Gulf, and in 1972 it rescued 17 downed pilots, helped destroy 14 enemy jet fighters, and directed 158 airstrikes against North Vietnam. Although they were heroes of the Vietnam War, the crew of the *Biddle* never set foot on Vietnamese soil.

At first, both the American press and people were at a loss to explain the early 1972 Nixon trip to China. Then most concluded that it was a wonderful thing, and the White House played it up big. Nixon, the great peacemaker, was heading to China. America was on the verge of a wonderful, new post-Vietnam era, said the State Department, and peace would rule the land for the rest of the century and beyond.

Without question, most Americans wanted to believe the spin doctors. Somehow, they hoped, the Vietnam War would end quicker because of all this. Somehow, all the death and misery over there had had a higher purpose, and maybe world peace would be the result. The Cold War, some even said, was on its last legs. Thank God for Richard Nixon, the great peacemaker.

Throughout the Watergate scandal, the Nixon team often pointed out that U.S. foreign policy would be in peril if "the man who opened

Shell Shock

Nixon's China policy and political dreams came together in 1973. His staff advocated repealing the 25th Amendment so he could run for a third term and continue his G.O.P. (Generation of Peace) efforts with China. (Passed after the death of Franklin Roosevelt, the 25th Amendment made it illegal for an incumbent president to seek a third term in office.)

China" were to fall. This argument was as exaggerated as the public version of Nixon's China policy. Kissinger's geopolitics had little impact on the Vietnam War, and time was not on Nixon's side.

Let's Go to Paris

In October 1972, Kissinger announced to the world press that "peace is at hand." Because of security reasons, he had no details. And the Nixon reelection campaign had an interesting question for the electorate. Why vote for McGovern and his New Left peacenik friends, when you can get a respectable "peace with honor" from a tried-and-true anticommunist?

Ask Saigon Sally

One of the sticking points in the 1972 peace negotiations involved the return of "all" U.S. prisoners of war. The North Vietnamese claimed that they weren't sure where they all were, and the Americans, for a time, wondered why. Many Americans interpreted North Vietnam's claim to mean that hundreds of American prisoners of war were being deliberately hidden or kept in Vietnam for whatever reason. Others might have been killed, and the North Vietnamese refused to admit it. American imaginations ran wild.

Kissinger hinted that all U.S. troops could be home immediately after an agreement with the North Vietnamese was signed. Because McGovern usually talked about a 90-day or so withdrawal if elected, the Nixon team would be ending the war faster than a longtime peace advocate. It was a masterful irony, and it would have an impact on Nixon's landslide win over McGovern.

Signed or unsigned, a full "peace is at hand" deal had not been finalized when Kissinger made his announcement. The National Security Council advisor had stretched the truth, although he later claimed that he meant no harm by it. A real deal had been in the wings, but signatures to it were months away.

As always, the scene of the diplomatic action was Paris. The leisurely schedule remained in place; the Americans and North Vietnamese would meet for a couple of hours in a given week or month. But the pace was stepped up in the fall of 1972. For the Americans, the promise of a Nixon reelection loomed. The great peacemaker rhetoric could not continue without some arrangement over Vietnam. For the North Vietnamese, a certain battlefield reality had settled in. Their 1972 attack into Quang Tri had been a major disappointment. A little too cocky and overconfident in the face of the usually laughable ARVN, the North Vietnamese had lost too many men. U.S. air power in an already devastated Quang Tri had played a ruthless and effective role.

Tales from the Front

From 1969 to 1973, Gary Larsen worked as a Foreign Service Officer (FSO) in the Mekong Delta. Attached to the district office of a corrupt Thieu regime official, Larsen was bilingual Vietnamese. Larsen claims that none of his American superiors in Vietnam spoke Vietnamese or knew a thing about Vietnamese culture. He counts that as a major reason the U.S. lost the Vietnam War. Today, Larsen is chairman of the board of International City Bank, headquartered in Long Beach, California. He also runs Operation California, an international relief group that works in Cambodia and Vietnam.

For North Vietnamese delegate Le Duc Tho, getting the United States out of Vietnam permanently was essential to victory. If U.S. forces merely temporarily withdrew to nearby bases in Thailand or elsewhere in the Asian/Pacific region, North Vietnamese plans for reunification with the south would be delayed.

President Thieu was an important consideration in the peace deal. Both Kissinger and Nixon agreed that there could be no U.S. withdrawal unless Thieu remained in power. A coalition government was still not possible, and Kissinger realized that some sort of U.S. concession was needed to make the peace deal happen. He agreed to recognize the Vietcong as a legitimate political force in South Vietnam, and agreed to a cease-fire whereby North Vietnamese or Vietcong-controlled areas would remain under their control after the peace accord was signed.

According to this arrangement, a Vietcong unit could control a village only one rice field away from an ARVN-controlled village. The Americans would pull out within 60 days, and a National Council of Reconciliation and Concord would be established to create a new political order in South Vietnam. Nobody knew how the latter was supposed to work, and neither Kissinger nor Tho thought it ever would. But it looked good to the war-weary public, and that was important to the diplomats in Paris.

Ask Saigon Sally

During the ending stages of the Paris peace negotiations, the Senate Foreign Relations Committee asked to be part of the process in the name of reason and democratic fair play. The White House rejected the request as both an intrusion and a security risk.

The peace deal created something of a political checkerboard in South Vietnam, and all the sides remained armed to the teeth. President Thieu, who was never personally present during any of the Paris talks, rejected it. Kissinger didn't care. He urged Nixon to sign the deal and move along. To Kissinger's shock, Nixon sided with Thieu. The peace plan, he said, was truly unworkable. Kissinger would have to do better, for the deal still made South Vietnam too vulnerable to communist takeover. Meanwhile, Thieu feared that the plan might result in a communist/noncommunist coalition government, and without him in it. And Nixon thought that something else must be done to pressure the North Vietnamese.

Shell Shock

Despite White House claims to the contrary, U.S. losses in the 1972 Christmas bombing were high. In 12 days, 26 aircraft were shot down.

Ask Saigon Sally

Although he had little to do with any of the negotiations with the North Vietnamese, Secretary of State William Rogers signed the Paris Peace Accords on behalf of the United States. He resigned shortly afterward, and Kissinger took his job.

Christmas Bombs Bring a New Year's Peace

Kissinger asked Le Duc Tho to recognize special political powers for Thieu in the final deal. This time it was Tho's turn to refuse. Kissinger got depressed. Had the Paris talks been for nothing?

In December 1972, Kissinger urged the freshly re-elected Nixon to bomb North Vietnam around-the-clock, taking out any target anywhere. Nixon responded and, during the Christmas holidays, the U.S. Air Force began the most ferocious bombing campaign of the war.

Le Duc Tho returned to the bargaining table, and the White House claimed that it was the Christmas bombing that did the trick. There was no doubt that Le Duc Tho went back to Paris in the interest of halting the bombing, but there would be no special arrangements for Thieu. The North Vietnamese never changed their position, and the previously arranged checkerboard cease-fire plan was finalized as the Paris Peace Accords of January 1973.

Secretly, Nixon and Kissinger promised Thieu the moon. As U.S. troops headed out of Vietnam, the White House authorized a $1 billion aid plan for the South Vietnamese government. Nixon also promised Thieu a swift American rescue should his government face a North Vietnamese offensive.

Thieu wasn't sure what to believe. He worried that the Americans had abandoned him, and that all he was left with were big promises from a guy known for his fibbing and corruption. But Thieu was no saint either, and he had little choice in the matter. Kissinger tried to ease his mind. Arguing that America's entire anticommunist commitment was still at stake in Vietnam, Kissinger insisted that Thieu had nothing to worry about when it came to U.S. military reliability.

Publicly, the press questioned the Nixon White House about secret commitments to Thieu. Were American troops poised for a quick return? Thousands appeared to be at the ready from Thailand to Guam. An outraged Kissinger denounced these questions as baseless and ridiculous. The American press needed to trust the Paris Peace Accords, he said, and even talk them up a bit. Nixon, meanwhile, went after the press directly, urging them to stop being conspiratorial and start being supportive of American peace policy. The public-versus-private games continued.

Shell Shock

Nixon was evasive when it came to precise military commitments to Thieu during a North Vietnamese invasion. Thieu expected full commitment. Nixon hoped to employ naval and air power only.

One month after the signing of the Paris Peace Accords, former American prisoners of war cheer after their aircraft takes off from an airfield near Hanoi.

National Archives Still Pictures Unit, College Park, Maryland.

The "Decent Interval" Begins

If the checkerboard of ARVN-controlled hamlets were added up, some three quarters of South Vietnam would be considered loyal to the Saigon regime. Nixon hoped that meant something, but his administration was prepared for the worst. They hoped for a "decent interval" between the end of Vietnam War, Part One and the beginning of Vietnam War, Part Two.

Vietnam's National Council of Reconciliation and Concord might have prevented the Part Two from beginning, but both the South and North Vietnamese governments did everything they could to delay and cancel meetings. According to the accords, the United States was required to pull out its troops, so the Nixon team played around with some semantics. More than 9,000 U.S. troops and CIA field agents remained in South Vietnam. They were labeled civilian "advisors" in the employ of the Saigon regime. But nobody was fooled. Hiding an army was easier said than done.

273

Ask Saigon Sally

Some 24,000 U.S. troops were still in Vietnam at the time of the Paris Peace Accords. Two weeks before its signing, a resounding majority of Americans, said the Gallup Poll, demanded an immediate military withdrawal.

A certain uneasy, surreal quiet ruled the day in Saigon. To convince Americans that all was well, the Thieu government even established an Office of Tourism. The American people were urged to vacation in "beautiful Vietnam." Travel brochures were printed, and even targeted TV audiences in the upper Midwest were told of balmy breezes and sandy beaches. There were no takers.

A Development Office was also established, urging American businessmen to invest in the soon-to-be booming economy of South Vietnam. But only the guns kept booming. Cease-fire violations were common. An International Commission of Control and Supervision arrived in the spring of 1973 to keep the rival sides from killing each other, but these Hungarian, Polish, Canadian, and Indonesian troops were too few and ineffective to halt the cease-fire violations.

From the beginning, CIA analysts at the U.S. Embassy warned of a slow-moving buildup of enemy reserves, preparedness, and invasion training. The U.S. ambassador, Graham Martin, dismissed the reports as alarmist and defeatist. Still an enthusiastic Cold Warrior, Martin had complete faith in the Saigon regime and America's continuing commitment to defend it. His faith was misplaced.

Ask Saigon Sally

As a Michigan congressman, Gerald Ford had opposed both the New Frontier and the Great Society. During his first year as president, he vetoed 39 bills passed by the Democratic Congress, including the Freedom of Information Act.

A Ford, Not a Lincoln

Watergate, Watergate, and more Watergate. President Thieu did not understand this scandal, and through it all, he worried that America had forgotten about South Vietnam and the anticommunist mission there. The lack of attention in the American government and media even triggered a moral crisis in the ARVN. It also set off the rumor that the United States would never lift a finger against a North Vietnamese invasion. By the time of Nixon's resignation, the number-one sport in South Vietnam, Saigon officials joked, was trying to find some way out of the country.

Declaring that the "long national nightmare is over," Gerald Ford took over a White House and society in disarray. His "nightmare" comment referred to Watergate, and not the Vietnam War. Hailing from Grand Rapids, Michigan, Ford embodied Midwestern values, good old-fashioned honesty, and clean living. A former University of Michigan football player and a Yale Law School graduate, Ford was a quiet, modest man with a reputation for Harry Truman–like candor. He was a refreshing contrast to the scheming, scamming Nixon. But he had no intention of being the president who lost Vietnam.

Likeable guy or not, Ford posed some interesting contradictions for the American people. He told the graduating class of the University of Michigan that the Vietnam War had been a "tragic mistake." Yet he kept Henry Kissinger as secretary of state and considered his Asian/Pacific-based troops a rescue force for South Vietnam. Although he said that he was always committed to doing the right thing, his quick, full pardon of Richard Nixon seemed wrong to most Americans.

According to the polls, the American people had already relegated Vietnam and Watergate to the history books. They expected the new president to do something about the neglected, collapsing domestic economy. Opposed to government interventionism in fiscal matters, the Ford administration printed up *WIN* buttons for its business supporters, and did little else.

Jarhead Jargon

The U.S. inflation rate was 11 percent in 1974, and oil prices had risen 350 percent in one year. Ford rejected wage-and-price controls, and urged American businesses to handle things themselves. Ford called it his **WIN** (or Whip Inflation Now) approach to noninterventionist government and volunteer business.

Ford was politically vulnerable from the start of his term, and the Democrats smelled blood. The political pundits even talked about a need for a post-Vietnam foreign policy, but they were jumping the gun. The last gasp of the Vietnam War had yet to come.

The Least You Need to Know

➤ Kissinger hoped the opening of U.S. relations with China would have an impact on the progress of the Vietnam War.

➤ The Paris Peace Accords created a difficult and bizarre cease-fire plan.

➤ The Christmas 1972 bombings did not change the North Vietnamese position on the Paris Peace Accords.

➤ Disguised as civilians, thousands of U.S. troops remained in South Vietnam after the signing of the Paris Peace Accords.

➤ Although a different political animal from Nixon, Gerald Ford did not want to be the president to lose South Vietnam.

Chapter 26

The Fall of Saigon

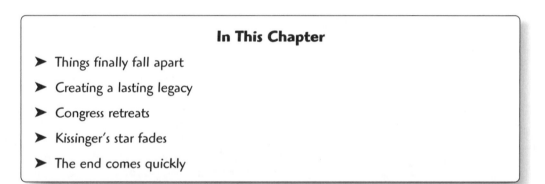

In This Chapter

➤ Things finally fall apart

➤ Creating a lasting legacy

➤ Congress retreats

➤ Kissinger's star fades

➤ The end comes quickly

Although it was called different things at different times, America's FEN (Far East Network) of the AFRTS (Armed Forces Radio and Television Service) had been a fact of life in South Vietnam. Meant to be a slice of Americana in an alien land, FEN radio was supposed to keep U.S. military personnel and expatriates up to date with pop culture, sports, and the news from home. In reality, it was as heavily censored as "The Five O'Clock Follies" (the press corp's nickname for the daily briefings by the U.S. high command and the Saigon regime).

FEN news was presented with a happy face. CBS-like reporting was not welcomed there. Labeled subversive, most of the Top 40 tunes from the United States were never played, and public service announcements asked its listeners to keep Saigon beautiful. The "safest" programming remained professional sports, and the baseball and football games were broadcast in their entirety and often. Of course, the time difference between America and South Vietnam often put the game on at an awkward hour. But at least somebody was speaking American, and even the South Vietnamese would listen to brush up on their English slang.

Tales from the Front

In 1964, Barry Zorthian came to Saigon from the U.S. Embassy in India. Originally put in charge of American propaganda efforts directed at the Vietnamese, Zorthian also became the coordinator of U.S. Embassy relations with the world press covering the Vietnam War. His daily afternoon briefings (nicknamed "Five O'Clock Follies" by reporters) put a positive spin on all American battle reports. Although he is targeted by historians and others for outright lying and deception, Zorthian claims that he held the line against bigger lies and deceptions insisted upon by Washington. Years after the war, Zorthian returned to the propaganda business as the news and information advisor to the Embassy of Oman in Washington, D.C.

Shell Shock

In December 1974, Soviet General Viktor Kulilov assured Hanoi that needed military supplies would be arriving shortly. That assurance helped determine the final push against the Saigon regime.

The FEN had remained on the outskirts of the war throughout its many years in South Vietnam. But in the spring of 1975, suddenly its broadcasts meant the difference between life and death. During the final North Vietnamese offensive on Saigon, the FEN played the old Bing Crosby classic "White Christmas." It was the signal for U.S. Embassy personnel and others to head for their evacuation points. The war was lost, and it was time to go home.

Final Days

The year 1974 had been a bad one for peace and sanity in Cambodia. Lon Nol's government continued to hang on by a thread, but forces loyal to him dwindled. By November 1974, the Khmer Rouge controlled the Mekong River, and the encirclement of Phnom Penh, Cambodia's capital, had begun.

The scene in surrounded Phnom Penh was surreal. The sidewalk cafes remained open for business, and the U.S. ambassador, John Gunther Dean, claimed that the enemy would never shell the city. Life was supposed to continue as usual, even though Phnom Penh had become one huge refugee camp. Close to three million refugees had fled to the capital city, and there was little for them to eat.

Chaos Rules

Dean claimed that the U.S. military had left Cambodia in 1970, and had no intention of returning; however, *The New York Times* and various television journalists had evidence to the contrary. B-52 raids on Khmer Rouge positions had taken place. While the U.S. press reported bombing operations and even "accidental" bombings on Cambodian soil, the official U.S. position ranged from "No comment" to outright denial. In August 1973, for instance, B-52s bombed the Cambodian village of Neak Luong. A mistake in navigation lead to this bombing, which killed 100 villagers. Ambassador Dean paid the survivors $100 each in compensation.

Tales from the Front

Thomas Polgar, the CIA station chief in Saigon from 1972 to 1975, remembered that after the fall of Saigon, the CIA held no debriefings, asked for no analysis or position papers, made no reports on mistakes made, and had nothing to say about future operations. "We just didn't believe," Polgar said, "that anything as 'bizarre' as Vietnam could ever happen again."

Privately, Dean reported to President Ford that Cambodia was in its death throes. The end was definitely near, and he worried that the Americans there might soon fall victim to a vengeful victor.

By March 1975, chaos also ruled nearby Laos. The capital city of Vientiane experienced daily antigovernment riots now, and Souvanna Phouma's efforts to halt the Pathet Lao had failed. Many of the Vientiane riots were organized by Pathet Lao troopers, and riots were repeated in smaller towns across the country. Meanwhile, the Laos-Thailand border was sealed by Pathet Lao fighters, and the battle threatened to spill over into Thailand.

Thailand had been spared the nightmares of Laos, Cambodia, and Vietnam. But the Thais had also hosted both the SEATO headquarters and a smattering of U.S. military bases. Washington worried that Thailand's fate might be sealed as well. They were wrong. The communists in Laos, Cambodia, and Vietnam concentrated on their home turf. It was the Americans who always worried about dominoes.

Ask Saigon Sally

One of Hanoi's chief strategists of the 1975 invasion, General Tran Van Tra, believed that ARVN's 1975 strength was more than one million men and that his own forces were less than one third that number. "Commitment and morale," he said, would win out over ARVN's superior strength.

Ask Saigon Sally

At the time of the North Vietnamese invasion, unemployment in South Vietnam was over 40 percent, inflation was over 60 percent, and the refugees in Saigon had upped the population from one million to four million.

Thieu's Suspicions

In South Vietnam, President Thieu continued to worry that the United States was not prepared to rescue his regime at a moment's notice. All the signals from Washington were bad. President Ford had become the most aloof and distant American leader that he had ever met. Ford's many years as a Michigan congressman had never put him in the forefront of the anticommunist crusade. He had issued the usual anticommunist statements, but what did that mean? Ford was a lukewarm anticommunist to Thieu, and he wanted assurances from the Americans that all was well in the Saigon-Washington relationship.

Thieu's suspicions were correct. Ford had little use for the Saigon regime, and his scaled-down military aid packages for them proved it. Thieu claimed that the lack of a massive aid plan would only help the North Vietnamese, and Ford, always the die-hard conservative, told him to make do. Thieu blamed Ford in advance for any ARVN setbacks on the battlefield.

Shortly after Christmas 1974, the opening bombardment of the North Vietnamese invasion began. Two divisions, with Soviet-made tanks, crossed into South Vietnam one week later. Thieu sent in a token force to stop them, expecting the Americans to rush in and crush the invasion. But no U.S. ground troops arrived and Ford ordered no U.S. air operations to cover the ARVN. Both Thieu and the North Vietnamese had just received an important message. The Americans were truly out of the fight.

You Storm, I'll Drizzle

During one of their famous "Road" pictures of the 1940s, Bing Crosby ordered Bob Hope to "storm" a heavily armed fortress. Hope answered, "You storm. I'll stay here and drizzle." In 1975, the U.S. Congress preferred to "drizzle," too.

What Nixon had called a "congressional revolution" gained steam in early 1975. In late January, dozens of young Democrats were sworn into office. The Republicans in both the House and the Senate had suffered a serious takedown in the November 1974 congressional elections. Given the Democrats' own contribution to the Vietnam nightmare, it wasn't easy labeling Republicans the "war party." Calling them the "Watergate party" worked better.

The new 1975 Congress was the youngest of the twentieth century, and most of these newcomers had learned their politics via the antiwar movement. Colorado's Gary Hart, for example, had worked his way up through the 1972 McGovern presidential campaign.

Opposing the Vietnam War had become an acceptable mainstream position by the time of the Paris Peace Accords, and during the height of the Watergate crisis, if anyone noticed, despising the Saigon regime became "in" politics, too. To new rabble-rousers like Hart, Pat Schroeder, Bella Abzug, and others, America's role in Vietnam had already ended. There would be no turning back the clock, and the Ford White House needed to accept that reality.

Shell Shock

Senator McGovern was still in office when Gary Hart was first elected. Hart kept his distance from his former mentor, preferring to accent his new moderate image and credentials.

The War Powers Act

To the 1975 Congress, it was irrelevant if the Paris Peace Accords included secret commitments to Thieu's South Vietnam. Only the War Powers Act was considered relevant. Carrying significant legal weight, the War Powers Act would be difficult for Ford to ignore. Disobeying an act of Congress could lead to his impeachment and jailing. Both the presidency and the American people had been through enough of that.

Authored by Clement Zablocki and tweaked by Senator Fulbright, the 1973 War Powers Act declared the Tonkin Gulf Resolution unconstitutional. Within 48 hours after dispatching U.S. troops overseas, the president now had to table a precise term paper to Congress explaining why he was putting troops in harm's way. The Congress could permit a maximum six-month intervention, and would meet now and then during this period to decide whether the military mission was a workable one.

Ask Saigon Sally

Gerald Ford was accident-prone, and comedian Chevy Chase built a career on it. Ford's slips and falls became the focus of Chase's slapstick comedy on NBC's surprise new hit of the 1975 television season, *Saturday Night Live*.

Both Nixon and Ford argued that there were too many commanders in chief now. National security had become a joke, they argued, and the Congress had overreacted to the situation in Vietnam. Public opinion strongly disagreed.

Ford had a hard time with the pro-Congress sentiment in the country. His two predecessors had been superpowerful, and according to most political scientists, since the

Jarhead Jargon

In 1975, the new Congress came up with the **Discomfort Index.** In domestic affairs, it combined the escalating unemployment and inflation rates. In foreign affairs, it kept close track of funding being "wasted" in Vietnam.

1930s a strong presidency was supposed to be a good thing. Maybe Johnson and Nixon had been abusive guys, but Ford said that he had little use for those kinds of abuses. He wanted the country to trust him and keep most foreign policy-making powers in the Oval Office. But America's trusting days were over.

Congress had been Jerry Ford's home for more than 25 years, but now it was a bad place in his view. It had pushed America into an eternal national security crisis, he said. Amazingly, public opinion polls noted that Ford, a decent guy, would restore a working relationship between Congress and the White House. Few believed that he shared the same views on "executive privilege" as Nixon and Kissinger. They were wrong.

To counter the hell and damnation from the White House, Congress insisted that they had taken a first step in removing America from the *Discomfort Index*. U.S. foreign policy was now declared more open and democratic. The days of lies and secrets, they argued, were gone for good.

In April 1975, President Ford meets in emergency session with his National Security Council to discuss the evacuation of the U.S. Embassy in Saigon.

Gerald R. Ford Library, Ann Arbor, Michigan, and photographer David Hume Kennerly.

But their War Powers Act had loopholes bigger than a 1975 Buick. The president could attach U.S. forces to a United Nations peace-keeping operation, for instance, and keep the boys overseas for as long as he wanted. Or he could just do his own thing and let the Justice Department argue the old executive privilege line in the Supreme Court. Ford and Kissinger threatened to go this latter route someday. A scowling Kissinger predicted a big win in that case, followed by a little presidential wrath on the Congress.

Bad Days for Henry

To Kissinger, the new Congress represented the old Isolationism. His biggest worry was that the Vietnam War would lead to a 1920s-like rejection of world affairs. The Cold War still raged, and an American retreat from it would be disastrous, he believed. The Congress was leading the country in the wrong direction, and the White House had a moral obligation to stop them.

Tales from the Front

In April 1975, when told by a reporter that the last helicopter had left Saigon, Secretary of State Henry Kissinger said that he now feared the return of 1920s-like U.S. isolationism, communist aggression everywhere, and anti-American backlashes from wavering allies. The U.S. had entered a new Dark Age, he believed, and it could have been avoided by standing firm behind the Saigon regime. His predictions were wrong.

Even before North Vietnam's final push, Kissinger was concerned about another potential brushfire war in a Third World country. In Angola, once a ruthless Portuguese colony in southwest Africa, independence had brought horrible violence and even the introduction of Cuban troops to help the procommunist movement there. Kissinger saw the makings of a new Vietnam in Angola, and the fact that Cuban troops were involved was especially embarrassing and disgusting to him. A tiny island only 90 miles south of Miami now had its own global policy, and America was heading into isolationism. What a sick irony. Or so Kissinger thought. It made him angry, and he displayed it all in front of Congress.

Ask Saigon Sally

In 1975, the Congress passed the Energy Policy and Conservation Act. Its most controversial provisions required a 27.5-mile-per-gallon average fuel economy from U.S. automobiles and set the national speed limit at the "double nickel" (55 miles per hour).

Appearing before the Senate Foreign Relations Committee, Kissinger told its new chairman, Frank Church, that the Ford administration could not rule out a U.S. military role in Angola. The communist world needed to know, he argued,

Shell Shock

In mid-March 1975, the North Vietnamese shelled fleeing civilians and retreating ARVN forces in South Vietnam's Central Highlands. Some 15,000 ARVN troops died and estimates for killed refugees numbered as high as 100,000.

that Vietnam was only a temporary problem for the United States in the Cold War. Angola might be the best place to make a new anticommunist stand in the Third World.

Although Kissinger picked his words carefully, he still sounded like he was lecturing the little men in Congress. It also sounded like he still didn't get it. America was fed up with brushfire wars in faraway places. Church asked Kissinger whether U.S. policy was at stake in Angola or just his academic-like thesis of foreign policy. Kissinger's reception on Capitol Hill was not friendly.

The years 1975 and 1976 would represent Kissinger's lowest days. Once the darling of the media, he was no longer seen as the good guy who hoped to tone down the Cold War. One of the few survivors of the Watergate scandal, Kissinger had lost his jaunty look of the early shuttle diplomacy days. He looked like the bad guy who would send your returning Vietnam veteran son or husband to Angola.

Kissinger had become increasingly bitter about Washington politics. He had lost the green light to conduct foreign policy in secret, and then tell the press whatever he felt like telling it. The times had changed very quickly, but events moved even quicker in Vietnam.

Don't Forget the Flag

In 1975, economic conditions in South Vietnam were considered four times worse than that of America during the Great Depression. Already struggling and hopelessly corrupt, the South Vietnamese economy lost 300,000 jobs when most of the Americans pulled out. As a result, there was little law and order. South Vietnamese military pilots charged infantry commanders high fees to fly their men to the battlefield. All the Thieu government needed was a push, and over the edge it would go. The North Vietnamese gave it a big push.

Hanoi's early 1975 military successes in the Central Highlands continued to answer important questions for them. The ARVN was weaker than ever, and the Ford administration didn't seem to care. This meant a grand offensive was destined to succeed, and the North Vietnamese finally saw victory on the not-too-distant horizon.

As North Vietnamese troops poured into the northern provinces of South Vietnam, Thieu ordered a full military withdrawal. It was not a popular decision with ARVN commanders. Any retreat would look like a rout, they argued, and the psychological impact on the country would be devastating. Thieu stuck to his guns, so to speak, and the withdrawal did indeed become a rout of scared-to-death ARVN troops and local residents. The coastal city of Danang, once a major U.S. base, was their first destination, and the city could not handle the arriving rabble of armed, desperate men and hungry refugees.

Ambassador Graham Martin refused to respond to the reports of imminent North Vietnamese victory, insisting that the Thieu regime would rally and prevail in the Saigon area. He urged his staff to conduct themselves with dignity, and to offer encouragement to their struggling ally. But embassy personnel spent night and day trying to arrange the safe passage out of the country for their closest South Vietnamese colleagues. Only a token number of South Vietnamese nationals could be taken in any fast-moving evacuation. Given the atrocities committed against pro-American South Vietnamese during the Tet Offensive, a horrible bloodbath was feared after the North Vietnamese arrived in Saigon.

Meanwhile, the U.S. Congress turned down a last-minute request from President Ford for $722 million in military aid. They did approve a budget for the evacuation of American citizens and some South Vietnamese. Ambassador Martin was going home.

A bitter President Thieu resigned on April 21, 1975, and fled the country. Tran Van Huong and then Big Minh would take charge, asking the North Vietnamese for a cease-fire. They refused. A hastily put-together helicopter evacuation operation (codenamed Frequent Wind) rescued 5,000 people from the U.S. Embassy and other rooftop pickup points in central Saigon. Nine hundred of those 5,000 were Americans, and all were brought to waiting aircraft carriers offshore. It was the end of April 1975, and the end of America's "great adventure" in Vietnam. Cambodia and Laos were now in the enemy's hands as well.

The FEN's last news broadcast from Saigon was written by the evacuating CIA personnel at the embassy. It declared the Vietnam War an American defeat that should not have happened, apologized to the people of South Vietnam, and asked for forgiveness. It was a moving commentary. Few heard it.

Ask Saigon Sally

ABC News scooped CBS News in the coverage of the evacuation of Americans from Dan ang. An ABC News film crew was on the last transport plane as American citizens fought off dozens of frightened ARVN troops in order for their overloaded plane to take off safely.

Tales from the Front

Lasting only two days (April 29 and 30, 1975), Operation Frequent Wind flew dozens of rescue helicopters (CH-53s and CH-46s) and a Marine protection force of 865 to downtown Saigon. The larger CH-53s picked up evacuating Americans near Saigon's Tan Son Nhut airport, and the smaller CH-46s landed on rooftops of the U.S. Embassy compound. The final evacuation helicopter left for an awaiting aircraft carrier offshore at 7:53 P.M., April 30, 1975.

Shell Shock

Author and former CIA agent Frank Snepp wrote that a drunken Thieu, cursing the Ford administration, left Saigon with American gold bars jiggling in his suitcase. Thieu denied the account. He made his first postwar homes in Taiwan and England, but later moved to Cambridge, Massachusetts.

The Least You Need to Know

➤ South Vietnam's economy, military, and political life collapsed even further following the U.S. withdrawal.

➤ The fall of Cambodia and Laos coincided with the end of the Saigon regime.

➤ The United States did not send a military rescue force to assist the South Vietnamese in 1975.

➤ The newly elected 1975 Congress took a strong stand against any further U.S. military role in South Vietnam.

➤ Without U.S. military aid, the fall of Saigon came quickly.

Chapter 27

Hollywood Goes to Vietnam

In This Chapter

➤ Vietnam is too ugly for the movies

➤ Anybody want to see my depressing Vietnam film?

➤ Chuck and Sly to the rescue

➤ Fantasy sells

➤ Reality can sell, too

Vietnam is a touchy subject. It divides, hurts, and disturbs people. A dirty, corrosive war is not a pleasant topic, and no one wants to be miserable. This was Hollywood's conclusion for years. It was echoed in America's universities.

Nearly a decade after the Vietnam War ended with the fall of Saigon, many of the country's finest institutions of higher learning still refused to teach courses about it. Academic administrators worried about resurrecting the old hawk versus dove fights in the classroom. The topic was too emotional, they argued, for objective study. But eventually Hollywood took the plunge, and there were plenty of veterans and others who wanted to know why there had been a Vietnam War. Concluding that a Chuck Norris movie or two was not how Americans should learn about the Vietnam War, academe changed its conservative ways.

Today most campuses offer Vietnam War history classes, and their curious students do not throw chairs at each other during a lecture. To the typical twenty-first-century college freshmen, the Vietnam War is ancient history. Few know that America fought on

Shell Shock

Arthur Penn, director of 1970's *Little Big Man*, claimed that his film about a survivor of the Indian wars was really about the "war of genocide" in Vietnam. Many viewers missed the connection.

the side of a country called South Vietnam. Those who do know took the course because it fulfilled three credits. Besides, if you watch old movies like *Platoon* or *Apocalypse Now,* you've learned what needs to be learned about Vietnam. Right?

The Taboo Topic

In contrast to both World War II and the Korean War, Hollywood was reluctant to make a movie about Vietnam while the war was being waged. The American people were divided over the conflict, and the nightly news brought horror into the country's living rooms night after night. Who would you make the movie for? Hadn't the country been through enough? A Vietnam film meant box office failure and public derision. Or so the Hollywood producers believed.

A notable exception was John Wayne's *The Green Berets*. Filmed in the U.S. South in 1968, *The Green Berets* was the usual gung-ho John Wayne war movie. This one happened to take place in Vietnam. A friend of both Barry Goldwater and Ronald Reagan, Wayne was proud of his conservative Republican credentials and pro–Vietnam War position. He had little use for antiwar protestors, and had complete faith in the U.S. military's ability to prevail in South Vietnam.

The Green Berets included a Wayne ensemble cast that went back decades. Veteran actors Bruce Cabot, Aldo Ray, Jim Hutton, and others portrayed kindly, all-American soldiers, while David Jansen, fresh from his hit TV series *The Fugitive,* played a doubting reporter. Georgia pines would appear now and then, and the entire cast was way too old to be playing combat soldiers. Yet Jansen's character would switch from dove to hawk by the film's end, and Wayne's character would have to admit that Vietnam was not a "normal war."

Leave it to the bull-in-the-china-shop Wayne to be the grand trailblazer of Vietnam films, but some of his best fans thought he should have stuck to Westerns and World War II heroics. Antiwar pickets of movie theaters showing the film were few, for student activists and others did not want to give the film additional publicity. In any event, *The Green Berets* did not open the door to more prohawk films, or prodove films for that matter. Wayne called *The Green Berets* an exercise in pure entertainment versus some sort of statement on Vietnam. Whatever it was, Hollywood wouldn't make any more of them for a while.

Television was better at taking on the Vietnam War topic, but with mixed results at first. As it did in its news coverage of the war, CBS led the way. *The Smothers Brothers Comedy Hour* dared to satirize the war and openly criticize the White House. Although a popular program, it was canceled in 1969 due to its overdose of controversy.

John Wayne was a frequent visitor to Vietnam. Here he signs PFC Fonsell Wofford's helmet during his visit to the 3rd Battalion, 7th Marines, at Chu Lai.

National Archives Still Pictures Unit, College Park, Maryland.

Two years later, CBS's *All in the Family* tried it again. This time, the venue was a half-hour sitcom about a working-class family with a hawk patriarch and a dove son-in-law. Their on-screen arguments over the war were brief, tame, and meant for comic relief, but many CBS affiliates saw the show as an attack on family values and the nation's war policy. Some refused to show it. Others compromised and aired it late at night for "mature audiences." Its producer, Norman Lear, expected the show's crude and rude prowar main character, Archie Bunker, to become something of the laughingstock. Instead, he won numerous fans and inspired bumper stickers with Bunker one-liners and even a tongue-in-cheek 1972 "Bunker for President" campaign.

Ask Saigon Sally

Carroll O'Connor, the star of TV's *All in the Family*, hated his Archie Bunker character. Campaigning for George McGovern in 1972, O'Connor went out of his way to prove his own antiwar credentials.

Shell Shock

During the late 1960s, when their senior officers removed rock and R&B records from a PX jukebox in Danang, young African American marines rioted to get them returned. The records had been labeled subversive.

Trailblazing Movies and TV

The first big-budget movie about the war, *The Deer Hunter* was released more than three years after the fall of Saigon. It was a long, moody film about struggling yet optimistic friends who leave their working-class drudgery and experience endless horrors in Vietnam. It brought back the old hawk versus dove arguments with a vengeance. Ned Tanen, then the president of Universal Pictures, was even tackled and beaten by an outraged hawk on the night of the film's premier.

The Deer Hunter even depicted captive American soldiers forced to play a grisly game of Russian roulette by their Vietcong captors. America lost its innocence in Vietnam, said the film's director Michael Cimino, and former antiwar activists claimed that his depiction of American life and culture was well done. The Academy Awards agreed with the antiwar activists, and the film was praised for its "bravery." Ironically, one of those awards was handed out by a sick and dying John Wayne.

In one way or another, all of the movie's main characters were changed, wounded, and disturbed by the Vietnam War. This lost innocence theme laid a foundation for other Vietnam films. The veteran emerged as a half-crazed loser who might never be able to adjust to life in *the world*. This image was powerfully presented in the low-budget movies *Coming Home* (1978) and *Heroes* (1977).

Jarhead Jargon

U.S. military slang for a trip back to CONUS (continental United States) was known as "going back to **the world.**" Such a phrase carried the connotation that after Vietnam, an adjustment to American life and culture might be difficult.

Tales from the Front

Nicknamed "the unofficial concierge of Hanoi," Chuck Searcy returned to Vietnam in 1995 to head the Vietnam Veterans of America Foundation's orthotics program. The latter provides corrective braces for Vietnamese children injured by leftover mines and other explosives from the Vietnam War. Searcy had been an Army intelligence analyst stationed in Saigon during the late 1960s. Today, he assists returning American veteran groups in Hanoi, consults with U.S. businessmen contemplating an entry into the Vietnamese economy, and offers advice to journalists arriving in Vietnam for the first time.

Coming Home was partially financed by Jane Fonda, and she costarred with Jon Voight in the film as well. Having gone to Hanoi during the war in order to make a more meaningful antiwar statement, Fonda was either loved or hated for her commitment. *Heroes* featured Henry Winkler, star of TV's nostalgic *Happy Days* sitcom about Midwest teen life in the 1950s. His character's nationwide efforts to get together with fellow Vietnam veterans constituted the sad plot of the movie. Both films portrayed returned veterans as former cogs in the wheel of an evil war machine. Now they were broken, forgotten, and discarded. Washington was to blame. The American people were to blame. And something had to be done. That something remained up to the viewers to decide.

Ask Saigon Sally

Jerome Hellman, who produced *Coming Home*, claims that all the Hollywood studios except United Artists rejected his project. When the film was completed, United Artists complained that it was too anti-American to be marketed successfully.

At first, veterans groups were divided over Hollywood's depiction of Vietnam veteran issues. Some welcomed the publicity and visibility. The Veteran's Administration had been underfunded for years, and any public outcry over that fact could only move Congress to do something about it. On the other hand, the movies continued to portray veterans as a collection of freaks and ex-baby killers. If Hollywood was a friend to the veteran, who needed enemies?

In contrast to the depressed and victimized Vietnam veteran theme, there was the upbeat and heroic antiwar activist theme. In 1970s films like *Getting Straight* with Elliot Gould, *The Strawberry Statement* with Anthony Quinn, and director Rob Cohen's autobiographical film about his days as an antiwar activist at Harvard, *Small Circle of Friends,* the antiwar activist was good-looking, steady, dedicated, and influential. One of the reasons for this contrast was the simple fact that many young Hollywood filmmakers were involved in the antiwar movement. They never knew any veterans.

A Few Good Superheroes

Time heals all wounds, the old saying goes, and it certainly rang true in the 1980s. Vietnam films and television programs became "in" for a while, and the Vietnam veteran went from half-crazed goofball to Superman in fatigues.

Magnum, P.I.

In 1980, CBS's *Magnum, P.I.* assumed the production facilities of the long-running *Hawaii Five-O.* Filmed entirely in Hawaii, the latter had been a Thursday night mainstay for CBS since 1968. Hawaii had been a primary rest and recreation (R and R) location for U.S. servicemen finishing off their Vietnam tour. In several episodes,

Shell Shock

A hot box–office draw in 1980, actor Burt Reynolds was offered the part of Thomas Magnum on CBS's *Magnum, P.I.* Reynolds turned it down, complaining that a show about Vietnam buddies in Hawaii would never make it. *Magnum, P.I.* ran for eight years, and continues in reruns more than a decade after its last filming.

Hawaii Five-O had depicted both veterans and R and R troopers as troubled, desperate men who turned to crime.

Magnum, P.I. might have retained the same locale and sets, but it did not carry on the *Hawaii Five-O* view of the Vietnam soldier. Its three main characters, Thomas Magnum (played by Tom Selleck), T. C. (played by Roger Mosley), and Rick Wright (played by Larry Manetti) were all Vietnam veterans who headed to Hawaii together, stuck together, and moved on with their lives together. None of them killed babies, robbed banks, wallowed in despair, or railed against Washington. They went about their business with a sense of humor, although the war remained the defining moment of their lives.

Although the pretty location, snappy writing, a red Ferrari 308, and handsome hunk Tom Selleck kept the show in the top 10 for years, veteran groups credited the show for giving Vietnam veterans an upbeat, positive image. Selleck's private detective character was more Three Stooges than Sherlock Holmes, but he was definitely the hero of the program. That was most unusual for its day, but the hero worship was just beginning.

Ask Saigon Sally

In *Missing in Action, I,* superhero Chuck Norris rescues dozens of American soldiers once presumed dead in Vietnam. Although panned by the critics, the film received rare standing ovations from audiences in theaters across the United States.

Norris and Stallone

Chuck Norris was an unlikely movie hero. Although an undefeated martial arts champion in the 1960s, he was a self-described lousy actor. Norris credited the commitment and dedication learned through martial arts training for his rise to movie stardom. Once a screen double for superstar Steve McQueen, Norris counted "chopsaki" film star Bruce Lee as a friend and sparring partner. Norris strove to be the American version of Hong Kong's Lee, and, although the critics never cared for him, 1980s audiences did.

In spite of being overshadowed by three 1980s films about Sylvester Stallone's fictional John Rambo, Norris made three films, too. All of them took place in Vietnam.

Norris's Colonel James Braddock character was featured in two films about rescuing American POW/MIAs.

A third had him saving Amerasian orphans and others in Vietnam. As in Stallone's *Rambo II,* Braddock did most of the rescuing on his own. He could wield heavy twin machine guns like they were twigs, take on company-strength enemy units with hand grenades and flying jump kicks, and apparently had no problem sneaking in and out of Vietnam whenever he felt like it.

Tales from the Front

"How do you ask a man to be the last man to die for a mistake?" Upon hearing this statement made by Vietnam Veterans Against the War (VVAW) activist and future Massachusetts Senator John Kerry, psychiatrist Robert Jay Lifton analyzed a number of Kerry's VVAW colleagues. His early 1970s analyses and observations led to his conclusion that many veterans suffered from what he called "post-traumatic stress disorder" (PTSD), or difficulty in returning to peacetime life after experiencing the horror of war. Lifton had already been well-known in medical circles for his work with American POWs of the Korean War, particularly those who had been the victims of psychological experiments by their captors. Lifton's conclusion that Vietnam veterans suffered more stress-related problems than veterans from other wars was accepted by the American Psychiatric Association in 1980. But debates over Lifton's work continued, for he had been an avowed antiwar activist during his early studies of PTSD.

Only one of the Rambo films had a Vietnam setting. In fact, the first Rambo film, *First Blood,* had Sylvester Stallone playing a disturbed Vietnam veteran of the 1970s Hollywood mold. He reverted to his Vietnam killing machine days when threatened by a sadistic small-town police department somewhere in the U.S. Northwest.

Stallone's inarticulate macho man turned one-man army, and Norris's quiet avenger-cum-rescuer, both struck a nerve in the United States. Their films presumed that American POW/MIAs were still trapped and abused by a vicious enemy in Vietnam. Some said that they were being used as slave labor. Others said that they were pawns in some sort of big political game. The more Congress and the Reagan administration denied

Shell Shock

In the mid-1980s, Congressman Bob Dornan (Republican, California) shocked his colleagues by calling for an immediate rescue of American POW/MIAs in Vietnam. He planned to accompany the rescue force himself, and won the nickname "Rambo Dornan" because of it.

these rumors, the more moviegoers cried coverup. For Hollywood, it was money in the bank. The producers had been wrong—Vietnam made money.

If only America had had these heroes in the field during the war, the Rambo and Braddock fans told themselves, there would have been no defeat in 1975. But they read a little too much into these flicks. Rambo and Braddock were comic-book characters on film, and little else. Some veterans said these new heroes made them feel proud to be American, but it usually took them a couple of six-packs to say it. Was America ready for a realistic depiction of warfare in the jungles of Vietnam?

Francis and Oliver Go to Vietnam

Nearly a quarter-century after it was filmed, Francis Ford Coppola's *Apocalypse Now* remains controversial. Taking years to complete and then more years to find a willing, suitable distributor, the movie had a strong cast (headed by Martin Sheen and Marlon Brando), a big budget, and a dark, bizarre script. Loosely based on Joseph Conrad's novel *Heart of Darkness, Apocalypse Now* excited the critics of 1979 and 1980. Although it had something of a cult following, the film broke no records at the box office.

Ask Saigon Sally

From Martin Sheen's on-set heart attack to typhoons and tropical diseases, the Philippines-based filming of *Apocalypse Now* had its share of problems. Director Coppola even made a documentary about it, entitled, of course, *Heart of Darkness*.

To veterans, *Apocalypse Now* was surreal, poetic, and just plain strange. To Coppola, those descriptions fit Vietnam quite well. Vietnam was "crazy" policy, a "crazy" place, and if viewers thought his film was "crazy," then they got the message. If the audience wanted a gritty, realistic depiction of men in combat, they were going to have to look elsewhere.

Fellow filmmaker Oliver Stone accepted Coppola's challenge. To Stone, Coppola had broken new ground in making a Vietnam War film that took place in Vietnam rather than on the American home front. The reality check time had arrived. Stone, a Vietnam veteran who claimed that he was forever traumatized by the war, wanted the moviegoer to see what he meant by trauma. If the movie stirred up old emotions and debates, then so much the better.

Platoon (1986) and *Born on the Fourth of July* (1989) defined the in-your-face style of Oliver Stone. Old hawks said he made the average foot soldier look less than glamorous, honorable, or heroic. The typical Vietnam veterans, they said, were not the foul-mouthed misfits portrayed in his films. Old doves praised Stone's depiction of the war's savagery, misery, and dehumanization. Right on, they shouted! Stone had exposed the evil of Vietnam.

The truth, of course, was somewhere in between. Stone's story of daily life for an isolated, forgotten, and struggling platoon combined a variety of actual and rumored events and atrocities reported by the press throughout the war years. One often-discussed report (depicted in the film) had an American soldier saving his own hide by using another soldier as a human shield. Drug use was also depicted as a matter of course, and always in Stone's platoon the simple desire for survival beat out military objectives and the desire for victory.

Born on the Fourth of July, based on Ron Kovic's highly acclaimed book of the same name, took the foot soldier out of Vietnam and into a stateside VA hospital. The film exposed the horrid conditions for returning veterans with war-related disabilities. It also traced the progress of one wounded veteran (played by Tom Cruise) whose politics shifted from hawk to dove because of his ordeal. In reaction, medical and government officials cried exaggeration and artistic license, while some veterans said that Stone was too polite to the VA and the government. As always, there was no resolution to all the charges and countercharges.

Ask Saigon Sally

The son of a World War II lieutenant colonel, Oliver Stone went to Vietnam in 1965 as a schoolteacher. He wrote a book about his experiences there, could not find a publisher, and ended up a combat soldier who, for a while, volunteered for the most dangerous search and destroy missions possible.

Shell Shock

Although some Vietnam veterans, such as Massachusetts senator John Kerry, confessed to some misgivings about a Hollywood comedy about Vietnam, it was inevitable that such a film would be made. In 1987, Touchstone Pictures released *Good Morning, Vietnam,* starring comedian Robin Williams. The film was a sensitive portrayal of American life in Saigon before the major escalation of the war, seen through the eyes of a funny deejay (based on the life of Adrian Cronauer) working for the "sanitized" Armed Forces Radio and Television Service (AFRTS).

Movie trends have a short shelf life, and the filmgoers' interest in Vietnam peaked in the early 1990s. Films with titles like *Full Metal Jacket* and *The Hanoi Hilton* were still being made, but the 1991 Gulf War proved that the U.S. military was no longer the Vietnam-era military. Perhaps it was time to move forward and stop dwelling on the ugly past. Stone didn't hear any of this. His *Between Heaven and Earth* was made in the 1990s, but in his classic 1980s approach.

Chronicling the horrors experienced by a Vietnamese woman during the war, her journey to the United States, and her new misery once she arrived, *Between Heaven and Earth,* like *Platoon,* combined dozens of facts and rumors into one wrenching tale of survival and redemption. For many film freaks, though, enough was enough. Not even box office sensation Tommy Lee Jones could save *Heaven and Earth* from a financial hell.

Be it Chuck Norris's Colonel Braddock or Tom Cruise's Ron Kovic, the big question has been always the same: Why were we in Southeast Asia? As long as the answer remains elusive, there will be movies about the Vietnam War.

The Least You Need to Know

➤ During and immediately after the Vietnam War, Hollywood considered Vietnam a wrenching topic that would never attract a film-going audience.

➤ The early film depictions of the Vietnam veteran were negative ones.

➤ Hollywood superhero films accented POW/MIA issues and suggested that America still had "the right stuff."

➤ Old 1960s hawk versus dove arguments lived on in the 1980s Vietnam War films.

➤ The popularity of realistic Vietnam War films faded after the Gulf War.

Chapter 28

The Road to Normalization

In This Chapter

➤ How to go nowhere

➤ POW/MIAs are the key

➤ Our new man in Vietnam

➤ Getting on with it

In early 2000, some wartime junk was found near a rice field in northern Vietnam. Finding this kind of stuff is not unusual there. As happened in the Pacific islands after World War II, yesterday's war materiel becomes today's scrap metal export. Scrap metal exporting remains an important business for impoverished Vietnam.

If the remains of American servicemen are suspected to be near a finding, the new U.S. Embassy in Vietnam requests the right to investigate. In mid-March 2000, it did just that, and drew some sad conclusions. The war materiel was believed to be the remains of an F-4B Phantom jet piloted by Navy Commander Richard N. Rich of Stamford, Connecticut. Two pieces of bone were found in the muddy earth. Rich's F-4B was shot down May 19, 1967, by a surface-to-air missile. The plane's radar intercept officer, Lieutenant Commander William Stark, parachuted from the diving aircraft. He was captured, imprisoned, and released in March 1973.

Secretary of Defense and Vietnam veteran William Cohen was visiting Vietnam when Rich's plane was found. He was the first senior White House official to visit Vietnam since the 1975 defeat. Although saddened by the discovery, Cohen had no intention of dwelling on what happened to Rich or the war that killed him. It was time to move forward, he insisted.

The "moving forward" theme was a favorite one of the U.S. ambassador there, Douglas "Pete" Peterson. But America and Vietnam had been trying to move forward for years. It's been a rocky road.

What Vietnam?

President Gerald Ford made it clear in 1975: As far as his administration was concerned, there was no country called Vietnam. Its leaders were evil, and America needed to sound as anticommunist as possible now that the Vietnam War was over. SEATO folded, Thailand and Taiwan kicked out the U.S. bases they had allowed, and the Soviets said that the imperialist Americans got what they deserved in tiny Vietnam. These were embarrassing days for lifelong American anticommunists. There could be no diplomatic connection to Hanoi because of it.

Jarhead Jargon

Nonrecognition is a diplomatic term referring to a complete U.S. ban on diplomatic, cultural, economic, or any other ties to a potential enemy. **Normalization** refers to the step-by-step process of reestablishing relations with the nonrecognized country.

At first, President Ford implied that *nonrecognition* was irreversible. During his tough 1976 reelection campaign, Ford budged a bit on that one. He said that *normalization* was possible when all POW/MIAs were home or at least accountable. He demanded that Hanoi get to work on it immediately.

Of course, the North Vietnamese government was not going to jump because Gerald Ford said so. He knew that, too. Yet even in defeat, the White House could win the support of old hawks by looking tough in the face of the Vietnamese, and Ford needed their support.

Jimmy Carter Looks for a Policy

Amazingly candid for a presidential candidate, Georgia's Jimmy Carter hounded Ford throughout the 1976 election. And he didn't have to do much to hound. He smiled a lot, said he would never tell a lie, and admitted that his only time spent in Washington was as a tourist. All of these things, usually kiss-of-death admissions of inexperience in other elections, were pluses in 1976. The outsider was coming to clean up Vietnam/Watergate-tainted Washington. He won handily, but a concerned press and electorate asked: "Jimmy who?"

Pointing out that America normalized its relations with both Japan and West Germany immediately after World War II, Carter had no problem with a healthy U.S.-Vietnam relationship "in principle." Like Ford, he wanted to know how many

Americans might be dead or alive in Vietnam, but unlike Ford he avoided a demanding tone.

Hoping to demonstrate American "goodness" in post-Vietnam foreign policy instead of strut-your-stuff "greatness," Carter preferred championing global human rights issues in his foreign policy. The Vietnamese could demonstrate their willingness to cooperate with this new, humbled, kindly America by answering questions on POW/MIA matters. They didn't respond.

During an international summit meeting in Tokyo, Carter asked America's allies to open their borders to the Southeast Asians fleeing the new communist governments that oppressed them. American immigration/refugee law was temporarily amended to admit thousands of people on the run, but thousands more lingered in refugee camps in the Philippines and Guam for years. Letting in great numbers of *boat people* during depressed economic times was not the most popular policy to some, and Carter hoped America's "humane" allies would respond to his human-rights appeal and help share the burden.

Carter also hoped that Hanoi would notice America's concerns for people rather than weapons. But the Vietnamese demanded reparations payments from the United States before any normalization deal could be struck, and few Americans liked demands from the Vietnamese. Carter's efforts failed, for he considered the demand for reparations an arrogant and unreasonable one. Carter's 1980 rival for the White House, Ronald Reagan, vowed to restore a powerful, successful presidency that, in the name of American pride and honor, would never try to make deals with the Vietnamese.

Ask Saigon Sally

In the year 2000, more than 2,000 U.S. servicemen were still listed as unaccounted for in Southeast Asia. That included 1,500 men on Vietnamese soil alone.

Jarhead Jargon

Millions of Southeast Asians, including tens of thousands of ethnic Chinese-Vietnamese, took to the ocean in anything that floated in order to escape the new communist regimes. Nicknamed the **boat people,** 250,000 of their ranks died at sea.

Overconfident and cocky from its victory over America and the Saigon regime, Vietnam also became an expansionist power after what it called the "American War." The NVA invaded Cambodia, eventually crushing the ruthless and bizarre Khmer Rouge government there. It also fought a border war with China that killed thousands. All of this confused the international community. The United States had wanted Pol Pot and the Khmer Rouge out of power, but now had to thank the Vietnamese? It was all very awkward.

Ronald Reagan Sees an "Evil Empire"

Ronald Reagan was not in a thankful mood. Carter managed to reestablish, at least on paper, cultural ties with Vietnam, and he had no opposition to seeing a Vietnamese delegate at the United Nations. To Reagan this was bowing to advancing communism, and, given Vietnam's connections to the Soviet Union, Hanoi was part of an "evil empire."

Shell Shock

Despite public denials, the U.S. government supported two of the three anti-Vietnamese resistance groups in Cambodia (temporarily renamed Kampuchea) throughout the 1980s. Pol Pot led the third guerrilla group, and all three factions shot at each other while shooting at the Vietnamese.

The Cold War took on a new confrontational tone with Reagan, but that was about all it did. American policy did not change. Nevertheless, Reagan's 1950s-like anticommunist speeches hadn't been heard in years. This stuff turned off most moderates and liberals who had been influenced by the defunct antiwar movement.

Others said Reagan relegated the Vietnam nightmare to history by making folks feel patriotic and decent again. Of course, this encouraged an anti-Vietnam opinion, making it difficult even to suggest the possibility of a U.S. Embassy over there someday. Added to this reality was the fact that Vietnam still had nothing of economic value to offer the capitalist United States. The Soviet navy took over some of America's old bases, and Hollywood went over the edge with the superhero movies that depicted Vietnamese being killed by the truckload.

It took the fall of the Soviet Union to produce any movement on the normalization front. Soviet aid to Vietnam was now a memory. The war in Cambodia and the border war with China had taken a heavy toll on Vietnam. As early as 1988, Hanoi's attitude toward America began to thaw a bit. In 1989 the Vietnamese government announced its willingness to cooperate with the Americans in locating the remains of American soldiers. This decision led Reagan's vice president turned president, George Bush, to permit American businesses to open shop in Vietnam if they dared. The nonrecognition days were over, but normalization was still controversial stuff for the many Americans who had been conditioned to hate the Vietnamese communists.

Bill Clinton Wants to Build an Embassy

Although he had made only two speeches in his 1992 campaign about foreign policy matters, President Bill Clinton said that normalization was inevitable. Shortly after making this statement, the press reported that archives from the old Soviet government indicated that hundreds of Americans had been held against their will in Vietnam long after the war ended. On the other hand, nothing could be found to back up these reports. The nervous North Vietnamese government denied them, and announced that it planned to be supercooperative in any U.S. effort to locate America's war dead in its country.

Tales from the Front

In 2000, 32-year-old Phuong Thao was labeled the "Mariah Carey of Vietnam" by her adoring Vietnamese fans. Her success as Vietnam's pop diva would have been impossible only a decade before. As the out-of-wedlock daughter of a South Vietnamese typist and an American serviceman, she was considered a social outcast when she was younger. Some 50,000 mixed-race children were left behind by American troops. Viewed as symbols of America's pollution of Vietnamese culture, many of these children were herded into crowded, poorly funded orphanages. Phuong Thao was lucky to be brought up by her mother, but destitution and derision was their fate. Thanks to her singing ability, well-publicized singing contest victories, and the changing attitudes among young Vietnamese who never experienced the Vietnam War, Phuong Thao's career took off in the mid-1990's.

The main issue for the Vietnamese was cash. Communist or not, they needed capitalist support. The International Monetary Fund organization had been banned from dealing with Vietnam, and the major economic giants of the world had no working trade policies with Hanoi. Clinton lifted the barriers and opposition, winning bipartisan support for the effort. But that support had serious limits.

The key to successful normalization was Vietnam's real and active cooperation in POW/MIA investigations. An American Embassy was also needed, Clinton said, and instantly won the wrath of the leftover Reaganite anticommunists in Congress. But the old-fashioned Congress-versus-the-presidency argument came down to the choice of ambassador, and Pete Peterson was hard to turn down.

Shell Shock

Leading an early 1990s Senate Special Investigative Committee into the possibility of American POW/MIAs trapped in Vietnam, Senator John Kerry (Democrat, Massachusetts), the former founding director of the Vietnam Veterans Against the War, found no evidence of Americans being held against their will.

Welcome Back to Vietnam

In 1997, Douglas "Pete" Peterson became the first U.S. ambassador to Vietnam in more than 22 years. He had spent three terms as a member of the House of Representatives, serving the Second Congressional District of Florida. Specializing in national defense and international relations matters, Peterson had been a consistent supporter of normalization.

Douglas "Pete" Peterson, U.S. Ambassador to the Socialist Republic of Vietnam.

Photograph courtesy of the U.S. Embassy, Hanoi.

Ask Saigon Sally

Pete Peterson first returned to Vietnam in 1991 as part of Senator Kerry's POW/MIA investigative committee. He quit Congress after the death of his first wife. The Clinton administration approached him for the ambassador job one day after he announced he was quitting.

Peterson's life was defined by his 26 years in the U.S. Air Force. As a fighter pilot and commander, he was a combat veteran of the Vietnam War who spent close to seven years as a POW in North Vietnam. Although a native of Nebraska, he lived in Florida for 40 years and founded CRT Computers, Inc., one of his adopted home state's first full-service computer facilities. His government service, business, and POW background won him immediate bipartisan support when nominated by President Clinton.

But that bipartisan support was for Peterson personally. Jesse Helms, chairman of the powerful Senate Foreign Relations Committee, used the Peterson nomination as a means to attack what he considered Clinton's lack of moral leadership in both foreign and domestic affairs. He specifically accused the president of stepping on the graves of America's war dead for even thinking about sending an ambassador to evil Vietnam. Certain Vietnamese American groups and POW/MIA organizations also opposed a U.S. Embassy there, and New Hampshire's Senator Bob Smith promised to work night and day against Clinton's "immoral foreign policy."

The political battle on Capitol Hill went on for more than a year, and on the night of the balloting, no one in the media could predict the outcome. Peterson smelled defeat, and was ready to praise the president for having tried his hand at U.S.-Vietnam reconciliation. To his surprise, his nomination moved forward. Too much press attention had been given to the anti-Clinton crowd.

Ask Saigon Sally

The final phase of the U.S. political battle over opening an embassy in Vietnam coincided with the latter's twentieth anniversary celebrations of victory over the Saigon regime. The celebrations were kept to a bare minimum in order not to influence the American debate.

Pete Peterson, POW

The Vietnamese leadership faced an obvious dilemma. They could remain dedicated to the old communist principles that would keep their country one of the world's poorest and most struggling. On the other hand, they could try to find some sort of compromise between diehard communism and the capitalist world, advance the economy, and probably keep themselves in power at the same time. Yesterday's enemy, with its unlimited economic resources, could kick-start things. Cooperating with the new ambassador was the key.

Peterson's POW background was worrisome to Hanoi, and the new ambassador was asked straightforwardly whether he held grudges against the North Vietnamese. His answer was neatly diplomatic. He said that he could never forget the bad old days, but that they should not stand in the way of the future.

Shell Shock

A recent opinion poll in Hanoi notes that a majority of Vietnamese academics and intellectuals believe that Ho Chi Minh's bloody war of liberation might have been unnecessary.

For Ambassador Peterson, the bad old days were 1966 to 1973. In 1966, during his sixty-seventh combat mission over North Vietnam, Peterson's F-4 was hit by anti-aircraft fire. He ejected from the burning plane and parachuted into a tree. Thanks to the huge white chute, he was discovered quickly by a militia group. As his future captors approached him, Peterson drew his .38 revolver. The only person he contemplated shooting was himself, but he decided to take his chances as a POW.

Tales from the Front

Although he graduated fifth from last in his U.S. Naval Academy class, John S. McCain III's leadership and in-flight skills won him the respect of fellow navy pilots. While flying an A4 Skyhawk over North Vietnam in October 1967, McCain was shot down. Perhaps the most severely injured pilot ever to enter Hoa Loa Prison (nicknamed the Hanoi Hilton), McCain refused the opportunity to be sent home in June 1968. Released at the end of the war, McCain won a seat in the U.S. House of Representatives in 1982, became a Senator (Republican, Arizona) in 1986, and ran an unsuccessful campaign for president in 2000. He was an early advocate for normalization of U.S.–Vietnamese relations.

En route to prison, the future ambassador was paraded through several villages. Angered by the American air war, the locals beat him up, but he made it intact to Hoa Loa prison. Nicknamed "the Hanoi Hilton," the prison had been built by the French to house Vietnamese prisoners.

Peterson spent his captivity in four different locations, including over three years in a tiny place its prisoners called "The Zoo." Forced to kneel with his hands in the air for hours on end, Peterson was tortured there. To this day, rope burns scar his elbows and his right hand goes numb from the many hours of wearing tight manacles.

The isolation, he remembered, was especially difficult. He had no idea who the president of the United States might have been. He had no idea a man had walked on the moon, and he had no idea about the level of antiwar demonstrations at home. His captors kept him informed about famous personalities in the United States speaking out against the war; however he discounted it all as enemy propaganda.

His family back home had no idea if their "Pete" was alive or dead until late 1970. Although weak and sickly, Peterson was cleaned up and taken with other prisoners to a church service on Christmas Eve 1969. He was glad to be there, but the North Vietnamese staged the event for propaganda purposes. A film of this special communion service was passed by a North Vietnamese diplomat to a U.S. congressman visiting the Paris Peace Talks several months later. Peterson was one of the 75 POWs clearly seen on the film, and it was the first confirmation that he had survived the 1966 crash.

Tales from the Front

In recognition of the fact that his city contributed more men and women to the Vietnam War than any other American community, New York City Mayor Ed Koch spent four years trying to fund and build a memorial to his city's veterans. Troubled economic times and the struggling condition of many Vietnam veterans delayed public and private funding efforts. But Vietnam Veterans Memorial Plaza (formerly Jeannette Park at 55 Water Street) was finally opened in May 1985. This event also marked the tenth anniversary of the end of the Vietnam War, and a Vietnam-veterans-only parade of over 25,000 accompanied it, cheered on by over one million New Yorkers. The event was christened the "Great Welcome Home," a welcome that never took place in the 1970s.

It would be more than three more years before Peterson was reunited with his family. At that time, he said that he had some important choices to make. He could stay bitter, angry, and depressed, or he could move forward and live a decent life. The past, Peterson explained to both the Vietnamese in 1997 and the U.S. Congress the year before, cannot be undone. The future is another matter, and U.S.-Vietnamese reconciliation made better sense than hatred.

Future Tense

As ambassador, Peterson's primary goal has involved building trade agreements with Vietnam. Like China, Vietnam is moving slowly toward a market economy, and economic connections between the United States and Vietnam would help cement the whole normalization process. Unfortunately, many American politicians and businessmen have not seen Vietnam as a priority trade partner.

Ask Saigon Sally

Officially, the U.S. reconciliation effort with Vietnam was on the outskirts of general U.S. foreign policy goals in the 1990s. In 1994, Secretary of State Warren Christopher said that today's best U.S. foreign policy stresses regions and countries where U.S. economic goals are "vitally important."

After three years on the job, Peterson had helped ease more than 200 U.S. companies into Vietnam, but this has not been satisfactory in his view. Old animosities live on.

His biggest problem has been convincing Americans that Vietnam is worth more than old war memories. It has been a hard sell, particularly in light of the twenty-fifth anniversary of the end of the war. Peterson remains optimistic, but there is a long way to go.

Years later, the Vietnam War still hurts. More people know about its myths and legends than they do about its history. Old doves still say they were right and everybody else was wrong. Old hawks say the same thing. Young people haven't a clue what everyone is yelling about, and politicians say let's move on and make some money. At least one thing is certain. The Vietnam War is finally over. May it rest in peace.

The Least You Need to Know

➤ Normalization was rejected by the Ford administration.

➤ Jimmy Carter toyed with normalization policies, but they went nowhere.

➤ Reagan's Cold War interests and Vietnam's conflicts with China and Cambodia delayed normalization in the 1980s.

➤ America's interest in finding all POW/MIAs has profoundly influenced the normalization issue.

➤ Ambassador Peterson's mission has improved U.S.-Vietnam relations, but much more needs to be done.

Casualty Figures for the Vietnam War

U.S. Military Casualties by Type and Service in Southeast Asia (Compiled in 1997)

Casualty Type	U.S. Army	U.S. Navy	U.S. Air Force	U.S. Marine Corps	U.S. Coast Guard	Total
Hostile (Combat Casualties)						
Killed	25,358	1,115	537	11,491	4	38,505
Died of wounds	3,566	150	49	1,476	1	5,242
Died while missing	1,960	325	1,130	108	0	3,523
Died while captured/ interned	45	36	25	10	0	116
Nonhostile (Non-Combat Casualties)						
Died of other causes	4,907	579	531	1,436	2	7,455
Died of illness/ injuries	1,437	69	170	314	0	1,990
Died while missing	928	281	141	3	0	1,353
TOTAL	38,196	2,555	2,583	14,837	7	58,178

Courtesy of Alan Oskvarek and The Vietnam Veterans Memorial Wall Page.

Jarhead Jargon Glossary

10/59 Law   The 10/59 (or October 1959) Law was the equivalent of a declaration of martial law over South Vietnam. President Diem conferred dictatorial authority upon himself and his family in the name of "national emergency." Even staunch American anticommunists questioned his reasoning in the matter, and the decision increased rather than lessened opposition to his regime.

Accord   The term accord in what is known as the 1954 Geneva Accords has an official U.S. diplomatic definition. If a president wants to negotiate a foreign affairs arrangement, but avoid the Constitutionally mandated treaty, his administration can negotiate an accord. This is based on "executive privilege" and does not require Congressional approval. Hence, America's earliest commitment to South Vietnam was done without formal Congressional approval.

agrovilles   In 1959, Diem ordered the removal of all peasants and villagers from areas most susceptible to communist penetration and general antigovernment activity. They were put in internment camps or fortified settlements known as agrovilles.

APC   A replacement for the M-113, the APC or Armored Personnel Carrier could carry more than 11 infantrymen plus a driver, and was constructed from aluminum armor welded over a watertight hull. It was designed to carry troops to combat, and it provided protection from small arms fire up to .50 caliber. Kennedy had authorized the creation of only two APC companies, but shortly after his assassination, and thanks to the quick transfer of former New Pacific Community funding to the military, over 2,100 APCs would soon be sent to South Vietnam.

ARVN   Founded by President Diem, the Army of the Republic of Vietnam was America's military ally in South Vietnam.

backwater nation   To Secretary of State Dean Rusk, Indonesia was a backwater nation. That meant it was supposed to be on the outskirts of America's major national security interests.

big tent   In February 1964, Johnson began to talk about his big tent. This was a reference to resurrecting the 1930s Grand Coalition of Franklin Roosevelt on the domestic scene. Abroad, the new Grand Coalition would include all noncommunist Third World nations. Under Johnson's big tent leadership, the downtrodden at home and overseas could be assured endless U.S. government support.

bipartisanship   No matter what party occupied the Oval Office, bipartisanship politics encouraged Republican and Democratic cooperation and unity in the march to Cold War victory.

boat people   Millions of Southeast Asians, including tens of thousands of ethnic Chinese-Vietnamese, took to the ocean in anything that could float in order to escape the new, 1970s communist regimes. Nicknamed the "boat people," 250,000 of their ranks died at sea.

brushfire war   A military confrontation in the Third World that avoids the use of nuclear weapons, strives to keep casualty figures low, and makes a political statement at the same time. The Americans put Vietnam in the brushfire category, and the Soviets put their 1979 invasion of Afghanistan in that same category as well.

clear and hold   The American military's effort to destroy a Vietcong sanctuary and make sure it never became one again was called clear and hold. Simply labeled, it was easier said than done.

Committee for the South   After the 1954 Geneva Accords, not all Vietminh activists moved north to form a new government. Those truly loyal to the new North Vietnamese regime were expected to stay put and work with the Committee for the South (an outgrowth of the Vietminh-run Central Office of South Vietnam, or COSVN during the Franco-Vietnamese War) in the heart of South Vietnam.

Congo Crisis   The Kennedy administration struggled with the Congo Crisis at the same time as Vietnam. From 1960 to 1963, the former Belgian Congo became a bloodbath. Kennedy authorized U.S. airlifts to assist U.N. troops in the field there. The violence ended in January 1963, and this was seen as a great example of U.N. cooperation and success.

credibility gap   The wide difference between official White House and Saigon regime statements about the progress of the war versus the facts reported by the news media and others in Vietnam.

de-escalation   During its Tet Offensive debates, the Johnson administration disagreed on a working definition of de-escalation. Some said it meant pulling out U.S. troops. Others said it meant maintaining current troop strength levels.

demobilization Literally meaning to "discharge from military service," the term demobilization was coined by the British government in the 1880s. Most often used to describe the return of troops to civilian life after a war, it is also associated with *isolationist* policies and antiwar causes when the recall of troops is demanded.

diplomatic hailstorm President Johnson's National Security Council predicted a diplomatic hailstorm should the United States attempt to win Japan to the "More Flags" effort. They were referring to the potentially strong, negative, and anti-American reaction of countries formerly occupied by Japan's World War II military.

Discomfort Index In 1975, the new Congress came up with the Discomfort Index. In domestic affairs, it combined the escalating unemployment and inflation rates. In foreign affairs, it kept close track of funding being "wasted" in Vietnam.

dominoes In 1946, President Truman dispatched a State Department expert on Asia, Abbot Low Moffat, to evaluate the Vietminh and its leader Ho Chi Minh. Moffat reported that Ho was "probably" a passionate communist, and that Vietnam, Laos, Cambodia, and Thailand would soon fall like "dominoes" to communism.

enclave strategy By mid-1965, the Johnson administration favored an enclave strategy for the thousands of fresh U.S. troops arriving in Vietnam. That meant protecting key coastal towns and existing U.S. military bases only.

existentialism In Jean-Paul Sartre's complicated theory of existentialism, traditional communism was morally bankrupt. It stifled the individual's natural tendency to do good things and share his talents with others.

firefight Often misused, even by the military, a firefight is a minor military engagement with the enemy at the platoon or company strength level.

fragging Fragging was a violent attack on an officer by his own men. Booby traps and grenades were the weapons of choice.

free-fire zones Because so many areas of South Vietnam had been evacuated of local residents, what they left behind was proclaimed free-fire zones. The U.S. military, sometimes offering warnings and sometimes not, would shoot at anything that moved in the free-fire zones.

Great Communicator During the early years of his presidency, Ronald Reagan, nicknamed the Great Communicator in the press, often praised another great communicator, John Kennedy. Generally, Reagan had no problem connecting his administration's foreign policies to the popular Kennedy agenda of 20 years earlier.

Great Society Although he was accused of borrowing his administration's title, the Great Society, from a socialist book, Lyndon Johnson first called for this new era of government activism and New Deal–like reform during his May 1964 commencement speech at the University of Michigan.

311

Hamburger Hill   The battle of Ap Bia. It was a play on General Abrams's "meat-grinder" approach against the North Vietnamese, and a recognition of their own high casualties in the effort.

hard hats   A mixture of World War II–era unionized blue-collar workers and younger like-thinking conservatives, the hard hats considered the antiwar movement pro-Hanoi, anti-American, and antiveteran.

hawk and dove   The term hawk dates back to the Congressional "War Hawks" of 1810–1812 who favored a war with Britain in the name of honor, pride, and a deep hatred for anything English. But according to Kathleen Thompson Hill and Gerald Hill's *The Real Life Dictionary of American Politics* (Los Angeles: General Publishing Group, 1994), the term dove is a product of 1967–1968 Vietnam War debates, and refers to the desire for a peaceful, nonviolent foreign policy. Its origin is not attributed to one person directly, such as Eugene McCarthy.

hedgehogs   Concerned about losing the isolated sections of Vietnam to the Vietminh, the French built military installations in those same sections. Called hedgehogs, these bases were supposed to destroy Vietminh supply lines and organizational efforts.

hippies   Characterized by their long hair, casual drug use, love of rock music, and promiscuity, the hippies were a social phenomenon of the late 1960s and early 1970s. Usually born into comfortable white middle-class families, these young Americans rejected their parents' values and questioned a government and society that encouraged their support of the Vietnam War. Many so-called mainstream Americans shared the hippies' revulsion for the war, but had little use for their lifestyle.

HUAC   Although its roots went back to 1938, the House Un-American Affairs Committee, or HUAC, was founded on January 3, 1945. Dedicated to probing communist subversion in the government, labor unions, and the press, HUAC continued its work into the 1970s.

incursion   Learning a lesson in semantics from Eugene McCarthy's 1968 presidential campaign, Nixon did not announce that the United States was invading Cambodia in 1970. Instead he said that the United States was involved in an incursion, thereby downplaying his widening of the war.

inevitable French defeat   At a time when French power seemed invincible, Ho predicted an inevitable French defeat. He asked for support and patience from the colonized Vietnamese.

Isolationism   Refers to America's post–World War I foreign policy of disarmament, endless peace talks, and general "take care of America first" politics. It was abandoned only after Japan's December 1941 attack on Pearl Harbor.

Kellogg-Briand Pact   The symbol of U.S. retreat from world responsibilities in the 1920s remains the Kellogg-Briand Pact. According to this 1928 diplomatic arrangement, the United States and France were to lead the world in the effort to "outlaw war as an instrument of national policy." In other words, war was declared illegal (except in matters of self-defense).

Khmer Rouge   This homegrown nationalist and radical communist movement was responsible for the Cambodian Holocaust of the 1970s.

lame duck   Dating back to the British Parliament of the 1760s, the term lame duck refers to the lapsing term of an outgoing elected official. Often a derogatory term, it also implies that that official is powerless to initiate new programs or policies, and is preoccupied with image-making and a respectable exit from office.

landslide   Political scientists, journalists, and historians continue to disagree over a universal figure for a presidential landslide election. Many consider 20 percent over an opponent an acceptable number, but others peg it as low as 12 percent.

MACV   America's Military Assistance Command in Vietnam (MACV) became a household term to most Americans by the November 1964 election.

mandarins   The French often referred to Vietnamese political leaders as mandarins. Although the French saw nothing wrong with the label, the Vietnamese did. Mandarin refers to one of the nine ranks of high officialdom in old imperial China.

mutual interference   For both appearance and security reasons, President Johnson preferred to keep any South Vietnamese commando operation into North Vietnam separate from American military/espionage activities there. Any American role in a South Vietnamese–led covert operation or vice versa would be labeled mutual interference.

neutralize   In the mid-1960s, President Charles de Gaulle of France hoped that a new China-France alliance would neutralize, or end, the fighting throughout France's old Indochina empire.

New Deal   The New Deal was President Franklin Roosevelt's frenetic legislative agenda to end the Great Depression of the 1930s. Consisting of dozens of new government agencies under the headings of Relief, Recovery, and Reform, the New Deal represented the height of government interventionism in the economy, elevated the powers of the presidency, and rescued a wounded capitalist system.

New Left   A peculiarly American phenomenon, the New Left welcomed the humanist and liberal side of socialist and communist philosophies. Borrowing from leftist thinkers ranging from Karl Marx to Mao Tse-tung, New Left adherents despised imperialism, capitalist excess and corruption, and preferred an isolationist U.S. foreign policy. The support for isolationism was reminiscent of conservative Republican views of the 1920s and 1930s. Hence, the New Left complicated the political scene, preferring political debate to political action. The New Left was more a state of mind than a political group.

new life villages   Hamlets administered by Republic of Korea (ROK) troops along with relocation centers for evacuated South Vietnamese villagers. Most of these villagers were forced into refugee status by ROK troops, and sometimes brutally, in the effort to keep them away from Vietcong influences.

New Look   Beginning with Eisenhower's 1954 State of the Union Address, the New Look became the official expression to describe 1950s U.S. defense policy. Its elements included a heavy reliance on nuclear weapons, a reduction in both ground and naval forces, and an emphasis on cost-cutting and strict fiscal conservatism.

nonalignment   The term nonalignment was invented to describe a newly independent government that determined its own destiny and thumbed its nose at both Washington and Moscow in the Cold War.

nonrecognition   A legitimate diplomatic term referring to a complete U.S. ban on diplomatic, cultural, economic, or any other ties to a potential enemy. Normalization refers to the step-by-step procedure of reestablishing relations with the nonrecognized country.

NVA and PAVN   A certain alphabet soup accompanies any study of the North Vietnamese military. Both NVA (North Vietnamese Army) and PAVN (People's Army of Vietnam) refer to North Vietnamese troops.

pacification   Involved the effort to secure U.S. and ARVN control over South Vietnamese villages, win the locals' allegiance to the Saigon regime, and deprive the enemy of all strongholds in the countryside.

paper tiger   Often applied to U.S. diplomacy issues during the heyday of the Cold War, the term "paper tiger" referred to threatening rhetoric, international agreements, and angry domestic politics focused against the communist enemy. It was not a flattering term, for it implied that meaningless rhetoric and do-nothing legal arrangements were being substituted for action, force, and victory.

Pathet Lao   This Laotian guerrilla force was also one of the first communist movements in Southeast Asia.

pay any price, bear any burden   This expression came out of John Kennedy's 1961 inaugural address. For years afterward, politicians, journalists, and historians said this one expression symbolized the entire Kennedy administration's commitment to the aging Truman Doctrine and to the anticommunist crusade in general.

plumbers   Called the plumbers because they were supposed to plug leaks, a White House team of ex-CIA and ex-FBI agents was created in 1971 to prevent security information from ending up in the hands of the press.

political stalking horse   Eugene McCarthy was once labeled a political stalking horse because it was assumed he was a weak, losing candidate testing the viability of an antiwar candidacy for allegedly stronger, winning candidates like Robert F. Kennedy or Hubert Humphrey.

Populist Party   Beginning in the rural U.S. South in the 1880s and spreading nationwide by 1892, the Populist Party favored government action to rescue the failing family farm, an activist economic foreign policy abroad, and anti-Big Business legislation at home. A powerful, unassailable president was supposed to initiate these reforms, but the Populists never won the White House.

power of the purse   James Madison, the senior writer of both the U.S. Constitution and the rules of Congress, always assumed that Congress should have the final say in the nation's financial policy-making. He called it the power of the purse.

punji stake   During 1947, terrorist tactics represented the heart and soul of the Vietminh war against the French. A sharpened bamboo pole tipped with poisons and even "night soil" (human manure), the punji stake was concealed near jungle trials, rice paddies, or wherever French troopers walked on patrol.

rapprochement   The Chinese premier and foreign minister, Chou En-lai, had sought a rapprochement with the Americans for years. *Rapprochement* refers to the first steps in reestablishing a relationship with a former enemy and ideological foe.

Road of Horrors   In the 1972 Easter Offensive, the North Vietnamese crossed the 17th parallel into Quang Tri province with T-54 and PT-76 tanks. Remembering the Tet Offensive massacres of four years earlier, the South Vietnamese fled south on Highway 1. Parts of the road were shelled by the advancing North Vietnamese and hundreds were killed. The Quang Tri section of the highway was known as "The Road of Horrors" for years afterward.

scorched earth   This term has been used to describe one opponent's effort to lay waste to the territory of another. Meant to break an enemy's will to fight as well as deprive him of anything and everything in a given area, scorched earth can be employed by both an attacking and a retreating army.

shuttle diplomacy   Henry Kissinger's effort to prove that America actually cared about the concerns of its allies and potential foes. Instead of urging them to come to Washington and discuss their differences, he flew to them.

Sino-Soviet rift   Known as the Sino-Soviet rift, pro-Chinese Maoist communists and pro-Soviet communists argued over ideological purity for years. The most difficult time was during the late 1950s and early 1960s when both Khrushchev and Mao threatened a major conflict over this debate.

student deferment   Any male student in an institution of higher learning could apply for student deferment status in the 1960s. By maintaining a B to B-plus average or above in his studies, he was spared from a military draft system that most likely would quickly send him to Vietnam.

"the world"   U.S. military slang for a trip back to CONUS (continental United States) was known as going back to the world. It carried the connotation that after Vietnam, an adjustment to American life and culture might be difficult.

315

thoi co   In Vietnamese, *thoi co* means waiting for the right moment to make the right move. Throughout the twentieth-century wars in Vietnam, thoi co became part of a winning military strategy against an always impatient enemy.

Vichy   More than a sleepy resort town in central France, the word Vichy became synonymous with collaboration and treason during World War II. Later, Vietnamese who sided with the French during the French phase of the Vietnam War would be labeled Vichyites by fellow Vietnamese who supported Ho Chi Minh.

Vietcong   Tracing its roots back to the Vietminh of the 1940s and early 1950s, the Vietcong were the Hanoi-backed armed opposition to the South Vietnamese government. American GI slang, such as Victor Charlie, VC, or simply Charlie and Chuck, comes from this title. The term Vietcong is slang even in Vietnamese. The official title for the anti-Saigon regime forces is National Liberation Front, or NLF.

walleye   Another sample of America's high-tech weaponry in Vietnam, a walleye was a missile fired from a fighter plane that reached its target courtesy of a TV camera and a pilot guiding its course from the comforts of his own aircraft.

Weathermen   One of the smallest and most extreme antiwar protest groups was the Weathermen. They got their name from a line from Bob Dylan's "Subterranian Homesick Blues": "You don't need a weatherman to know which way the wind blows."

WIN   The U.S. inflation rate was 11 percent in 1974, and oil prices had risen 350 percent in one year. President Ford rejected wage-and-price controls and urged American business to handle things themselves. Ford called it his WIN (Whip Inflation Now) approach to noninterventionist government and volunteer business.

Yalta sellout   During early 1945, President Roosevelt made concessions to Stalin at the Yalta conference. In fact, some said that he made too many concessions. To American anticommunists, the term Yalta sell-out was synonymous with treason, appeasement, and unpatriotic behavior.

Yippies   Led by Abbie Hoffman and Jerry Rubin, the Youth International Party, or Yippies, championed an anarchist agenda that favored an immediate end to the Vietnam War, capitalism, drug laws, work, and the police.

Recommended Reading

There was a time when publishers and bookstore owners believed that no one in his right mind would read a book about the misery of Vietnam. Boy, were they wrong. There aren't as many Vietnam books as there are World War II or Civil War books, but they are catching up fast. There are thousands of titles now, and few of these works will cure your insomnia problems.

The following list of books represents some of the better trailblazing stuff, the hottest new analyses, and just darn good reading. Most of the authors noted here embrace controversy rather than reject it. Vietnam should never be a boring tale, and the following writers prove the point.

Atkinson, Rick. *The Long Gray Line: The American Journey of West Point's Class of 1966*. New York: Henry Holt & Company, 1999.

Brands, H.W. *The Wages of Globalism: Lyndon Johnson and the Limits of American Power*. New York: Oxford University Press, 1995.

Bundy, William. *A Tangled Web: The Making of Foreign Policy in the Nixon Presidency*. New York: Hill and Wang, 1988.

Caputo, Philip. *A Rumor of War*. New York: Henry Holt & Company, 1996.

Carroll, Peter N. *It Seemed Like Nothing Happened: The Tragedy and Promise of America in the 1970s*. New York: Holt, Rinehart & Winston, 1982.

Carter, Dan T. *The Politics of Rage: George Wallace, the Origins of the New Conservatism, and the Transformation of American Politics*. New York: Simon & Schuster, 1995.

Chanoff, David, and Doan Van Toai. *Portrait of an Enemy*. New York: Random House, 1986.

Clancy, Tom. *Without Remorse*. New York: Putnam, 1993.

Diggins, John Patrick. *The Rise and Fall of the American Left*. New York: Norton, 1992.

Donahue, James C. *Mobile Guerrilla Force*. New York: St. Martin's Press, 1997.

Duiker, William J. *U.S. Containment Policy and the Conflict in Indochina*. Stanford, Calif.: Stanford University Press, 1994.

Dunnigan, James F., and Albert Nofi. *Dirty Little Secrets of the Vietnam War: Military Information You're Not Supposed to Know*. New York: St. Martin's Press, 2000.

Faas, Horst, and Tim Page, eds. *Requiem: By the Photographers Who Died in the Vietnam and Indochina War*. New York: Random House, 1997.

Fall, Bernard. *Hell in a Very Small Place*. Philadelphia: J.B. Lippincott, 1967.

Farber, David. *The Age of Great Dreams: America in the 1960s*. New York: Hill & Wang, 1994.

Fawcett, Bill, ed. *Hunters and Shooters: An Oral History of the U.S. Navy SEALs in Vietnam*. New York: Morrow, 1996.

Fitzgerald, Francis. *Fire in the Lake: The Vietnamese and the Americans in Vietnam*. New York: Random House, 1973.

Gitlin, Todd. *The Sixties: Years of Hope, Days of Rage*. New York: Bantam Books, 1987.

Greene, Graham. *The Quiet American*. New York: Penguin, 1991.

Guarino, Larry. *A POW's Story: 2,801 Days in Hanoi*. New York: Ballantine Books, 1990.

Hackworth, David H., and Julie Sherman. *About Face: The Odyssey of an American Warrior*. New York: Simon & Schuster, 1990.

Halberstam, David. *The Best and the Brightest*. New York: Ballantine Books, 1993.

Hamby, Alonzo L. *Liberalism and its Challengers: F.D.R. to Reagan*. New York: Oxford University Press, 1985.

Hammer, Ellen J. *A Death in November: America in Vietnam, 1963*. New York: Dutton, 1987.

Hayslip, Le Ly, with Jay Wurts. *When Heaven and Earth Changed Places: A Vietnamese Woman's Journey from War to Peace*. New York: Penguin USA, 1990.

Herr, Michael, and Marty Asher, ed. *Dispatches*. New York: Random House, 1991.

Herring, George. *America's Longest War: The United States and Vietnam, 1950–1975*. New York: McGraw Hill, 1994.

Isaacson, Walter. *Kissinger: A Biography*. New York: Simon & Schuster, 1992.

Isserman, Maurice, and Michael Kazin. *America Divided: The Civil War of the 1960s.* New York: Oxford University Press, 2000.

Just, Ward. *A Dangerous Friend.* Boston: Houghton Mifflin, 1999.

Kaiser, David. *American Tragedy: Kennedy, Johnson, and the Origins of the Vietnam War.* Cambridge, Mass.: Harvard University Press, 2000.

Karnow, Stanley. *Vietnam: A History.* New York: Viking Penguin, 1997.

Kruger, Ed. *Dead Center: A Marine Sniper's Two-Year Odyssey in the Vietnam War.* New York: Ballantine Publishing Group, 1995.

Lacouture, Jean. *Ho Chi Minh: A Political Biography.* New York: Random House, 1968.

Lind, Michael. *Vietnam: The Necessary War: Grand Strategy, Domestic Politics, and the American War for Indochina.* New York: Simon & Schuster, 1999.

Maga, Timothy P. *John F. Kennedy and the New Pacific Community, 1961-1963.* London: Macmillan, 1990.

———. *The Perils of Power: Crises in American Foreign Relations Since World War II.* West Haven, Conn.: University of New Haven Press, 1995.

Mailer, Norman. *Miami and the Siege of Chicago.* New York: World Publishing Company, 1968.

Mangold, Tom, and John Penycate. *The Tunnels of Cu Chi.* New York: Berkeley Publishing Group, 1997.

Mason, Robert. *Chickenhawk.* New York: Viking Penguin, 1984.

McMaster, H.R. *Dereliction of Duty: Johnson, McNamara, the Joint Chiefs of Staff, and the Lies That Led to Vietnam.* New York: HarperCollins, 1998.

McNamara, Robert S., with Brian Vandemark. *In Retrospect: The Tragedy and Lessons of Vietnam.* New York: Times Books, 1995.

Moore Harold G., and Joseph Galloway. *We Were Soldiers Once-and-Young: Ia Drang, the Battle That Changed the War in Vietnam.* New York: Harper, 1993.

Nolan, Keith William. *Operation Buffalo: USMC Fight for the DMZ.* New York: Bantam Doubleday Dell Publishing Group, 1992.

Norman, Elizabeth. *Women at War: The Story of Fifty Military Nurses Who Served in Vietnam.* Philadelphia: University of Pennsylvania Press, 1990.

Oberdorfer, Don. *Tet.* New York: Doubleday, 1971.

O'Nan, Stewart, ed. *The Vietnam Reader: The Definitive Collection of American Fiction and Nonfiction on the War.* New York: Doubleday & Company, 1998.

Pike, Douglas. *Vietnam and the Soviet Union: Anatomy of an Alliance.* Boulder, Colo.: Westview Press, 1987.

319

Pimlott, John, ed. *NAM: The Vietnam Experience, 1965–75.* London: Barnes and Noble Books, 1995.

Plaster, John L. *SOG: The Secret Wars of America's Commandos in Vietnam.* New York: Penguin Putnam Inc., 1998.

Rochester, Stuart I., and Frederick Kiley, *Honor Bound: American Prisoners of War in Southeast Asia, 1961–1973.* Annapolis: Naval Institute Press, 1999.

Rowe, James N. *Five Years to Freedom.* New York: Ballantine, 1984.

Sheehan, Neil. *A Bright Shining Lie: John Paul Vann and America in Vietnam.* New York: Random House, 1989.

Sherwood, John Darrell. *Fast Movers: Jet Pilots and the Vietnam Experience.* New York: Simon & Schuster, 2000.

Shultz, Richard. *The Secret War Against Hanoi: Kennedy and Johnson's Use of Spies, Saboteurs, and Covert Warriors in North Vietnam.* New York: HarperCollins Publishers, 1999.

Sorley, Lewis. *A Better War: The Unexamined Victories and Final Tragedy of America's Last Years in Vietnam.* Fort Worth, TX: Harcourt Brace, 1999.

Spector, Ronald H. *After Tet: The Bloodiest Year in Vietnam.* New York: Free Press, 1993.

Stacewicz, Richard. *Winter Soldiers: An Oral History of the Vietnam Veterans Against the War.* New York: Twayne Publishers, 1997.

Stone, Robert. *Dog Soldiers.* Boston: Houghton Mifflin, 1997.

Summers, Harry G. *Historical Atlas of the Vietnam War.* Boston: Houghton Mifflin, 1995.

Templer, Robert. *Shadows and Wind: A View of Modern Vietnam.* New York: Viking Penguin, 1999.

Veith, George J. *Code-Name Bright Light: The Untold Story of U.S. POW Rescue Efforts During the Vietnam War.* New York: Free Press, 1997.

Vetter, Lawrence. *Never Without Heroes: Marine Third Reconnaissance Battalion in Vietnam, 1965–1970.* New York: Random House, 1996.

Walsh, Michael J., and Eric Tobias, ed., with Greg Walker. *Seal!: From Vietnam's Phoenix Program to Central America's Drug Wars: Twenty-six Years with a Special Operations Warrior.* New York: Simon & Schuster, 1994.

Ward, Joseph T. *Dear Mom: A Sniper's Vietnam.* New York: Ballantine, 1991.

Wicker, Tom. *One of Us: Richard Nixon and the American Dream.* New York: Random House, 1991.

Index

323